Mungo Park

Travels in the Interior Districts of Africa

With an Introduction and Notes
by Bernard Waites

WORDSWORTH CLASSICS
OF WORLD LITERATURE

Readers who are interested in other titles from
Wordsworth Editions are invited to visit our website at
www.wordsworth-editions.com

For our latest list and a full mail-order service, contact
Bibliophile Books, 5 Thomas Road, London E14 7BN
Tel: +44 (0)20 7515 9222 Fax: +44 (0)20 7538 4115
E-mail: orders@bibliophilebooks.com

This edition published 2002 by Wordsworth Editions Limited
8B East Street, Ware, Hertfordshire SG12 9HJ

ISBN 1 84022 601 3

Text © Wordsworth Editions Limited 2002
Introduction and Notes © Bernard Waites 2002

Wordsworth® is a registered trademark of
Wordsworth Editions Limitd

Typeset in Great Britain by Antony Gray
Printed and bound by Clays Ltd, St Ives plc

CONTENTS

INTRODUCTION

Mungo Park's *Travels in the Interior Districts of Africa performed under Direction and Patronage of the Afrcian Association in the Years 1795, 1796 and 1797* is a classic record of European exploration that affords its readers three distinct pleasures. There is the pleasure that comes from careful, unprejudiced observation of other cultures and other lands and, incidental to it, of ethnography, geography and humane social science. There is the pleasure of making vicarious acquaintance with a man of stoic, Christian virtue, whose resourcefulness and humanity shine through a studied reserve. Autobiographies of the good are rarely much fun to read, but Mungo Park's account of himself in the African interior is a splendid exception. He was, by most accounts, not easy to know in person. But the character that emerges from his book is, taken in the round, very attractive to modern sensibilities. Finally, there is the pleasure that comes from good writing. Park's prose is never ostentatiously stylish, but it is always lucid. As his first biographer, John Whishaw, acknowledged, 'the distinguished success' of the *Travels* was due 'not only to the interesting nature of its subject, but in a certain degree also to the merits of the work as a composition; to the clearness of the descriptions, the natural and easy flow of the narration, and the general elegance of the style'.

Whether these literary qualities were due entirely to Park's authorship is an intriguing question that I will return to later in this Introduction.

Park was born on 11 September 1771 at Foulshiels, near Selkirk, the seventh of thirteen children of a tenant farmer, also called Mungo. The family home was a modest cottage, but Park's father was a man of sufficient substance to hire a private tutor for his children, and three of his sons were educated for the professions. Young Mungo attended Selkirk Grammar School, and was originally intended for the Ministry of the Secession Church, a strict Calvinist sect that had split from the Church of Scotland in 1733. However, the lad had 'no calling' and by his own choice was apprenticed to a local physician, Dr Thomas Anderson. In the autumn of 1788, he enrolled at Edinburgh University to study medicine and developed a particular passion for botany, at that time taught in the medical faculty. His studies exposed him – at least in a general way – to the ideas of the Scottish Enlightenment: though he never lapsed into scepticsm, he believed that the Divinely created natural order could be best understood through empirical, scientific enquiry. He brought the same attitude of mind to the observation of foreign cultures.

The most important relationship in deciding the young man's future was with his brother-in-law James Dickson, a self-educated botanist of some distinction and a founding fellow of the Linnaean Society, set up in 1788 and named after the great Swedish naturalist, Carl Linnaeus. Park accompanied Dickson on a botanical expedition to the Scottish Highlands in the summer of 1792. We can only speculate as to what passed between them, but it seems that Park determined on some alternative career to medical practice in Scotland. Through Dickson, he was given an introduction to Sir Joseph Banks, a co-founder of the Linnaean Society and president of the Royal Society from 1778 to his death in 1820. Park was elected an associate of the Linnaean Society in November 1792, thanks to Dickson's nomination. In January 1793, he completed his professional training by oral examination at the Company of Surgeons. In February, he was appointed, on Banks's recommendation, assistant surgeon on an East Indiamen, the *Worcester*, bound for Sumatra, and sailed from Portsmouth in April. His reading matter on the voyage included Dugald Stewart's *Elements of the Philosophy of the Human Mind*. The first sentence of Park's *Travels* has misled generations of readers into believing that he returned from the East Indies in 1793, but this was a slip of the pen. The ship's log shows that the return voyage ended at Gravesend on 2 May 1794. It is a fair presumption that Banks had recommended Park on the understanding that he would carry out botanical and zoological research, for shortly after his return he presented Banks with some plant specimens, as well as anatomical watercolours of fish species. After his discharge from the *Worcester*, Park had no immediate professional prospects. Either on his own initiative or – as seems more likely – at Banks's prompting, he offered his services as an explorer to the African Association. Finding him 'a young man of no mean talents, who had been regularly educated in the medical line . . . [and] sufficiently instructed in the use of Hadley's Quadrant to make the necessary observations, and geographer enough to track out the path through the wilderness, and not unacquainted with natural history . . . ', the association accepted his offer.

The Association for Promoting the Discovery of the Inland Parts of the Continent of Africa had been established by Banks and eight other wealthy patrons of science in the summer of 1788. Apart from Banks, its most active member was its secretary, Henry Beaufoy, a Quaker MP and strong supporter of the campaign for the abolition of the slave trade until his death in 1795. In his plan for the association, Beaufoy reviewed the state of European knowledge of African geography and concluded that, notwithstanding the progress of discovery on its coasts and borders, the map of the vast continent's interior 'is still but a wide extended blank on which the Geographer . . . has traced with a hesitating hand a few names of unexplored rivers and of uncertain nations'. Europeans had been trading with West Africa since the mid-fifteenth century, but their direct knowledge of the Sudan stopped at the limits of navigation on the Senegal and Gambia Rivers in the west and the highlands of Christian Abyssinia in the east. Francis Moore, one of the Royal African Company's factors, had published a most informative account of the riverine states and peoples of the Gambia in 1738, based on a three-year stint as a slave-trader on the river (*Travels in the Inland Parts of Africa*). In Moore's day, the British had never gone higher up the river than the kingdom of Woolli, which lay about 180 miles inland from James Island in the estuary. For their knowledge of the interior, they relied mainly on Leo Africanus's *Description of Africa,* first issued in Italian in 1526. Its author, otherwise known Johannes Leo, was a Spanish Arab who had travelled widely in Muslim Africa (including Timbuktu and the Niger basin) before being taken captive in 1520 and presented to Pope Leo X. Moore included substantial translated extracts from the *Description* . . . in his own book, and this was almost certainly how Leo Africanus's work was known to Park. We can judge just how exiguous European knowledge of African geography was in 1790 from the map drawn for the African Association by Major James Rennell, a talented cartographer. Only one West African town, Timbuktu, was located with any accuracy; the Niger was shown as a pathetic remnant, flowing from the north east to the south west, and petering out in the wilderness.

Soon after its formation, the association had recruited two adventurers for journeys of exploration: the first, the American John Ledyard, intended to approach Timbuktu by the caravan route from the Blue Nile, but took a fatal dose of an emetic after a bilious sickness; the second, Simon Lucas, hoped to reach the Niger basin from Tripoli but his way was barred by tribal rebellion. The association then enlisted the services of a third traveller, Major Daniel Houghton, to penetrate to the Niger by way of the Gambia. Houghton had wide experience, having served with the British consul in Morocco and as fort major on the island of Goree, off Dakar, and was evidently determined to fulfil his instructions to ascertain the course of the Niger and visit 'the cities of Tombuctoo and Houssa'. (The latter was a confusion with Hausa, a language diffused across what is now Northern Nigeria and neighbouring Niger. The principal town in Hausaland was Kano.) Houghton set out from the Gambia in November 1790 and sent a last pencilled note from Simbing, in Ludamar, on 1 September 1791, saying that he was on his way to Timbuktu, and in good health, but had been robbed of all his trade goods by the son of the local potentate. Rumours of his death seeped back to the coast, but his fate was not known for certain until Park passed through Ludamar in February 1796 and heard that Houghton had been robbed and stripped by Moors, who either killed him or left him to die of thirst and exposure. Though he had not reached the Niger, Houghton had been given accurate information about its upper reaches by an old Moroccan acquaintance he met by chance in the interior, and his dispatches had conveyed this intelligence to the African Association. When Park was recruited, it was already known that the river ran south to north before it reached Jennie (or Djenné), the capital of Bambara, and then eastward to Timbuktu.

The most formidable obstacle to European penetration of West Africa was the disease barrier, and Park took the precaution of 'seasoning' himself on the Gambia before embarking on his journey. This did not ward off a 'smart fever', but made recovery more likely because he was in the good care of Dr Laidley, the main British slave trader on the river. Park used his time to learn Mandingo (now more usually called Malinke), the principal language of the western Sudan. He began his travels with an interpreter, but by their end had spent months relying on his own linguistic skills and must have become very proficient. Houghton was thought to have invited robbery and extortion by setting out from the Gambia richly laden with trade goods, so Park was either instructed or advised to travel light. When he left Pisania, on 2 December 1795, he had provisions for two days and only 'a small assortment of beads, amber and tobacco, for the purchase of a fresh supply'. This did not, unfortunately, save him from the predatory ways of African rulers. He entered a region of small, but territorially well-defined polities, whose monarchs expected to levy tribute on travellers and traders. By mid-January, three-quarters of Park's goods had been extorted from him. During the latter half of his journey, he was reduced to itinerant beggary and was dependent on the charity of African villagers, usually womenfolk. In all his wanderings and wretchedness, he found African women uniformly kind and compassionate.

Park travelled mostly through monotonous, undulating scrubland with few natural landmarks, but his experiences were 'shaped' by crossing the ecological, socio-cultural and linguistic frontiers that inter-meshed in the western Sudan. South of the Senegal River lived Negro speakers of the Mande languages (such as Malinke) or the West Atlantic languages (such as Wolof which Park refers to as Jaloff). These peoples were sedentary agriculturists with ancient political traditions of kingship, administration and taxation. The only markedly pastoral Negro people were the Fulani (whom Park calls Foulahs) who lived in scattered communities throughout the savanna. The sedentary peoples frequently dwelt in towns, practised a wide range of pre-industrial crafts, including high quality iron-making, but had no indigenous writing. Since the eighth century, Islam had been peacefully transmitted to the West African savanna by trans-Saharan traders. Some dynasties had converted and courtly advisers and urban merchants were often Muslims, but in Park's day West African Negroes were predominantly pagan. Their basic religious tenets were consistent with Islam: all pagans believed in one

God, the creator and preserver of all things, and in a future state of reward and punishment. Many practices – such as circumcision and child-naming ceremonies – were common to both religious cultures. What separated them was the austerity of the Islamic way of life, the consciousness Muslims had of belonging to a vast community of believers, and the Muslims' monopoly on writing. Park held the usual European prejudices against Islam, but they were softened by appreciating its vital role in disseminating literacy and schooling. From the Muslim schoolmaster at Kamalia, Park discovered that the Negroes were in possession of an Arabic version of the Pentateuch, and he heard the story of Adam and Eve related in Malinke 'with tolerable exactness'.

North of the Senegal River, on the fringes of the desert, the peoples were fairer skinned (to Park they resembled West Indian Mulattos). They spoke Arabic, or sometimes Berber, and were fiercely Muslim. Park followed normal usage in calling them 'Moors', but this unsatisfactory term could refer to all inhabitants of Morocco or North African Muslims in general. They were cattle drovers who shifted north and south according to the season: when the Saharan winds burnt off the pastures in February they moved to the savanna; when the rains came in July they moved back towards the desert. The free men amongst them were mounted warriors and they regularly raided the sedentary peoples for slaves, who were bartered for weapons on the Senegal or marched across the desert to the North African slave markets. Some slaves were put to work mining rock salt (a major item of trade in West Africa). Park was forcibly detained for over two months by Ali, King of Ludamar, in a desert-edge camp at Benowm, where he suffered physical privation as well as 'the insults of the rudest savages on earth'. The abuse was, it would seem, worse than he cared to tell his readers; in 1804, he became friendly with Walter Scott and confided in him that certain shocking incidents had been omitted from his account. When Park was eventually released by Ali, the slave boy Demba – who had faithfully accompanied him from Dr Laidley's and been promised his freedom – was enslaved by the Moors. Not surprisingly, Park detested them. Yet his description of their way of life still manages to be detached, and sometimes delightfully ironic. After a wedding, an old woman dashed a bowl of the bride's pee in his face. Apparently, young unmarried Moors always received this nuptial benediction as a mark of distinguished favour. 'This being the case, I wiped my face and sent my acknowledgements to the lady.'

When Park came to write up his *Travels* . . . he undoubtedly had some literary assistance. He returned with extensive notes (now unfortunately lost) but at first laboured to turn these into a manuscript fit for publication. Travellers' accounts were not uncommonly 'polished' for publication by professional authors (a Dr Hawkesworth had assisted Captain Cook) and Park had a distinguished helpmate in Bryan Edwards MP. Edwards was a former West Indian planter who made his literary reputation with a *Civil and Commercial History of the British Colonies in the West Indies* (1793) and succeeded Beaufoy as Secretary of the African Association in 1795. But unlike Beaufoy, Edwards opposed the abolition of the slave trade and was a highly plausible spokesman for the West Indian interest. Soon after Park's return to England, Edwards had prepared an abstract of his journey for the African Association on the basis of information given him by Park, which was incorporated wholesale into the published *Travels* . . . According to John Whishaw, Edwards was consulted upon every part of the work, and revised and corrected the whole manuscript before it was sent to press. A later secretary of the African Association, Sir William Young, credited Edwards with 'the judicious compilation and elegant recital of the travels of Mungo Park'. When Park angrily protested, Young retracted this in a fulsome letter of apology, which he gave Park permission to use publicly. We have Edwards's word that his contribution to the manuscript from about Chapter X onwards was editorial rather than co-authorial. In a letter informing Banks on the progress of the work. Edwards wrote: 'Park goes on triumphantly – He improves in his style so much by practice, that his journal now requires but little correction; and some parts, which he has lately sent me, are equal to any thing in the English language . . . '

This does not entirely settle Edwards's role in the writing of Chapter XXII, 'On Slavery in Africa' – a chapter that had considerable import for contemporary political and moral argument. The *Travels* . . . were published when the campaign for the abolition of the slave trade was mobilising enlightened public opinion in a quite unprecedented way. It was an article of faith among abolitionists that halting the slave trade was the key to moral and social progress *within* Africa: it would create a demand for wage labour, encourage the spread of a money economy and enlarge the market for imported European manufactures. In concluding his observations on slavery in Africa, Park rejected this progressive scenario. He believed that the institution of African slavery pre-dated the Atlantic slave trade and that it would persist after its abolition. This was not what the enlightened public wanted to read, and many believed that Edwards had foisted his own views on Park or that the young man had deferred to his social and intellectual superior in this key chapter. Whishaw asserted that 'considerable parts [of] . . . the observations on the state of slavery in Africa may be confidently pronounced, from the peculiar character both of the style and sentiments, to have proceeded from the pen of Mr Edwards'. → limitation

This seems most unlikely. Park did not repeat the spurious justifications for the Atlantic slave trade to be found in Edwards's *History of the British West Indies* (where we learn that, by being sold to the whites, the wretched victims were removed to a far more desirable situation than that of the most fortunate slaves in Africa, and, besides, if the British forswore the trade, the French would snaffle up their market share). It is much more likely that Park's unpalatable views (in progressive circles) came from observing just how entrenched human bondage was in the West African regional economy and its native societies. He reckoned that slaves outnumbered the free by three to one, though he stressed that slavery was a differentiated condition. Domestic slaves enjoyed certain rights denied to slaves who had been captured in war or purchased on the slave marts. He appreciated that commercial slavery and social violence formed a vicious circle, yet he was sufficiently detached to recognise that the evil was not totally unmitigated. The treatment of captives who were being held in Kamalia prior to being marched to the coast was, he noted, far from harsh or cruel. Rather than the influence of Edwards, one may discern in Park's account of African slavery and slave trading the moral ambiguities of his own experiences. He began and ended his journey indebted to the slave trader Dr Laidley, on whose credit he had drawn hundreds of miles inland. He owed his life to another slave trader, the Muslim Karfa Taura, who befriended him when he was sick and destitute, and cared for him for seven months. Park was able to return to the Gambia only by joining Karfa and a coffle of slaves who were to be sold on the river. Karfa became so devoted to Park that he would not leave him until he had been safely delivered into European hands. As it transpired, Park's assessment that abolishing the Atlantic slave trade would do little to affect slavery in Africa proved entirely accurate. When export markets dried up, masters put their slaves to work in the production of such commodities as palm oil that were the staples of 'legitimate commerce'.

Park's *Travels* . . . is a splendid record of what was, in terms of its original objectives, an unsuccessful journey of exploration. He did not reach Timbuktu, and he mapped the course of the Niger for only a relatively short distance. Nevertheless, his safe return from that hitherto elusive river was regarded as little short of miraculous. His account of his solitary wanderings was a great success with the reading public, and was quickly translated into other European languages.

The *Journal* he kept of his 1805 mission to the interior is the partial record of a different type of expedition that ended in disaster. The British Government had become interested in supporting the exploration of West Africa, partly for commercial reasons but also to thwart French expansion in the

region. A plan was conceived in the War Office to dispatch a
column of men from Pisania to Bammakoo on the upper Niger,
with sufficient equipment to build and rig two shallow-
draught, forty-foot boats that were to be sailed downriver to
the sea. It was not supposed to be a military expedition. Park –
the obvious choice for leader – was instructed to use
conciliatory measures on every occasion, and quite lavish
funds were spent in Britain on the necessary presents for
African kings (including 460 yards of cloth). In all, forty-five
Europeans left Pisania on 4 May and headed due east. Only
eleven arrived at Bammakoo on 19 August; the rest had
succumbed to disease. The party had blundered its way
through the worst months for travel, when every stream was
swollen by the rains and clouds of mosquitoes tormented the
flesh. Dysentery, malaria and yellow fever did their worst. The
men became too weak to defend the loads on their pack asses
from pillaging natives. Park wore himself out trying to keep his
column together and it is astonishing that he managed to keep
a journal at all. Though lacking the literary quality of the
Travels . . . , it nevertheless has a compelling immediacy.
When the expedition finally set sail from Sansanding on 16
November in the schooner HMS *Joliba,* there were only five
European survivors, accompanied by three slaves and a native
guide and interpreter, Amadi Fatouma. Park gave his *Journal*
and his last letters into the keeping of Isaaco, a trader who had
acted as a guide on the journey from the Gambia and who
carried the papers back to the coast. The only testimony we
have as to Park's fate comes from a deposition made around
1810 by Amadi Fatouma, who had been engaged to travel in
the *Joliba* only as far as Hausaland. Shortly after he left

Park's service, the expedition was attacked when the schooner became stuck in rocks on the Boussa rapids. To save themselves, Park and his white companions jumped into the river but were drowned. One slave survived. Memories of Park, six feet tall, broad-shouldered and big-bearded, persisted in the local lore until the last years of the nineteenth century. In his humanity, he remains a man for our times.

BERNARD WAITES
The Open University

BIBLIOGRAPHY

The most scholarly biography of Park is Kenneth Lupton's *Mungo Park, the African Traveler* (Oxford University Press, 1979). This excellent account draws upon all the relevant archival sources and a great deal of secondary literature. Neither of the biographies that appeared in 1934 – Lewis Grassic Gibbon's *Niger: The Life of Mungo Park* (The Porpoise Press) and Stephen Gwynn's *Mungo Park and the Quest of the Niger* (John Lane, The Bodley Head) – has a scholarly apparatus. Gibbon's is, in places, a work of pure speculation, and absurdly hostile to Park; Gwynn's is more informative and sympathetic. John Whishaw's biographical memoir remains extremely useful; it is best read in the 1815 edition of the combined *Travels . . .* and *Journal*, which contains important addenda and appendices relating to the composition of Park's work. A broader perspective on Park's place in the exploration of Africa and the formation of British ideas about the continent and its people can be gained from Robin Hallett, *The Penetration of Africa: European Enterprise and Exploration Principally in Northern and Western Africa up to 1830* (Routledge and Kegan Paul, 1965): and Philip Curtin, *The Image of Africa: British Ideas and Action, 1780–1850* (Macmillan, 1965). Those wanting to know more about the economy and societies of the region through which Park travelled should consult Curtin's *Economic Change in Precolonial Africa: Senegambia in the Era of the Slave Trade* (University of Wisconsin Press, 1975).

AUTHOR'S PREFACE

The following Journal, drawn up from original minutes and notices made at the proper moment, and preserved with great difficulty, is now offered to the Public by the direction of my noble and honourable employers, the Members of the African Association. I regret that it is so little commensurate to the patronage I have received. As a composition, it has nothing to recommend it but *truth*. It is a plain unvarnished tale, without pretensions of any kind, except that it claims to enlarge, in some degree, the circle of African geography. For this purpose my services were offered, and accepted by the Association; and I trust I have not laboured altogether in vain. The work, however, must speak for itself; and I should not have thought any preliminary observations necessary if I did not consider myself called upon, both by justice and gratitude, to offer those which follow.

Immediately after my return from Africa, the Acting Committee of the Association,* taking notice of the time it

---

* Consisting of the following noblemen and gentlemen: Earl of Moira; Lord Bishop of Landaff; Right Hon. Sir Joseph Banks, President of the Royal Society; Andrew Stewart, Esq., F.R.S.; and Bryan Edwards, Esq., F.R.S. Concerning the original institution of the Society itself, and the progress of discovery previous to my expedition, the fullest information has already been given in the various publications of the Society.

would require to prepare an account in detail, as it now appears, and being desirous of gratifying, as speedily as possible, the curiosity which many of the Members were pleased to express concerning my discoveries, determined that an epitome, or abridgement, of my travels should be forthwith prepared from such materials and oral communications as I could furnish, and printed for the use of the Association, and also that an engraved map of my route should accompany it. A memoir, thus supplied and improved, was accordingly drawn up in two parts by members of the Association and distributed among the Society: the first consisting of a narrative, in abstract, of my travels, by Bryan Edwards, Esq.; the second, of geographical illustrations of my progress, by Major James Rennell, F.R.S. Major Rennell was pleased also to add a map of my route, constructed in conformity to my own observations and sketches, freed from those errors which the Major's superior knowledge and distinguished accuracy in geographical researches enabled him to discover and correct.

Availing myself, therefore, on the present occasion, of assistance like this, it is impossible that I can present myself before the public without expressing how deeply and gratefully sensible I am of the honour and advantage which I derive from the labours of those gentlemen; for Mr. Edwards has kindly permitted me to incorporate, as occasion offered, the whole of his narrative into different parts of my work; and Major Rennell, with equal good will, allows me to embellish and elucidate my travels with the map before mentioned.

Thus aided and encouraged, I should deliver this volume to the world with that confidence of a favourable reception which no merits of my own could authorise me to claim, were I not apprehensive that expectations have been formed by some of my subscribers of discoveries to be unfolded which I have not made and of wonders to be related of which I am utterly ignorant. There is danger that those who feel a disappointment of this nature, finding less to astonish and amuse in my book than they had promised to themselves beforehand, will not even allow me the little merit which I really possess. Painful as this circumstance may prove to my feelings, I shall console myself under it if the distinguished persons under whose auspices I entered on my mission shall allow that I have executed the duties of it to their satisfaction; and that they consider the Journal, which I have now the honour to present to them, to be, what I have endeavoured to make it, an honest and faithful report of my proceedings and observations in their service, from the outset of my journey to its termination.

M. P.

TRAVELS IN AFRICA.

——◆——

CHAPTER I.

Passion for Travel—Instructions and Departure—Jillifree, on the Gambia—Kingdom of Barra—Vintain—The Feloops—Voyage up the Gambia—Jonkakonda—Arrival at Dr. Laidley's—Pisania, and the British Factory—Employment at Pisania—Fever.

OON after my return from the East Indies in 1793, I learnt that the Association for the purpose of prosecuting discoveries in the interior of Africa were desirous of engaging a person to explore that continent by the way of the Gambia river. I therefore took occasion, through means of the President of the Royal Society, to whom I had the honour to be known, of offering myself for that service. I had been informed that a Captain Houghton, formerly fort-major at Goree, had already sailed to the Gambia, under the direction of the Association, and that there was reason to apprehend he had fallen a sacrifice to the climate, or perished in some contest with the natives : but this intelligence, instead of deterring me from my purpose, animated me to persist in the offer of my services with the greater solicitude.

I had a passionate desire to examine into the productions of a country so little known, and to become experimentally acquainted with the modes of life and character of the natives. I knew that I was able to bear fatigue ; and I relied on my youth and the strength of my constitution to preserve me from the effects of the climate. The salary which the committee allowed was sufficiently large, and I made no stipulation for future reward. If I should perish in my journey, I was willing that my hopes and expectations should perish with me ; and if I should succeed in rendering the geography of Africa more familiar to my countrymen, and in opening to their ambition and industry new sources of wealth and new channels of commerce, I knew that I was in the hands of men of honour, who would not fail to bestow that remuneration which my successful services should appear to them to merit. The Committee of the Association, having made such inquiries as they thought necessary, declared themselves satisfied with my qualifications ; and with that liberality which on all occasions distinguished their conduct, gave me every encouragement which it was in their power to grant, or which I could with propriety ask.

It was at first proposed that I should accompany Mr. James Willis, who was then recently appointed Consul at Senegambia, and whose countenance in that capacity it was thought might have served and protected me ; but Government afterwards rescinded his appointment, and I lost that advantage. The kindness of the Committee, however, supplied all that was necessary. The Secretary of the Association, the late Henry Beaufoy, Esq., favoured me with a recommendation to Dr. John Laidley (a gentleman who had resided many years at an English factory on the banks of the Gambia), and a letter of credit on him for £200. I then became impatient for my departure, and took my passage in the brig *Endeavour*, a small vessel trading to the Gambia for bees'-wax and ivory, commanded by Captain Richard Wyatt.

My instructions were very plain and concise. I was directed, on my arrival in Africa, "to pass on to the river Niger, either by the way of Bambouk, or by such other route as should be found most convenient. That I should ascertain the course, and, if possible, the rise and termination of that river. That I should use my utmost exertions to visit the principal towns or cities in its neighbourhood, particularly Timbuctoo and Houssa ; and that I should be afterwards at liberty to return to Europe, either by the way of the Gambia, or by such other route as, under all the then existing circumstances of my situation and prospects, should appear to me to be most advisable."

We sailed from Portsmouth on the 22d day of May 1795. On the 4th of June we saw the mountains over Mogadore, on the coast of Africa ; and on the 21st of the same month, after a pleasant voyage of thirty days, we anchored at Jillifree, a town on the northern bank of the river Gambia, opposite to James's Island, where the English had formerly a small port.

The kingdom of Barra, in which the town of Jillifree is situated, produces great plenty of the necessaries of life ; but the chief trade of the inhabitants is in salt ; which commodity they carry up the river in canoes as high as Barraconda, bringing down in return Indian corn, cotton cloths, elephants' teeth, and small quantities of gold dust. The number of canoes and

people constantly employed in this trade makes the king of
Barra more formidable to Europeans than any other chieftain
on the river ; and this circumstance probably encouraged him
to establish those exorbitant duties which traders of all nations
are obliged to pay at entry, amounting to nearly £20 on every
vessel, great and small.   These duties or customs are generally
collected in person by the Alkaid, or governor of Jillifree, and
he is attended on these occasions by a numerous train of de-
pendents, among whom are found many who, by their frequent
intercourse with the English, have acquired a smattering of
our language ; but they are commonly very noisy and very
troublesome,—begging for everything they fancy with such
earnestness and importunity, that traders are frequently
obliged to grant their requests in order to get quit of them.

On the 23d we departed from Jillifree, and proceeded to
Vintain, a town situated about two miles up a creek on the
southern side of the river.   This is much resorted to by
Europeans, on account of the great quantities of bees'-wax
which are brought hither for sale.   The wax is collected in
the woods by the Feloops, a wild and unsociable race of people ;
who also supply the traders, both on the Gambia and Cassa-
mansa rivers, with goats and poultry, on very reasonable terms.
The honey which they collect is chiefly used by themselves in
making a strong intoxicating liquor, much the same as the
mead which is produced from honey in Great Britain.   Their
country, which is of considerable extent, abounds in rice.

In their traffic with Europeans the Feloops generally employ a factor or agent, of the Mandingo nation, who speaks a
little English, and is acquainted with the trade of the river.
This broker makes the bargain ; and, with the connivance of the

European, receives a certain part only of the payment, which he gives to his employer as the whole ; the remainder (very truly called the *cheating-money*) he receives when the Feloop is gone, and appropriates to himself, as a reward for his trouble.

The language of the Feloops is appropriate and peculiar ; and as their trade is chiefly conducted by Mandingoes, the Europeans have no inducement to learn it. The numerals are as follow : One—*Enory ;* Two—*Sickaba* or *Cookaba ;* Three —*Sisajee ;* Four—*Sibakeer ;* Five—*Footuck ;* Six—*Footuck-Enory ;* Seven—*Footuck-Cookaba ;* Eight—*Footuck-Sisajee ;* Nine—*Footuck-Sibakeer ;* Ten—*Sibankonyen.*

On the 26th we left Vintain, and continued our course up the river, anchoring whenever the tide failed us, and frequently towing the vessel with the boat. The river is deep and muddy, the banks are covered with impenetrable thickets of mangrove, and the whole of the adjacent country appears to be flat and swampy.

The Gambia abounds with fish, some species of which are excellent food ; but none of them that I recollect are known in Europe. At the entrance from the sea sharks are found in great abundance ; and higher up, alligators and the hippopotamus (or river-horse) are very numerous. The latter might with more propriety be called the river-elephant, being of enormous and unwieldy bulk, and its teeth furnish good ivory. This animal is amphibious, with short and thick legs, and cloven hoofs : it feeds on grass and such shrubs as the banks of the river afford, boughs of trees, etc., seldom venturing far from the water, in which it seeks refuge on hearing the approach of man. I have seen many, and always found them of a timid and inoffensive disposition.

In six days after leaving Vintain we reached Jonkakonda, a place of considerable trade, where our vessel was to take in part of her lading. The next morning the several European traders came from their different factories to receive their letters, and learn the nature and amount of the cargo; and the captain dispatched a messenger to Dr. Laidley to inform him of my arrival. He came to Jonkakonda the morning following, when I delivered him Mr. Beaufoy's letter, and he gave me a kind invitation to spend my time at his house until an opportunity should offer of prosecuting my journey. This invitation was too acceptable to be refused; and being furnished by the Doctor with a horse and guide, I set out from Jonkakonda at daybreak on the 5th of July, and at eleven o'clock arrived at Pisania, where I was accommodated with a room and other conveniences in the Doctor's house.

Pisania is a small village in the king of Yany's dominions, established by British subjects as a factory for trade, and inhabited solely by them and their black servants. It is situated on the banks of the Gambia, sixteen miles above Jonkakonda. The white residents, at the time of my arrival consisted only of Dr. Laidley and two gentlemen who were brothers, of the name of Ainslie, but their domestics were numerous. They enjoyed perfect security under the king's protection; and being highly esteemed and respected by the natives at large, wanted no accommodation or comfort which the country could supply; and the greatest part of the trade in slaves, ivory, and gold, was in their hands.

Settled now for some time at my ease, my first object was to learn the Mandingo tongue, the language in almost general use throughout this part of Africa, and without which I was fully convinced I never could acquire an extensive knowledge of the country or its inhabitants. In this pursuit I was greatly assisted by Dr. Laidley, who, by a long residence in the country, and constant intercourse with the natives, had made himself completely master of it. Next to the language, my great object was to collect information concerning the countries I intended to visit. I was referred to certain traders called Slatees — free black merchants, of great consideration in this part of Africa, who come down from the interior countries chiefly with enslaved negroes for sale ; but I soon discovered that very little dependence could be placed on the accounts they gave, for they contradicted each other in the most important particulars, and all of them seemed extremely unwilling that I should prosecute my journey. These circumstances increased my anxiety to ascertain the truth from my own personal observations.

In researches of this kind, and in observing the manners and customs of the natives in a country so little known to the nations of Europe, and furnished with so many striking and uncommon objects of nature, my time passed not unpleasantly ; and I began to flatter myself that I had escaped the fever, or seasoning, to which Europeans, on their first arrival in hot climates, are generally subject. But, on the 31st of July, I imprudently exposed myself to the night dew, in observing an eclipse of the moon, with a view to determine the longitude of the place ; the next day I found myself attacked with a smart fever and delirium ; and such an illness followed as confined me to the house during the greatest part of August. My recovery was very slow ; but I embraced every short interval of convalescence to walk out and make myself ac-

quainted with the productions of the country. In one of
those excursions, having rambled further than usual in a hot
day, I brought on a return of my fever, and on the 10th of
September I was again confined to my bed. The fever, however, was not so violent as before ; and in the course of three
weeks I was able, when the weather would permit, to renew
my botanical excursions ; and when it rained, I amused myself
with drawing plants, etc., in my chamber. The care and
attention of Dr. Laidley contributed greatly to alleviate my
sufferings ; his company and conversation beguiled the tedious
hours during that gloomy season when the rain falls in
torrents, when suffocating heats oppress by day, and when
the night is spent by the terrified traveller in listening to the
croaking of frogs (of which the numbers are beyond imagination), the shrill cry of the jackal, and the deep howling of
the hyæna—a dismal concert, interrupted only by the roar of
such tremendous thunder as no person can form a conception
of but those who have heard it.

The country itself, being an immense level and very
generally covered with woods, presents a tiresome and gloomy
uniformity to the eye ; but, although nature has denied to the
inhabitants the beauties of romantic landscapes, she has
bestowed on them, with a liberal hand, the more important
blessings of fertility and abundance. A little attention to
cultivation procures a sufficiency of corn ; the fields afford a
rich pasturage for cattle ; and the natives are plentifully
supplied with excellent fish, both from the Gambia river and
the Walli creek.

The grains which are chiefly cultivated are Indian corn
(*Zea mays*) ; two kinds of *Holcus spicatus*, called by the natives

soono and *sanio ; Holcus niger*, and *Holcus bicolor ;* the former of which they have named *bassi woolima*, and the latter *bassiqui.* These, together with rice, are raised in considerable quantities ; besides which the inhabitants in the vicinity of the towns and villages have gardens which produce onions, calavances, yams, cassavi, ground-nuts, pompions, gourds, water-melons, and some other esculent plants.

I observed, likewise, near the towns, small patches of cotton and indigo. The former of these articles supplies them with clothing, and with the latter they dye their cloth of an excellent blue colour, in a manner that will hereafter be described.

In preparing their corn for food the natives use a large wooden mortar called a *paloon*, in which they bruise the seed until it parts with the outer covering, or husk, which is then separated from the clean corn by exposing it to the wind ; nearly in the same manner as wheat is cleared from the chaff in England. The corn thus freed from the husk is returned to the mortar and beaten into meal, which is dressed variously in different countries ; but the most common preparation of it among the nations of the Gambia is a sort of pudding, which they call *kouskous.* It is made by first moistening the flour with water, and then stirring and shaking it about in a large calabash or gourd, till it adheres together in small granules resembling sago. It is then put into an earthen pot, whose bottom is perforated with a number of small holes ; and this pot being placed upon another, the two vessels are luted together, either with a paste of meal and water or with cows' dung, and placed upon the fire. In the lower vessel is commonly some animal food and water, the steam or vapour of which ascends through the perforations in the bottom of the upper vessel, and softens and prepares the *kouskous*, which is very much esteemed throughout all the countries that I visited. I am informed that the same manner of preparing flour is very generally used on the Barbary coast, and that the dish so prepared is there called by the same name. It is therefore probable that the Negroes borrowed the practice from the Moors.

respect

For gratifying a taste of variety, another sort of pudding called *nealing* is sometimes prepared from the meal of corn ; and they have also adopted two or three different modes of dressing their rice. Of vegetable food, therefore, the natives have no want ; and although the common class of people are but sparingly supplied with animal food, yet this article is not wholly withheld from them.

Their domestic animals are nearly the same as in Europe. Swine are found in the woods, but their flesh is not esteemed ; probably the marked abhorrence in which this animal is held by the votaries of Mahomet has spread itself among the pagans. Poultry of all kinds (the turkey excepted) is everywhere to be had. The Guinea fowl and red partridge abound in the fields ; and the woods furnish a small species of antelope, of which the venison is highly and deservedly prized.

Of the other wild animals in the Mandingo countries, the most common are the hyæna, the panther, and the elephant. Considering the use that is made of the latter in the East Indies, it may be thought extraordinary that the natives of Africa have not, in any part of this immense continent, acquired the skill of taming this powerful and docile creature, and applying his strength and faculties to the service of man.

Needs a European mind

When I told some of the natives that this was actually done in the countries of the East, my auditors laughed me to scorn, and exclaimed, *Tobaubo fonnio* (a white man's lie) ! The Negroes frequently find means to destroy the elephant by fire-arms ; they hunt it principally for the sake of the teeth, which they transfer in barter to those who sell them again to the Europeans. The flesh they eat, and consider it as a great delicacy.

The usual beast of burthen in all the Negro territories is the ass. The application of animal labour to the purposes of agriculture is nowhere adopted ; the plough, therefore, is wholly unknown. The chief implement used in husbandry is the hoe, which varies in form in different districts ; and the labour is universally performed by slaves.

On the 6th of October the waters of the Gambia were at the greatest height, being fifteen feet above the high-water mark of the tide ; after which they began to subside—at first slowly, but afterwards very rapidly, sometimes sinking more than a foot in twenty-four hours; by the beginning of November the river had sunk to its former level, and the tide ebbed and flowed as usual. When the river had subsided, and the atmosphere grew dry, I recovered apace, and began to think of my departure—for this is reckoned the most proper season for travelling : the natives had completed their harvest, and provisions were everywhere cheap and plentiful.

Dr. Laidley was at this time employed in a trading voyage at Jonkakonda. I wrote to him to desire that he would use his interest with the Slatees, or slave-merchants, to procure me the company and protection of the first *coffle* (or caravan) that might leave Gambia for the interior country ; and in the meantime I requested him to purchase for me a horse and two asses. A few days afterwards the Doctor returned to Pisania, and informed me that a coffle would certainly go for the interior in the course of the dry season ; but that as many of the merchants belonging to it had not yet completed their assortment of goods, he could not say at what time they would set out.

The characters and dispositions of the Slatees and people that composed the caravan were also entirely unknown to me, and as they seemed rather averse to my purpose, and unwilling to enter into any positive engagements, and the time of their departure being withal very uncertain, I resolved, on further deliberation, to avail myself of the dry season, and proceed without them.

Dr. Laidley approved my determination, and promised me every assistance in his power to enable me to prosecute my journey with comfort and safety.

This resolution having been formed, I made preparations accordingly. And now, being about to take leave of my hospitable friend (whose kindness and solicitude continued to the moment of my departure),* and to quit, for many months, the countries bordering on the Gambia, it seems proper, before I proceed with my narrative, that I should, in this place, give some account of the several Negro nations which inhabit the banks of this celebrated river, and the commercial intercourse that subsists between them and such of the nations of Europe as find their advantage in trading to this part of Africa.

* Dr. Laidley, to my infinite regret, has since paid the debt of nature. He left Africa in the latter end of 1797, intending to return to Great Britain by way of the West Indies, and died soon after his arrival at Barbadoes.

CHAPTER II.

Negro Nations inhabiting the Banks of the Gambia: the Feloops, the Jaloffs, the Foulahs, and Mandingoes—Trade of the Gambia— Slaves and Slave-Merchants.

THE natives of the countries bordering on the Gambia, though distributed into a great many distinct governments, may, I think, be divided into four great classes: the Feloops, the Jaloffs, the Foulahs, and the Mandingoes. Among all these nations the religion of Mahomet has made, and continues to make, considerable progress; but in most of them, the body of the people, both free and enslaved, persevere in maintaining the blind but harmless superstitions of their ancestors, and are called by the Mahomedans *kafirs*, or infidels.

Of the Feloops I have little to add to what has been observed concerning them in the former chapter. They are of a gloomy disposition, and are supposed never to forgive an injury. They are even said to transmit their quarrels as deadly feuds to their posterity; insomuch that a son considers it as incumbent on him, from a just sense of filial obligation, to become the avenger of his deceased father's wrongs. If a man loses his life in one of those sudden quarrels, which perpetually occur at their feasts, when the whole party is intoxicated with mead, his son, or the eldest of his sons (if he has more than one), endeavours to procure his father's sandals, which he wears *once a-year*, on the anniversary of his father's death, until a fit opportunity offers of avenging his fate, when the object of his resentment seldom escapes his pursuit. This fierce and unrelenting disposition is, however, counterbalanced by many good qualities; they display the utmost gratitude and affection towards their benefactors; and the fidelity with which they preserve whatever is intrusted to them is remarkable. During the present war they have more than once taken up arms to defend our merchant vessels from French privateers; and English property, of considerable value, has frequently been left at Vintain, for a long time, entirely under the care of the Feloops, who have uniformly manifested on such occasions the strictest honesty and punctuality.

How greatly is it to be wished that the minds of a people so determined and faithful could be softened and civilised by the mild and benevolent spirit of Christianity!

The Jaloffs (or Yallofs) are an active, powerful, and warlike race, inhabiting great part of that tract which lies between the river Senegal and the Mandingo states on the Gambia; yet they differ from the Mandingoes, not only in language, but likewise in complexion and features. The noses of the Jaloffs are not so much depressed, nor the lips so protuberant, as among the generality of Africans; and although their skin is of the deepest black, they are considered by the white traders as the most sightly Negroes in this part of the continent.

They are divided into several independent states or kingdoms, which are frequently at war, either with their neighbours or with each other. In their manners, superstitions, and government, however, they have a greater resemblance to the

Mandingoes than to any other nation ; but excel them in the
manufacture of cotton cloth—spinning the wool to a finer
thread, weaving it in a broader loom, and dyeing it of a better
colour. Their language is said to be copious and significant,
and is often learnt by Europeans trading to Senegal.

The Foulahs (or Pholeys), such of them at least as reside
near the Gambia, are chiefly of a tawny complexion, with
soft silky hair and pleasing features. They are much attached
to a pastoral life, and have introduced themselves into all the
kingdoms on the windward coast as herdsmen and husbandmen,
paying a tribute to the sovereign of the country for the lands
which they hold.

The Mandingoes constitute in truth the bulk of the
inhabitants in all those districts of Africa which I visited ;
and their language, with a few exceptions, is universally
understood, and very generally spoken, in that part of the
continent.

They are called Mandingoes, I conceive, as having originally migrated from the interior state of Manding, of which
some account will hereafter be given ; but, contrary to the
present constitution of their parent country, which is re-
publican, it appeared to me that the government in all the
Mandingo states, near the Gambia, is monarchical. The power
of the sovereign is, however, by no means unlimited. In all
affairs of importance, the king calls an assembly of the
principal men, or elders, by whose councils he is directed, and
without whose advice he can neither declare war nor conclude
peace.

In every considerable town there is a chief magistrate,
called the *Alkaid*, whose office is hereditary, and whose busi-

ness it is to preserve order, to levy duties on travellers, and to preside at all conferences in the exercise of local jurisdiction and the administration of justice. These courts are composed of the elders of the town (of free condition), and are termed *palavers ;* and their proceedings are conducted in the open air with sufficient solemnity. Both sides of a question are freely canvassed, witnesses are publicly examined, and the decisions which follow generally meet with the approbation of the surrounding audience.

As the Negroes have no written language of their own, the general rule of decision is an appeal to *ancient custom ;* but since the system of Mahomet has made so great progress among them, the converts to that faith have gradually introduced, with the religious tenets, many of the civil institutions of the Prophet ; and where the Koran is not found sufficiently explicit, recourse is had to a commentary called *Al Sharra*, containing, as I was told, a complete exposition or digest of the Mahomedan laws, both civil and criminal, properly arranged and illustrated.

This frequency of appeal to written laws, with which the pagan natives are necessarily unacquainted, has given rise in their palavers to (what I little expected to find in Africa) professional advocates, or expounders of the law, who are allowed to appear and to plead for plaintiff or defendant, much in the same manner as counsel in the law courts of Great Britain. They are Mahomedan Negroes who have made, or affect to have made, the laws of the Prophet their peculiar study ; and if I may judge from their harangues, which I frequently attended, I believe that in the forensic qualifications of procrastination and cavil, and the arts of confounding and perplexing a cause, they are not always surpassed by the ablest pleaders in Europe. While I was at Pisania a cause was heard which furnished the Mahomedan lawyers with an admirable opportunity of displaying their professional dexterity.

The case was this : An ass belonging to a Serawoolli Negro (native of an interior country near the river Senegal) had broken into a field of corn belonging to one of the Mandingo inhabitants, and destroyed great part of it. The Mandingo, having caught the animal in his field, immediately drew his knife and cut its throat. The Serawoolli thereupon called a *palaver* (or in European terms, *brought an action*) to recover damages for the loss of his beast, on which he set a high value. The defendant confessed he had killed the ass, but pleaded a *set-off*, insisting that the loss he had sustained by the ravage in his corn was equal to the sum demanded for the animal. To ascertain this fact was the point at issue, and the learned advocates contrived to puzzle the cause in such a manner, that after a hearing of three days the court broke up without coming to any determination upon it ; and a second palaver was, I suppose, thought necessary.

The Mandingoes, generally speaking, are of a mild, sociable, and obliging disposition. The men are commonly above the ~~Slaves~~ middle size, well shaped, strong, and capable of enduring great labour ; the women are good-natured, sprightly, and agreeable. The dress of both sexes is composed of cotton cloth, of their own manufacture ; that of the men is a loose frock, not unlike a surplice, with drawers which reach half-way down the leg ; and they wear sandals on their feet and white cotton caps on their heads. The women's dress consists of two pieces of cloth which they wrap round the waist, which, hanging down to the

Two word for African clothing

ankles, answers the purpose of a petticoat; the other is thrown negligently over the shoulders.

This account of their clothing is indeed nearly applicable to the natives of all the different countries in this part of Africa; a peculiar national mode is observable only in the head-dresses of the women.

Thus, in the countries of the Gambia, the females wear a sort of bandage, which they call *Jalla*. It is a narrow stripe of cotton cloth, wrapped many times round, immediately over the forehead. In Bondou, the head is encircled with strings of white beads, and a small plate of gold is worn in the middle of the forehead. In Kasson, the ladies decorate their heads in a very tasteful and elegant manner, with white sea-shells. In Kaarta and Ludamar, the women raise their hair to a great height by the addition of a pad (as the ladies did formerly in Great Britain), which they decorate with a species of coral, brought from the Red Sea by pilgrims returning from Mecca, and sold at a great price.

In the construction of their dwelling-houses, the Mandingoes also conform to the general practice of the African nations on this part of the continent, contenting themselves with small and incommodious hovels. A circular mud wall about four feet high, upon which is placed a conical roof, composed of the bamboo cane, and thatched with grass, forms alike the palace of the king and the hovel of the slave. Their household furniture is equally simple. A hurdle of canes placed upon upright stakes about two feet from the ground, upon which is spread a mat or bullock's hide, answers the purpose of a bed; a water-jar, some earthen pots for dressing their food, a few wooden bowls and calabashes, and one or two low stools, compose the rest.

As every man of free condition has a plurality of wives, it is found necessary (to prevent, I suppose, matrimonial dispute) that each of the ladies should be accommodated with a hut to herself; and all the huts belonging to the same family are surrounded by a fence, constructed of bamboo canes split and formed into a sort of wicker-work. The whole enclosure is called a *sirk* or *surk*. A number of these enclosures, with narrow passages between them, form what is called a town; but the huts are generally placed without any regularity, according to the caprice of the owner. The only rule that seems to be attended to, is placing the door towards the southwest, in order to admit the sea-breeze.

In each town is a large stage called the *Bentang*, which answers the purpose of a public hall or town-house; it is composed of interwoven canes, and is generally sheltered from the sun by being erected in the shade of some large tree. It is here that all public affairs are transacted, and trials conducted; and here the lazy and indolent meet to smoke their pipes and hear the news of the day. In most of the towns the Mahomedans have also a *missura*, or mosque, in which they assemble and offer up their daily prayers, according to the rules of the Koran.

In the account which I have thus given of the natives, the reader must bear in mind that my observations apply chiefly to persons of *free condition*, who constitute, I suppose, not more than one-fourth part of the inhabitants at large; the other three-fourths are in a state of hopeless and hereditary slavery, and are employed in cultivating the land, in the care of cattle, and in servile offices of all kinds, much in the same manner as the slaves in the West Indies. I was told, however, that the Mandingo master can neither deprive his slave of life, nor sell him to a stranger, without first calling a palaver on his conduct, or, in other words, bringing him to a public trial ; but this degree of protection is extended only to the native or domestic slave.   Captives taken in war, and those unfortunate victims who are condemned to slavery for crimes or insolvency, and, in short, all those unhappy people who are brought down from the interior countries for sale, have no security whatever, but may be treated and disposed of in all respects as the owner thinks proper.   It sometimes happens, indeed, when no ships are on the coast, that a humane and considerate master incorporates his purchased slaves among his domestics ; and their offspring at least, if not the parents, become entitled to all the privileges of the native class.

The earliest European establishment on this celebrated river (the Gambia) was a factory of the Portuguese, and to this must be ascribed the introduction of the numerous words of that language still in use among the Negroes.   The Dutch, French, and English, afterwards successively possessed themselves of settlements on the coast ; but the trade of the Gambia became, and continued for many years, a sort of monopoly in the hands of the English.   In the travels of Francis Moore[5] is preserved an account of the Royal African Company's establishments in this river in the year 1730, at which time James' factory alone consisted of a governor, deputy-governor, and two other principal officers ; eight factors, thirteen writers, twenty inferior attendants and tradesmen ; a company of soldiers, and thirty-two Negro servants, besides sloops, shallops, and boats, with their crews ; and there were no less than eight subordinate factories in other parts of the river.

The commodities exported to the Gambia from Europe consist chiefly of firearms and ammunition, ironware, spirituous liquors, tobacco, cotton caps, a small quantity of broad cloth, and a few articles of the manufacture of Manchester; a small assortment of Indian goods, with some glass beads, amber, and other trifles; for which are taken in exchange, slaves, gold-dust, ivory, bees'-wax, and hides. Slaves are the chief article. Most of these unfortunate victims are brought to the coast in periodical caravans, many of them from very remote inland countries, for the language which they speak is not understood by the inhabitants of the maritime districts. In a subsequent part of my work I shall give the best information I have been able to collect concerning the manner in which they are obtained. On their arrival at the coast, if no immediate opportunity offers of selling them to advantage, they are distributed among the neighbouring villages until a slave-ship arrives, or until they can be sold to black traders, who sometimes purchase on speculation. In the meanwhile, the poor wretches are kept constantly fettered, two and two of them being chained together, and employed in the labours of the field; and, I am sorry to add, are very scantily fed, as well as harshly treated. The price of a slave varies according to the number of purchasers from Europe and the arrival of caravans from the interior; but, in general, I reckon that a young and healthy male, from sixteen to twenty-five years of age, may be estimated on the spot from £18 to £20 sterling.

The Negro slave-merchants, as I have observed in the former chapter, are called *Slatees;* who, besides slaves and the merchandise which they bring for sale to the whites,

supply the inhabitants of the maritime districts with native
iron, sweet-smelling gums and frankincense, and a commodity
called *sheatoulou*, which, literally translated, signifies *tree-butter*.
This commodity is extracted, by means of boiling water,
from the kernel of a nut, as will be more particularly described
hereafter ; it has the consistence and appearance of butter,
and is in truth an admirable substitute.   It forms an important article in the food of the natives, and serves also for
every domestic purpose in which oil would otherwise be used.
The demand for it is therefore very great.

In payment of these articles, the maritime states supply
the interior countries with salt, a scarce and valuable commodity, as I frequently and painfully experienced in the
course of my journey.   Considerable quantities of this article,
however, are also supplied to the inland natives by the Moors,
who obtain it from the salt-pits in the Great Desert, and
receive in return corn, cotton cloth, and slaves.

In thus bartering one commodity for another, many in-
conveniencies must necessarily have arisen at first from the
want of coined money, or some other visible and determinate
medium to settle the balance or difference of value between
different articles, to remedy which the natives of the interior
make use of small shells called *cowries*, as will be shown hereafter.   On the coast, the inhabitants have adopted a practice
which I believe is peculiar to themselves.

In their early intercourse with Europeans, the article that
attracted most notice was iron.   Its utility, in forming the
instruments of war and husbandry, made it preferable to all
others ; and iron soon became the measure by which the
value of all other commodities was ascertained.   Thus, a

certain quantity of goods, of whatever denomination, appearing to be equal in value to a bar of iron, constituted, in the trader's phraseology, a bar of that particular merchandise. Twenty leaves of tobacco, for instance, were considered as a *bar* of tobacco; and a gallon of spirits (or rather half-spirits and half-water) as a *bar* of rum; a bar of one commodity being reckoned equal in value to a bar of another commodity.

As, however, it must unavoidably happen that, according to the plenty or scarcity of goods at market in proportion to the demand, the relative value would be subject to continual fluctuation, greater precision has been found necessary; and at this time the current value of a single bar of any kind is fixed by the whites at two shillings sterling. Thus a slave, whose price is £15, is said to be worth 150 bars.

In transactions of this nature, it is obvious that the white trader has infinitely the advantage over the African, whom, therefore, it is difficult to satisfy; for, conscious of his own ignorance, he naturally becomes exceedingly suspicious and wavering; and indeed, so very unsettled and jealous are the Negroes in their dealings with the whites, that a bargain is never considered by the European as concluded, until the purchase-money is paid, and the party has taken leave.

Having now brought together such general observations on the country and its inhabitants as occurred to me during my residence in the vicinage of the Gambia, I shall detain the reader no longer with introductory matter, but proceed, in the next chapter, to a regular detail of the incidents which happened, and the reflections which arose in my mind, in the course of my painful and perilous journey, from its commencement until my return to the Gambia.

CHAPTER III.

COMMENCEMENT OF AUTHOR'S PERILOUS JOURNEY.

Departure from Pisania—Reach Jindey—Story-telling—Medina, Capital of Woolli—Interview with the King—Saphies or Charms— Koler—Mumbo Jumbo—Koojar—Wrestling-match—Crossing the Wilderness—Tallika—Kingdom of Bondou.

ON the 2d of December 1795 I took my departure from the hospitable mansion of Dr. Laidley. I was fortunately provided with a Negro servant, who spoke both the English and Mandingo tongues. His name was *Johnson.* He was a native of this part of Africa; and having in his youth been conveyed to Jamaica as a slave, he had been made free, and taken to England by his master, where he had resided many years; and at length found his way back to his native country. As he was known to Dr. Laidley, the Doctor recommended him to me, and I hired him as my interpreter, at the rate of ten bars monthly to be paid to himself, and five bars a-month to be paid to his wife during his absence. Dr. Laidley further- more provided me with a Negro boy of his own, named *Demba;* a sprightly youth, who, besides Mandingo, spoke the language of the Serawoollies, an inland people (of whom mention will hereafter be made) residing on the banks of the Senegal; and to induce him to behave well, the Doctor promised him his freedom on his return, in case I should report favourably of his fidelity and services. I was furnished with a horse for myself (a small, but very hardy and spirited beast, which cost me to the value of £7 : 10s.), and two asses for my interpreter and servant. My baggage was light, consisting chiefly of provisions for two days ; a small assortment of beads, amber, and tobacco, for the purchase of a fresh supply, as I proceeded ; a few changes of linen, and other necessary apparel ; an umbrella, a pocket sextant, a magnetic compass, and a thermometer ; together with two fowling-pieces, two pairs of pistols, and some other small articles.

A freeman (a Bushreen or Mahomedan), named Madiboo, who was travelling to the kingdom of Bambarra, and two Slatees or slave-merchants of the Serawoolli nation, and of the same sect, who were going to Bondou, offered their services as far as they intended respectively to proceed ; as did likewise a Negro named Tami (also a Mahomedan), a native of Kasson, who had been employed some years by Dr. Laidley as a blacksmith, and was returning to his native country with the savings of his labours. All these men travelled on foot, driving their asses before them.

Thus I had no less than six attendants, all of whom had been taught to regard me with great respect, and to consider that their safe return hereafter to the countries on the Gambia would depend on my preservation.

Dr. Laidley himself, and Messrs. Ainsley, with a number of their domestics, kindly determined to accompany me the first two days ; and, I believe, they secretly thought they should never see me afterwards.

We reached Jindey the same day, having crossed the Walli creek, a branch of the Gambia, and rested at the house of a black woman, who had formerly been the *chere amie* of a white trader named Hewett; and who, in consequence thereof, was called, by way of distinction, *Seniora*. In the evening we walked out to see an adjoining village, belonging to a Slatee named Jemaffo Mamadoo, the richest of all the Gambia traders. We found him at home; and he thought so highly of the honour done him by this visit that he presented us with a fine bullock, which was immediately killed, and part of it dressed for our evening's repast.

The Negroes do not go to supper till late, and in order to amuse ourselves while our beef was preparing, a Mandingo was desired to relate some diverting stories; in listening to which, and smoking tobacco, we spent three hours. These stories bear some resemblance to those in the Arabian Nights' Entertainments; but, in general, are of a more ludicrous cast. I shall here abridge one of them for the reader's amusement.

STORY OF CATCHING A LIVE LION.

"Many years ago the people of Doomasansa (a town on the Gambia) were much annoyed by the visit of a lion, that nightly preyed upon their cattle. By continuing his depredations, the people were at length so enraged, that a party of them resolved to go out and hunt the monster. They accordingly proceeded in search of the common enemy, whom they found concealed in a thicket. They immediately fired at him, and were lucky enough to wound him in such a manner that, in springing from the thicket towards the people, he fell down among the grass and was unable to rise. The animal, however, showed such appearance of vigour that nobody cared to approach him singly; and a consultation was held as to the best means of taking him alive. This plan, it was thought, would not only furnish undeniable proof of their prowess, but have the additional advantage of enabling them to sell him to the Europeans, it being resolved to convey him to the coast. While some persons proposed one plan, and some another, an old man offered the following scheme: —'Strip the roof of a house of its thatch, and carry the bamboo frame (the pieces of which are well secured together by thongs), and throw it over the lion. If in approaching him he should attempt to spring upon us, then will we have nothing to do but to let down the roof upon ourselves and fire at the lion through the rafters.'

"This proposition was approved and adopted. The thatch was taken from the roof of a hut, and the lion-hunters, supporting the fabric, marched courageously to the field of battle ; each person carrying a gun in one hand and bearing his share of the roof on the opposite shoulder. In this manner they approached the enemy ; but the beast had by this time recovered his strength ; and such was the fierceness of his countenance, that the hunters, instead of proceeding any further, thought it prudent to provide for their own safety by covering themselves with the roof. Unfortunately, the lion was two nimble for them ; for, making a spring while the roof was setting down, both the beast and his pursuers were caught in the same cage, and the lion devoured them at his leisure, to the great astonishment and mortification of the people of Doomasansa." As might be expected the story became the subject of laughter and derision in the neighbouring countries, and nothing will enrage an inhabitant so much as to ask him, " Can you catch a lion alive ?"

About one o'clock in the afternoon of the 3d of December I took my leave of Dr. Laidley and Messrs. Ainsley, and rode slowly into the woods. I had now before me a boundless forest, and a country, the inhabitants of which were strangers to civilised life, and to most of whom a white man was the object of curiosity or plunder. I reflected that I had parted from the last European I might probably behold, and perhaps quitted for ever the comforts of Christian society. Thoughts like these would necessarily cast a gloom over the mind, and I rode musing along for about three miles, when I was awakened from my reverie by a body of people, who came running up and stopped the asses, giving me to understand that I must go with them to Peckaba, to present myself to the king of Walli, or pay customs to them. I endeavoured to make them comprehend that as the object of my journey was not traffic, I ought not to be subjected to a tax like the Slatees and other merchants who travel for gain ; but I reasoned to no purpose. They said it was usual for travellers of all descriptions to make a present to the king of Walli, and without doing so I could not be permitted to proceed. As they were more numerous than my attendants, and withal very noisy, I thought it prudent to comply with their demand, and having presented them with four bars of tobacco for the king's use, I was permitted to continue my journey, and at sunset reached a village near Kootacunda, where we rested for the night.

In the morning of December 4th I passed Kootacunda, the last town of Walli, and stopped about an hour at a small adjoining village to pay customs to an officer of the king of Woolli. We rested the ensuing night at a village called

Tabajang, and at noon the next day (December 5th) we reached Medina, the capital of the king of Woolli's dominions.

The kingdom of Woolli is bounded by Walli on the west, by the Gambia on the south, by the small river Walli on the north-west, by Bondou on the north-east, and on the east by the Simbani wilderness.

The country everywhere rises into gentle acclivities, which are generally covered with extensive woods, and the towns are situated in the intermediate valleys. Each town is surrounded by a tract of cultivated land, the produce of which, I presume, is found sufficient to supply the wants of the inhabitants ; for the soil appeared to me to be everywhere fertile except near the tops of the ridges, where the red ironstone and stunted shrubs sufficiently marked the boundaries between fertility and barrenness. The chief products are cotton, tobacco, and esculent vegetables ; all which are raised in the valleys, the rising grounds being appropriated to different sorts of corn.

trade lands

The inhabitants are Mandingoes ; and, like most of the Mandingo nations, are divided into two great sects—the Mahomedans, who are called *Bushreens*, and the Pagans, who are called indiscriminately *Kafirs* (unbelievers) and *Sonakies* (*i.e.* men who drink strong liquors). The Pagan natives are by far the most numerous, and the government of the country is in their hands, for though the most respectable among the Bushreens are frequently consulted in affairs of importance, yet they are never permitted to take any share in the executive government, which rests solely in the hands of the *Mansa*, or sovereign, and great officers of the state. Of these the first in point of rank is the presumptive heir of the crown, who is called the *Farbanna ;* next to him are the *Alkaids*, or provin-

Pays attention to sects

cial governors, who are more frequently called *Keamos*. Then
follow the two grand divisions of freemen and slaves ; of the
former, the Slatees, so frequently mentioned in the preceding
pages, are considered as the principal ; but in all classes great
respect is paid to the authority of aged men.

On the death of the reigning monarch, his eldest son (if he
has attained the age of manhood) succeeds to the regal authority. If there is no son, or if the son is under the age of
discretion, a meeting of the great men is held, and the late
monarch's nearest relation (commonly his brother) is called to
the government, not as regent, or guardian to the infant son,
but in full right, and to the exclusion of the minor. The
charges of the government are defrayed by occasional tributes
from the people, and by duties on goods transported across the
country. Travellers, on going from the Gambia towards the
interior, pay customs in European merchandise. On returning
they pay in iron and *shea-toulou ;* these taxes are paid at
every town.

Medina,* the capital of the kingdom, at which I was now
arrived, is a place of considerable extent, and may contain
from eight hundred to one thousand houses. It is fortified in
the common African manner, by a surrounding high wall
built of clay, and an outward fence of pointed stakes and
prickly bushes ; but the walls are neglected, and the outward
fence has suffered considerably from the active hands of busy
housewives, who pluck up the stakes for firewood. I obtained
a lodging at one of the king's near relations, who apprised me
that at my introduction to the king I must not presume *to*

---

* Medina, in the Arabic, signifies a city. The name is not uncommon
among the Negroes, and has probably been borrowed from the Mahomedans.

shake hands with him. It was not usual, he said, to allow this liberty to strangers. Thus instructed, I went in the afternoon to pay my respects to the sovereign and ask permission to pass through his territories to Bondou. The king's name was *Jatta.* He was the same venerable old man of whom so favourable an account was transmitted by Major Houghton.⁶ I found him seated upon a mat before the door of his hut; a number of men and women were arranged on each side, who were singing and clapping their hands. I saluted him respectfully, and informed him of the purport of my visit. He graciously replied, that he not only gave me leave to pass through his country, but would offer up prayers for my safety. On this, one of my attendants, seemingly in return for the king's condescension, began to sing, or rather to roar, an Arabic song ; at every pause of which, the king himself, and all the people present, struck their hands against their foreheads, and exclaimed, with devout and affecting solemnity, *Amen, Amen.** The king told me, furthermore, that I should have a guide the day following, who would conduct me safely to the frontier of his kingdom. I then took my leave, and in the evening sent the king an order upon Dr. Laidley for three gallons of rum, and received in return great store of provisions. *reciprocity*

Early next morning (Dec. 6th) I went to the king a second time, to learn if the guide was ready. I found his majesty

---

* It may seem from hence that the king was a Mahomedan; but I was assured to the contrary. He joined in prayer on this occasion probably from the mere dictates of his benevolent mind; considering perhaps that prayers to the Almighty, offered up with true devotion and sincerity, were equally acceptable whether from Bushreen or Pagan.

sitting upon a bullock's hide, warming himself before a large fire ; for the Africans are sensible of the smallest variation in the temperature of the air, and frequently complain of cold when a European is oppressed with heat. He received me with a benevolent countenance, and tenderly entreated me to desist from my purpose of travelling into the interior, telling me that Major Houghton had been killed in his route, and that, if I followed his footsteps, I should probably meet with his fate. He said that I must not judge of the people of the eastern country by those of Woolli ; that the latter were acquainted with white men and respected them ; whereas the people of the east had never seen a white man, and would certainly destroy me. I thanked the king for his affectionate solicitude, but told him that I had considered the matter, and was determined, notwithstanding all dangers, to proceed. The king shook his head, but desisted from further persuasion, and told me the guide should be ready in the afternoon.

About two o'clock, the guide appearing, I went and took my last farewell of the good old king, and in three hours reached Konjour, a small village, where we determined to rest for the night. Here I purchased a fine sheep for some beads, and my Serawoolli attendants killed it with all the ceremonies prescribed by their religion ; part of it was dressed for supper, after which a dispute arose between one of the Serawoolli Negroes and Johnson, my interpreter, about the sheep's horns. The former claimed the horns as his perquisite, for having acted the part of our butcher, and Johnson contested the claim. I settled the matter by giving a horn to each of them. This trifling incident is mentioned as introductory to what follows ; for it appeared on inquiry that these horns were highly valued as being easily convertible into portable sheaths, or cases, for containing and keeping secure certain charms or amulets called *saphies*, which the Negroes constantly wear about them. These saphies are prayers, or rather sentences from the Koran, which the Mahomedan priests write on scraps of paper, and sell to the simple natives, who consider them to possess very extraordinary virtues. Some of the Negroes wear them to guard themselves against the bite of snakes or alligators, and on this occasion the saphie is commonly enclosed in a snake's or alligator's skin, and tied round the ankle. Others have recourse to them in time of war to protect their persons against hostile weapons ; but the common use to which these amulets are applied is to prevent or cure bodily diseases, to preserve from hunger and thirst, and generally to conciliate the favour of superior powers under all the circumstances and occurrences of life.*

In this case it is impossible not to admire the wonderful contagion of superstition ; for notwithstanding that the majority of the Negroes are pagans, and absolutely reject the doctrines of Mahomet, I did not meet with a man, whether a Bushreen or Kafir, who was not fully persuaded of the powerful efficacy of these amulets. The truth is, that all the natives of this part of Africa consider the art of writing as bordering on magic ; and it is not in the doctrines of the Prophet, but in the arts of the magician, that their confidence is placed. It will hereafter be seen that I was myself lucky enough, in circumstances of distress, to turn the popular credulity in this respect to good account.

* I believe that similar charms or amulets, under the names of *domini*, *grigri*, *fetich*, etc. etc., are common in all parts of Africa.

On the 7th * I departed from Konjour, and slept at a
village called Malla (or Mallaing); and on the 8th, about
noon, I arrived at Kolor, a considerable town, near the entrance
into which I observed, hanging upon a tree, a sort of mas-
querade habit, made of the bark of trees, which I was told on
inquiry belonged to

MUMBO JUMBO.[7]

This is a strange bugbear, common to all the Mandingo
towns, and much employed by the pagan natives in keeping
their women in subjection ; for, as the Kafirs are not restricted
in the number of their wives, every one marries as many as he
can conveniently maintain ; and as it frequently happens that
the ladies disagree among themselves, family quarrels sometimes rise to such a height that the authority of the husband
can no longer preserve peace in his household. In such cases,
the interposition of Mumbo Jumbo is called in, and is always
decisive.

This strange minister of justice (who is supposed to be
either the husband himself, or some person instructed by him),
disguised in the dress that has been mentioned, and armed
with the rod of public authority, announces his coming
(whenever his services are required) by loud and dismal
screams in the woods near the town. He begins the panto-
mime at the approach of night; and as soon as it is dark he
enters the town, and proceeds to the Bentang, at which all
the inhabitants immediately assemble.

It may be easily supposed that this exhibition is not
much relished by the women ; for as the person in disguise is

* December 1795.

MUMBO JUMBO.—Page 34.

entirely unknown to them, every married female suspects that the visit may possibly be intended for herself; but they dare not refuse to appear when they are summoned; and the ceremony commences with songs and dances, which continue till midnight, about which time Mumbo fixes on the offender. This unfortunate victim being thereupon immediately seized, is stripped naked, tied to a post, and severely scourged with Mumbo's rod, amidst the shouts and derision of the whole assembly; and it is remarkable that the rest of the women are the loudest in their exclamations on this occasion against their unhappy sister. Daylight puts an end to this indecent and unmanly revel. *Opinion*

As there was no water to be procured on the road, we travelled with great expedition until we reached Tambacunda; and departing from thence early the next morning (the 10th), we reached in the evening Kooniakary, a town of nearly the same magnitude as Kolor. About noon on the 11th we arrived at Koojar, the frontier town of Woolli towards Bondou, from which it is separated by an intervening wilderness of two days' journey.

The guide appointed by the king of Woolli was now to return, and I presented him with some amber for his trouble. I was now informed that it was not possible at all times to procure water in the wilderness. I therefore made inquiry for men who would serve both as guides and water-bearers during my journey across it. Three Negroes (elephant-hunters) offered their services for these purposes, which I accepted, and paid them three bars each in advance. The day being far spent, I determined to pass the night in my present quarters.

White supremacy

The inhabitants of Koojar, though not wholly unaccustomed to the sight of Europeans (most of them having occasionally visited the countries on the Gambia), beheld me with a mixture of curiosity and reverence ; and in the evening invited me to see a *neobering,* or wrestling-match, at the Bentang. This is an exhibition very common in all the Mandingo countries. The spectators arranged themselves in a circle, leaving the intermediate space for the wrestlers, who were strong active young men, full of emulation, and accustomed, I suppose, from their infancy to this sort of exertion. Stripped of their clothing, except a short pair of drawers, and having their skin anointed with oil or *shea* butter, the combatants approached each other on all fours, parrying with and occasionally extending a hand for some time, till at length one of them sprang forward and caught his rival by the knee. Great dexterity and skill were now displayed, but the contest was decided by superior strength ; and I think that few Europeans would have been able to cope with the conqueror. The combatants were animated by the music of a drum, by which their actions were in some measure regulated.

The wrestling was succeeded by a dance, in which many performers assisted, all of whom were provided with little bells, which were fastened to their legs and arms ; and here, too, the drum regulated their motions. It was beaten with a crooked stick, which the drummer held in his right hand, occasionally using his left to deaden the sound, and thus vary the music. The drum is likewise applied on these occasions to keep order among the spectators, by imitating the sound of certain Mandingo sentences : for example, when the wrestling-match is about to begin, the drummer strikes what is understood to signify *ali bœ see,*—sit all down ; upon which the spectators immediately seat themselves ; and when the combatants are to begin he strikes *amuta amuta*—take hold, take hold.

In the course of the evening I was presented, by way of refreshment, with a liquor which tasted so much like the strong beer of my native country (and very good beer, too) as to induce me to inquire into its composition ; and I learnt, with some degree of surprise, that it was actually made from corn which had been previously malted, much in the same manner as barley is malted in Great Britain. A root yielding a grateful bitter was used in lieu of hops, the name of which I forgot ; but the corn which yields the wort is the *Holcus spicatus* of botanists.

Early in the morning (the 12th) I found that one of the elephant-hunters had absconded with the money he had received from me in part of wages ; and in order to prevent the other two from following his example I made them instantly fill their calabashes (or gourds) with water, and as the sun rose I entered the wilderness that separates the kingdoms of Woolli and Bondou.

We had not travelled more than a mile before my attendants insisted on stopping, that they might prepare a saphie or charm, to insure us a safe journey. This was done by muttering a few sentences and spitting upon a stone, which was thrown before us on the road. The same ceremony was repeated three times, after which the Negroes proceeded with the greatest confidence ; every one being firmly persuaded that the stone (like the scape-goat) had carried with it everything that could induce superior powers to visit us with misfortune.

We continued our journey without stopping any more till noon, when we came to a large tree, called by the natives *Meema Taba.* It had a very singular appearance, being decorated with innumerable rags or scraps of cloth, which persons travelling across the wilderness had at different times tied to the branches; probably, at first, to inform the traveller that water was to be found near it; but the custom has been so greatly sanctioned by time, that nobody now presumes to pass without hanging up something. I followed the example, and suspended a handsome piece of cloth on one of the boughs; and being told that either a well or pool of water was at no great distance, I ordered the Negroes to unload the asses that we might give them corn, and regale ourselves with the provisions we had brought. In the meantime I sent one of the elephant-hunters to look for the well, intending, if water was to be obtained, to rest here for the night. A pool was found, but the water was thick and muddy, and the Negro discovered near it the remains of a fire recently extinguished, and the fragments of provisions; which afforded a proof that it had been lately visited either by travellers or banditti. The fears of my attendants supposed the latter; and believing that robbers lurked near us I was persuaded to change my resolution of resting here all night, and proceed to another watering-place, which, I was assured, we might reach early in the evening.

We departed accordingly, but it was eight o'clock at night before we came to the watering-place; and, being now sufficiently fatigued with so long a day's journey, we kindled a large fire and lay down, surrounded by our cattle, on the bare ground, more than a gunshot from any bush—the Negroes agreeing to keep watch by turns to prevent surprise.

I know not indeed that any danger was justly to be dreaded, but the Negroes were unaccountably apprehensive of banditti during the whole of the journey. As soon, therefore, as daylight appeared, we filled our *soofroos* (skins) and calabashes at the pool, and set out for Tallika, the first town in Bondou, which we reached about eleven o'clock in the forenoon (the 13th of December). I cannot, however, take leave of Woolli without observing that I was everywhere well received by the natives, and that the fatigues of the day were generally alleviated by a hearty welcome at night; and, although the African mode of living was at first unpleasant to me, yet I found at length that custom surmounted trifling inconveniences, and made everything palatable and easy.

CHAPTER IV.

Tallika—A refractory Ass—Cross the Neriko—Arrival at Koorkarany—Fishery on the River Falemé—Naye or Nayemow—Cross the Falemé, and arrive at Fatteconda, Capital of Bondou—Interview with the King—Introduction to the Seraglio—Depart on friendly terms—Description of Bondou and the Foulahs.

TALLIKA, the frontier town of Bondou towards Woolli, is inhabited chiefly by Foulahs of the Mohamedan religion, who live in considerable affluence, partly by furnishing provisions to the *coffles*, or caravans, that pass through the town, and partly by the sale of ivory, obtained by hunting elephants; in which employment the young men are generally very successful. Here an officer belonging to the king of Bondou constantly resides, whose business it is to give timely information of the arrival of the caravans, which are taxed according to the number of loaded asses that arrive at Tallika.

I took up my residence at this officer's house, and agreed with him to accompany me to Fatteconda, the residence of the king, for which he was to receive five bars; and before my departure I wrote a few lines to Dr. Laidley,[8] and gave my letter to the master of a caravan bound for the Gambia. This caravan consisted of nine or ten people, with five asses loaded with ivory. The large teeth are conveyed in nets, two on each side of the ass; the small ones are wrapped up in skins and secured with ropes.

We left Tallika (Dec. 14th) and rode on very peaceably for about two miles, when a violent quarrel arose between two of my fellow-travellers—one of whom was the blacksmith—in the course of which they bestowed some opprobrious terms upon each other ; and it is worthy of remark, that an African will sooner forgive a blow than a term of reproach applied to his ancestors.

"Strike me, but do not curse my mother," *African morals* *Humour* is a common expression even among the slaves. This sort of abuse, therefore, so enraged one of the disputants that he drew his cutlass upon the blacksmith, and would certainly have ended the dispute in a very serious manner if the others had not laid hold of him and wrested the cutlass from him. I was obliged to interfere and put an end to this disagreeable business, by desiring the blacksmith to be silent, and telling the other, who I thought was in the wrong, that if he attempted in future to draw his cutlass, or molest any of my attendants, I should look upon him as a robber, and shoot him without further ceremony. This threat had the desired effect, and we marched sullenly along till the afternoon, when we arrived at a number of small villages scattered over an open and fertile plain. At one of these, called Ganado, we took up our residence for the night. Here an exchange of presents and a good supper terminated all animosities among my attendants ; and the night was far advanced before any of us thought of going to sleep. We were amused by an itinerant *singing-man*,* who told a number of diverting stories, and played some sweet airs, by

* These are a sort of travelling bards and musicians, who sing extempore songs in praise of those who employ them. A fuller account of them will be given hereafter.

blowing his breath upon a bowstring, and striking it at the same time with a stick.

At daybreak (Dec. 15th) my fellow-travellers, the Sera-woollies, took leave of me, with many prayers for my safety. About a mile from Ganado we crossed a considerable branch of the Gambia, called Neriko. The banks were steep and covered with *mimosas;* and I observed in the mud a number of large mussels, but the natives do not eat them. About noon, the sun being exceedingly hot, we rested two hours in the shade of a tree, and purchased some milk and pounded corn from some Foulah herdsmen, and at sunset reached a town called Koorkarany, where the blacksmith had some relations ; and here we rested two days.

Koorkarany is a Mahomedan town surrounded by a high wall, and is provided with a mosque. Here I was shown a number of Arabic manuscripts, particularly a copy of the book before mentioned, called *Al Shara.* The *Maraboo,*[9] or priest, in whose possession it was, read and explained to me in Man-dingo many of the most remarkable passages ; and in return I showed him Richardson's Arabic grammar,[10] which he very much admired.

On the evening of the second day (Dec. 17th) we departed from Koorkarany. We were joined by a young man who was travelling to Fatteconda for salt ; and as night set in we reached Dooggii, a small village about three miles from Koor-karany.

Provisions were here so cheap that I purchased a bullock for six small stones of amber ; for I found my company increase or diminish according to the good fare they met with.

Early in the morning (Dec. 18th) we departed from Dooggii.

Reciprocity of literature!

An accession of Foulahs and other people gave us a formidable appearance, and we were now under no apprehension of being plundered in the woods. On the way the Negroes took a curious method to make a very refractory ass tractable. They cut a forked stick, and put the forked part into the ass's mouth, like the bit of a bridle, tied the two smaller parts together above his head, leaving the lower part of the stick of sufficient length to strike against the ground if the ass should attempt to put his head down. After this, the ass walked along quietly and gravely enough, taking care, after some practice, to hold his head sufficiently high to prevent the stones or roots of trees from striking against the end of the stick, which experience had taught him would give a severe shock to his teeth. This contrivance produced a ludicrous appearance, but my fellow-travellers told me it was constantly adopted by the Slatees, and always proved effectual.

In the evening we arrived at a few scattered villages surrounded with extensive cultivation ; at one of which, called Buggil, we passed the night in a miserable hut, having no other bed than a bundle of corn-stalks, and no provisions but what we brought with us. The wells here are dug with great ingenuity, and are very deep. I measured one of the bucket-ropes, and found the depth of the well to be twenty-eight fathoms.

We departed from Buggil (Dec. 19th) and travelled along a dry, stony height covered with *mimosas*, till mid-day, when the land sloped towards the east, and we descended into a deep valley, in which I observed abundance of whinstone and white quartz. Pursuing our course to the eastward, along this valley, in the bed of an exhausted river-course, we came to a large village, where we intended to lodge. We found many of the natives dressed in a thin French gauze, which they called *byqui;* this being a light airy dress and well calculated to display the shape of their persons, is much esteemed by the ladies. The manners of these females, however, did not correspond with their dress, for they were rude and troublesome in the highest degree ; they surrounded me in numbers, begging for amber, beads, etc., and were so vehement in their solicitations that I found it impossible to resist them. They tore my cloak, cut the buttons from my boy's clothes, and were proceeding to other outrages, when I mounted my horse and rode off, followed for half-a-mile by a body of these harpies.

In the evening we reached Soobrudooka, and as my company was numerous (being fourteen) I purchased a sheep and abundance of corn for supper; after which we lay down by the bundles, and passed an uncomfortable night in a heavy dew.

We departed from Soobrudooka (Dec. 20th), and at two o'clock reached a large village situated on the banks of the Falemé river, which is here rapid and rocky. The natives were employed in fishing in various ways. The large fish were taken in long baskets made of split cane, and placed in a strong current which was created by walls of stone built across the stream, certain open places being left through which the water rushed with great force. Some of these baskets were more than twenty feet long, and when once the fish had entered one of them, the force of the stream prevented it from returning. The small fish were taken in great numbers in hand-nets, which the natives weave of cotton and use with great dexterity. The fish last mentioned are about the size of sprats, and are prepared for sale in different ways ; the most common is by pounding them entire as they come from the stream in a wooden mortar, and exposing them to dry in the sun, in large lumps like sugar-loaves. It may be supposed that the smell is not very agreeable; but in the Moorish countries to the north of the Senegal, where fish is scarcely known, this preparation is esteemed as a luxury, and sold to considerable advantage. The manner of using it by the natives is by dissolving a piece of this black loaf in boiling water, and mixing it with their *kouskous*.

I thought it very singular, at this season of the year, to find the banks of the Falemé everywhere covered with large and beautiful fields of corn, but on examination I found it was not the same species of grain as is commonly cultivated on the Gambia; it is called by the natives *Manio*, and grows in the dry season, is very prolific, and is reaped in the month of January. It is the same which, from the depending position of the ear, is called by botanical writers *Holcus cernuus.*[12]

On returning to the village, after an excursion to the riverside to inspect the fishery, an old Moorish shereef came to bestow his blessing upon me, and beg some paper to write saphies upon. This man had seen Major Houghton in the kingdom of Kaarta, and told me that he died in the country of the Moors. I gave him a few sheets of paper, and he levied a similar tribute from the blacksmith; for it is customary for young Mussulmans to make presents to the old ones in order to obtain their blessing, which is pronounced in Arabic and received with great humility.

About three in the afternoon we continued our course along the bank of the river to the northward, till eight o'clock, when we reached Nayemow; here the hospitable master of the town received us kindly, and presented us with a bullock. In return, I gave him some amber and beads.

In the morning, having agreed for a canoe to carry over my bundles, I crossed the river, which came up to my knees as I sat on my horse; but the water is so clear, that from the high bank the bottom is visible all the way over.

About noon we entered Fatteconda, the capital of Bondou; and in a little time received an invitation to the house of a respectable Slatee; for as there are no public-houses in Africa, it is customary for strangers to stand at the Bentang, or some other place of public resort, till they are invited to a lodging by some of the inhabitants. We accepted the offer, and in an hour afterwards a person came and told me that he was sent on purpose to conduct me to the king, who was very desirous of seeing me immediately, if I was not too much fatigued.

I took my interpreter with me, and followed the messenger till we got quite out of the town and crossed some corn-fields; when suspecting some trick, I stopped and asked the guide whither he was going. Upon which he pointed to a man sitting under a tree at some little distance, and told me that the king frequently gave audience in that retired manner, in order to avoid a crowd of people, and that nobody but myself and my interpreter must approach him. When I advanced, the king desired me to come and sit by him upon the mat; and after hearing my story, on which he made no observation, he asked if I wished to purchase any slaves or gold: being answered in the negative, he seemed rather surprised, but desired me to come to him in the evening and he would give me some provisions.

This monarch was called Almami, a Moorish name, though

I was told that he was not a Mahomedan, but a Kafir, or
Pagan.   I had heard that he had acted towards Major
Houghton with great unkindness, and caused him to be plundered.   His behaviour, therefore, towards myself at this interview, though much more civil than I expected, was far from
freeing me from uneasiness.   I still apprehended some double
dealing ; and as I was now entirely in his power I thought
it best to smooth the way by a present ; accordingly I took
with me in the evening one canister of gunpowder, some
amber, tobacco, and my umbrella ; and as I considered that
my bundles would inevitably be searched, I concealed some
few articles in the roof of the hut where I lodged, and I put
on my new blue coat in order to preserve it.

All the houses belonging to the king and his family are
surrounded by a lofty mud wall, which converts the whole
into a kind of citadel.   The interior is subdivided into different
courts.   At the first place of entrance I observed a man
standing with a musket on his shoulder ; and I found the
way to the presence very intricate, leading through many
passages, with sentinels placed at the different doors.   When
we came to the entrance of the court in which the king resides,
both my guide and interpreter, according to custom, took off
their sandals ; and the former pronounced the king's name
aloud, repeating it till he was answered from within.   We
found the monarch sitting upon a mat, and two attendants
with him.   I repeated what I had before told him concerning
the object of my journey, and my reasons for passing through
his country.   He seemed, however, but half satisfied.   The
notion of travelling for curiosity was quite new to him.   He
thought it impossible, he said, that any man in his senses

would undertake so dangerous a journey, merely to look at the country and its inhabitants; however, when I offered to show him the contents of my portmanteau, and everything belonging to me, he was convinced; and it was evident that his suspicion had arisen from a belief that every white man must of necessity be a trader. When I had delivered my presents, he seemed well pleased, and was particularly delighted with the umbrella, which he repeatedly furled and unfurled, to the great admiration of himself and his two attendants, who could not for some time comprehend the use of this wonderful machine. After this I was about to take my leave, when the king, desiring me to stop awhile, began a long preamble in favour of the whites, extolling their immense wealth and good dispositions. He next proceeded to an eulogium on my blue coat, of which the yellow buttons seemed particularly to catch his fancy; and he concluded by entreating me to present him with it, assuring me, for my consolation under the loss of it, that he would wear it on all public occasions, and inform every one who saw it of my great liberality towards him. The request of an African prince in his own dominions, particularly when made to a stranger, comes little short of a command. It is only a way of obtaining by gentle means what he can, if he pleases, take by force; and as it was against my interest to offend him by a refusal, I very quietly took off my coat, the only good one in my possession, and laid it at his feet.

In return for my compliance he presented me with great plenty of provisions, and desired to see me again in the morning. I accordingly attended, and found him sitting upon his bed. He told me he was sick, and wished to have a little blood taken from him; but I had no sooner tied up his arm and displayed the lancet, than his courage failed, and he begged me to postpone the operation till the afternoon, as he felt himself, he said, much better than he had been, and thanked me kindly for my readiness to serve him. He then observed that his women were very desirous to see me, and requested that I would favour them with a visit. An attendant was ordered to conduct me, and I had no sooner entered the court appropriated to the ladies, than the whole seraglio surrounded me, some begging for physic, some for amber, and all of them desirous of trying that great African specific, *blood-letting*. They were ten or twelve in number, most of them young and handsome, and wearing on their heads ornaments of gold and beads of amber.

They rallied me with a good deal of gaiety on different subjects, particularly upon the whiteness of my skin and the prominency of my nose. They insisted that both were artificial. The first, they said, was produced when I was an infant, by dipping me in milk; and they insisted that my nose had been pinched every day till it had acquired its present unsightly and unnatural conformation. On my part, without disputing my own deformity, I paid them many compliments on African beauty. I praised the glossy jet of their skins, and the lovely depression of their noses; but they said that flattery, or (as they emphatically termed it) *honey mouth*, was not esteemed in Bondou. In return, however, for my company or my compliments (to which, by the way, they seemed not so insensible as they affected to be), they presented me with a jar of honey and some fish, which were sent to my

Women's thoughts of him

lodging, and I was desired to come again to the king a little before sunset.

I carried with me some beads and writing paper, it being usual to present some small offering on taking leave, in return for which the king gave me five drachms of gold, observing that it was but a trifle, and given out of pure friendship, but would be of use to me in travelling for the purchase of provision. He seconded this act of kindness by one still greater, politely telling me that though it was customary to examine the baggage of every traveller passing through his country, yet, in the present instance, he would dispense with that ceremony ; adding, I was at liberty to depart when I pleased.

Accordingly, on the morning of the 23d we left Fatteconda, and about eleven o'clock came to a small village, where we determined to stop for the rest of the day.

In the afternoon, my fellow-travellers informed me that as this was the boundary between Bondou and Kajaaga, and dangerous for travellers, it would be necessary to continue our journey by night, until we should reach a more hospitable part of the country. I agreed to the proposal, and hired two people for guides through the woods ; and as soon as the people of the village were gone to sleep (the moon shining bright) we set out. The stillness of the air, the howling of the wild beasts, and the deep solitude of the forest, made the scene solemn and impressive. Not a word was uttered by any of us but in a whisper ; all were attentive, and every one anxious to show his sagacity, by pointing out to me the wolves and hyænas as they glided like shadows from one thicket to another. Towards morning we arrived at a village

Not a word was uttered by any of us but in a whisper; and every one was anxious to show his sagacity by pointing out to me the wolves and hyenas as they glided like shadows from one thicket to another.—Page 50.

called Kimmoo, where our guides awakened one of their acquaintances, and we stopped to give the asses some corn and roast a few ground-nuts for ourselves. At daylight we resumed our journey, and in the afternoon arrived at Joag in the kingdom of Kajaaga.

Being now in a country and among people differing in many respects from those that have as yet fallen under our observation, I shall, before I proceed further, give some account of Bondou (the territory we have left) and its inhabitants, the Foulahs, the description of whom I purposely reserved for this part of my work.

Bondou is bounded on the east by Bambouk ; on the southeast and south by Tenda and the Sambani wilderness ; on the south-west by Woolli ; on the west by Foota Torra ; and on the north by Kajaaga.

The country, like that of Woolli, is very generally covered with woods, but the land is more elevated, and towards the Falemé river rises into considerable hills. In native fertility the soil is not surpassed, I believe, by any part of Africa.

From the central situation of Bondou, between the Gambia and Senegal rivers, it is become a place of great resort ; both for the Slatees, who generally pass through it in going from the coast to the interior countries, and for occasional traders, who frequently come hither from the inland countries to purchase salt.

These different branches of commerce are conducted principally by Mandingoes and Serawoollies, who have settled in the country. These merchants likewise carry on a considerable trade with Gedumah and other Moorish countries, bartering corn and blue cotton cloths for salt, which they again barter in Dentilla and other districts for iron, shea butter, and small quantities of gold-dust. They likewise sell a variety of sweet-smelling gums packed up in small bags, containing each about a pound. These gums, being thrown on hot embers, produce a very pleasant odour, and are used by the Mandingoes for perfuming their huts and clothes.

The customs or duties on travellers are very heavy ; in almost every town an ass-load pays a bar of European merchandise ; and at Fatteconda, the residence of the king, one Indian baft, or a musket, and six bottles of gunpowder, are exacted as a common tribute. By means of these duties, the king of Bondou is well supplied with arms and ammunition ; a circumstance which makes him formidable to the neighbouring states.

The inhabitants differ in their complexions and national manners from the Mandingoes and Serawoollies, with whom they are frequently at war. Some years ago the king of Bondou crossed the Falemé river with a numerous army, and after a short and bloody campaign totally defeated the forces of Samboo, king of Bambouk, who was obliged to sue for peace, and surrender to him all the towns along the eastern bank of the Falemé.

The Foulahs in general (as has been observed in a former chapter) are of a tawny complexion, with small features and soft silky hair : next to the Mandingoes they are undoubtedly the most considerable of all the nations in this part of Africa. Their original country is said to be Fooladoo, which signifies the country of the Foulahs ; but they possess at present many other kingdoms at a great distance from each other. Their complexion, however, is not exactly the same in the different districts ; in Bondou and the other kingdoms which are situated in the vicinity of the Moorish territories, they are of a more yellow complexion than in the southern states.

The Foulahs of Bondou are naturally of a mild and gentle disposition, but the uncharitable maxims of the Koran have made them less hospitable to strangers, and more reserved in their behaviour, than the Mandingoes. They evidently consider all the Negro natives as their inferiors ; and when talking of different nations, always rank themselves among the white people.

Their government differs from that of the Mandingoes chiefly in this, that they are more immediately under the influence of the Mahomedan laws ; for all the chief men (the king excepted) and a large majority of the inhabitants of Bondou are Mussulmans, and the authority and laws of the Prophet are everywhere looked upon as sacred and decisive. In the exercise of their faith, however, they are not very intolerant towards such of their countrymen as still retain their ancient superstitions. Religious persecution is not known among them, nor is it necessary ; for the system of Mahomet is made to extend itself by means abundantly more efficacious. By establishing small schools in the different towns, where many of the Pagan as well as Mahomedan children are taught to read the Koran and instructed in the tenets of the Prophet, the Mahomedan priests fix a bias on the minds, and form the character of their young disciples, which no accidents of life can ever afterwards remove or alter. Many of these little schools I visited in my progress through the country, and observed with pleasure the great docility and submissive deportment of the children, and heartily wished they had had better instructors and a purer religion.

Excuse for misinterpretation

With the Mahomedan faith is also introduced the Arabic language, with which most of the Foulahs have a slight acquaintance. The native tongue abounds very much in liquids, but there is something unpleasant in the manner of pronouncing it. A stranger, on hearing the common conversation of two Foulahs, would imagine that they were scolding each other.

The industry of the Foulahs, in the occupations of pasturage and agriculture, is everywhere remarkable. Even on the banks of the Gambia, the greater part of the corn is raised by them; and their herds and flocks are more numerous and in better condition than those of the Mandingoes; but in Bondou they are opulent in a high degree, and enjoy all the necessaries of life in the greatest profusion. They display great skill in the management of their cattle, making them extremely gentle by kindness and familiarity. On the approach of night they are collected from the woods and secured in folds, called korrees, which are constructed in the neighbourhood of the different villages. In the middle of each korree is erected a small hut, wherein one or two of the herdsmen keep watch during the night, to prevent the cattle from being stolen, and to keep up the fires which are kindled round the korree to frighten away the wild beasts.

The cattle are milked in the mornings and evenings: the milk is excellent, but the quantity obtained from any one cow is by no means so great as in Europe. The Foulahs use the milk chiefly as an article of diet, and that not until it is quite sour. The cream which it affords is very thick, and is converted into butter by stirring it violently in a large calabash. This butter, when melted over a gentle fire and freed from impurities, is preserved in small earthen pots, and forms a part in most of their dishes ; it serves likewise to anoint their heads, and is bestowed very liberally on their faces and arms.

But although milk is plentiful, it is somewhat remarkable that the Foulahs, and indeed all the inhabitants of this part of Africa, are totally unacquainted with the art of making cheese. A firm attachment to the customs of their ancestors makes them view with an eye of prejudice everything that looks like innovation. The heat of the climate and the great scarcity of salt are held forth as unanswerable objections ; and the whole process appears to them too long and troublesome to be attended with any solid advantage.

Besides the cattle, which constitute the chief wealth of the Foulahs, they possess some excellent horses, the breed of which seems to be a mixture of the Arabian with the original African.

CHAPTER V.

*Kingdom of Kajaaga—Manners and Language of the Serawoollies—
Account of Joag—Arrested by King Batcheri—Robbed of half
his Goods—Commiseration of a Female Slave—Dembo Sego,
nephew of the King of Kasson, offers a Safe-conduct—Samee,
on the banks of the Senegal—Journey to Kayee, and, crossing
the Senegal, to the kingdom of Kasson.*

THE kingdom of Kajaaga, in which I was now arrived, is
called by the French Gallam ; but the name that I have
adopted is universally used by the natives. This country is
bounded on the south-east and south by Bambouk ; on the
west by Bondou and Foota Torra ; and on the north by the
river Senegal. The air and climate are, I believe, more pure
and salubrious than at any of the settlements towards the
coast ; the face of the country is everywhere interspersed with
a pleasing variety of hills and valleys ; and the windings of
the Senegal river, which descends from the rocky hills of the
interior, make the scenery on its banks very picturesque and
beautiful.

The inhabitants are called Serawoollies,[13]or (as the French
write it) *Seracolets.* Their complexion is a jet black ; they are
not to be distinguished in this respect from the Jaloffs.

The government is monarchical ; and the regal authority,
from what I experienced of it, seems to be sufficiently formid-

able. The people themselves, however, complain of no oppression, and seemed all very anxious to support the king in a contest he was going to enter into with the sovereign of Kasson. The Serawoollies are habitually a trading people; they formerly carried on a great commerce with the French in gold and slaves, and still maintain some traffic in slaves with the British factories on the Gambia. They are reckoned tolerably fair and just in their dealings, but are indefatigable in their exertions to acquire wealth, and they derive considerable profits by the sale of salt and cotton cloth in distant countries. When a Serawoolli merchant returns home from a trading expedition the neighbours immediately assemble to congratulate him upon his arrival. On these occasions the traveller displays his wealth and liberality by making a few presents to his friends; but if he has been unsuccessful, his levee is soon over, and every one looks upon him as a man of no understanding, who could perform a long journey, and (as they express it) *bring back nothing but the hair upon his head.*

Their language abounds much in gutturals, and is not so harmonious as that spoken by the Foulahs; it is, however, well worth acquiring by those who travel through this part of the African continent; it being very generally understood in the kingdoms of Kasson, Kaarta, Ludamar, and the northern parts of Bambarra. In all these countries the Serawoollies are the chief traders.

We arrived at Joag, the frontier town of this kingdom, on the 24th of December, and took up our residence at the house of the chief man, who is here no longer known by the title of *Alkaid,* but is called the *Dooty.* He was a rigid Mahomedan. but distinguished for his hospitality. This town may be supposed, on a gross computation, to contain two thousand inhabitants. It is surrounded by a high wall, in which are a number of portholes for musketry to fire through in case of an attack. Every man's possession is likewise surrounded by a wall—the whole forming so many distinct citadels; and amongst a people unacquainted with the use of artillery these walls answer all the purposes of stronger fortifications. To the westward of the town is a small river, on the banks of which the natives raise great plenty of tobacco and onions.

The same evening Madiboo Bushreen, who had accompanied me from Pisania, went to pay a visit to his father and mother, who dwelt at a neighbouring town called Dramanet. He was joined by my other attendant the blacksmith; and as soon as it was dark I was invited to see the sports of the inhabitants, it being their custom, on the arrival of strangers, to welcome them by diversions of different kinds. I found a great crowd surrounding a party who were dancing, by the light of some large fires, to the music of four drums, which were beat with great exactness and uniformity. The dances, however, consisted more in wanton gestures than in muscular exertion or graceful attitudes. The ladies vied with each other in displaying the most voluptuous movements imaginable.

About two o'clock next morning a number of horsemen came into the town, and having awakened my landlord, talked to him for some time in the Serawoolli tongue, after which they dismounted and came to the Bentang, on which I had made my bed. One of them, thinking that I was asleep, attempted to steal the musket that lay by me on the mat; but finding that he could not effect his purpose undiscovered, he desisted, and the strangers sat down by me till daylight.

I could now easily perceive, by the countenance of my interpreter Johnson, that something very unpleasant was in agitation. I was likewise surprised to see Madiboo and the blacksmith so soon returned. On inquiring the reason, Madiboo informed me, that as they were dancing at Dramanet, ten horsemen belonging to Batcheri, king of the country, with his second son at their head, had arrived there, inquiring if the white man had passed, and on being told that I was at Joag, they rode off without stopping. Madiboo added, that on hearing this he and the blacksmith hastened back to give me notice of their coming. Whilst I was listening to this narrative, the ten horsemen mentioned by Madiboo arrived ; and coming to the Bentang, dismounted and seated themselves with those who had come before, the whole being about twenty in number, forming a circle round me, and each man holding his musket in his hand. I took this opportunity to observe to my landlord, that as I did not understand the Serawoolli tongue, I hoped, whatever the men had to say, they would speak in Mandingo. To this they agreed ; and a short man, loaded with a remarkable number of saphies, opened the business in a very long harangue, informing me that I had entered the king's town without having first paid the duties or given any present to the king, and that, according to the laws of the country, my people, cattle, and baggage, were forfeited. He added, that they had received orders from the king to conduct me to Maana,* the place of his residence, and if I refused to come with them, their orders were to bring me by force ; upon his saying which, all of them rose up and asked me if I was

* Maana is within a short distance of the ruins of Fort St. Joseph, on the Senegal river, formerly a French factory.

ready. It would have been equally vain and imprudent in me to have resisted or irritated such a body of men. I therefore affected to comply with their commands, and begged them only to stop a little until I had given my horse a feed of corn and settled matters with my landlord. The poor blacksmith, who was a native of Kasson, mistook this feigned compliance for a real intention, and taking me away from the company, told me that he had always behaved towards me as if I had been his father and master, and he hoped I would not entirely ruin him by going to Maana ; adding, that as there was every reason to believe a war would soon take place between Kasson and Kajaaga, he should not only lose his little property, the savings of four years' industry, but should certainly be detained and sold as a slave, unless his friends had an opportunity of paying two slaves for his redemption. I saw this reasoning in its full force, and determined to do my utmost to preserve the blacksmith from so dreadful a fate. I therefore told the king's son that I was ready to go with him, upon condition that the blacksmith, who was an inhabitant of a distant kingdom, and entirely unconnected with me, should be allowed to stay at Joag till my return. To this they all objected, and insisted that, as we had all acted contrary to the laws, we were all equally answerable for our conduct.

I now took my landlord aside, and giving him a small present of gunpowder, asked his advice in so critical a situation. He was decidedly of opinion that I ought not to go to the king. He was fully convinced, he said, that if the king should discover anything valuable in my possession, he would not be over scrupulous about the means of obtaining it. This made me the more solicitous to conciliate matters with the king's people; and I began by observing that what I had done did not proceed from any want of respect towards the king, nor from any wish to violate his laws, but wholly from my own inexperience and ignorance, being a stranger, totally unacquainted with the laws and customs of their country. I had indeed entered the king's frontier without knowing that I was to pay the duties beforehand, but I was ready to pay them now, which I thought was all they could reasonably demand. I then tendered them as a present to the king the five drachms of gold which the king of Bondou had given me; this they accepted, but insisted on examining my baggage, which I opposed in vain. The bundles were opened, but the men were much disappointed in not finding in them so much gold and amber as they expected. They made up the deficiency, however, by taking whatever things they fancied; and after wrangling and debating with me till sunset, they departed, having first robbed me of half my goods.

These proceedings dispirited my people, and our fortitude was not strengthened by a very indifferent supper, after a long fast. Madiboo begged me to turn back, Johnson laughed at the thoughts of proceeding without money, and the blacksmith was afraid to be seen, or even to speak, lest any one should discover him to be a native of Kasson. In this disposition we passed the night by the side of a dim fire, and our situation the next day was very perplexing. It was impossible to procure provisions without money, and I knew that if I produced any beads or amber the king would immediately hear of it, and I should probably lose the few effects I had concealed. We therefore resolved to combat hunger for the day, and wait some favourable opportunity of purchasing or begging provisions.

humour

Towards evening, as I was sitting upon the Bentang chewing straws, an old female slave passing by with a basket upon her head asked me *if I had got my dinner.* As I thought she only laughed at me, I gave her no answer ; but my boy, who was sitting close by, answered for me, and told her that the king's people had robbed me of all my money. On hearing this, the good old woman, with a look of unaffected benevolence, immediately took the basket from her head, and showing me that it contained ground-nuts, asked me if I could eat them ; being answered in the affirmative, she presented me with a few handfuls, and walked away before I had time to thank her for this seasonable supply. This trifling circumstance gave me peculiar satisfaction. I reflected with pleasure on the conduct of this poor untutored slave, who, without examining into my character or circumstances, listened implicitly to the dictates of her own heart. Experience had taught her that hunger was painful, and her own distresses made her commiserate those of others.

The old woman had scarcely left me when I received information that a nephew of Demba Sego Jalla, the Mandingo king of Kasson, was coming to pay me a visit. He had been sent on an embassy to Batcheri, king of Kajaaga, to endeavour to settle the disputes which had arisen between his uncle and the latter ; but after debating the matter four days without success he was now on his return ; and hearing that a white man was at Joag, on his way to Kasson, curiosity brought him to see me. I represented to him my situation and distresses, when he frankly offered me his protection, and said he would be my guide to Kasson (provided I would set out the next morning), and be answerable for my safety. I readily and gratefully accepted his offer, and was ready, with my attendants, by day-light on the morning of the 27th of December.

My protector, whose name was Demba Sego, probably after his uncle, had a numerous retinue. Our company at leaving Joag consisted of thirty persons and six loaded asses ; and we rode on cheerfully enough for some hours, without any remark-able occurrence, until we came to a species of tree, for which my interpreter Johnson had made frequent inquiry. On finding it he desired us to stop ; and producing a white chicken, which he had purchased at Joag for the purpose, he tied it by the leg to one of the branches, and then told us we might now safely pro-ceed, for that our journey would be prosperous. This circum-stance is mentioned merely to illustrate the disposition of the Negroes, and to show the power of superstition over their minds ; for although this man had resided seven years in England, it was evident that he still retained the prejudices and notions he had imbibed in his youth. He meant this ceremony, he told me, as an offering or sacrifice to the spirits of the woods, who were, he said, a powerful race of beings of a white colour, with long flowing hair. I laughed at his folly, but could not con-demn the piety of his motives.

At noon we had reached Gungadi, a large town, where we stopped about an hour, until some of the asses that had fallen behind came up. Here I observed a number of date-trees, and a mosque built of clay, with six turrets, on the pinnacles of which were placed six ostrich eggs. A little before sunset we arrived at the town of Samee, on the banks of the Senegal, which is here a beautiful but shallow river, moving slowly over a bed of sand and gravel. The banks are high and covered with verdure, the country is open and cultivated, and the rocky hills of Felow and Bambouk add much to the beauty of the landscape.

We departed from Samee (Dec. 28th), and arrived in the afternoon at Kayee, a large village, part of which is situated on the north, and part on the south side of the river. A little above this place is a considerable cataract, where the river flows over a ledge of whinstone rock with great force ; below this, the river is remarkably black and deep ; and here it was proposed to make our cattle swim over. After hallooing and firing some muskets the people on the Kasson side observed us, and brought over a canoe to carry our baggage. I did not, however, think it possible to get the cattle down the bank, which is here more than forty feet above the water ; but the Negroes seized the horses, and launched them, one at a time, down a sort of trench or gully that was almost perpendicular, and seemed to have been worn smooth by this sort of use. After the terrified cattle had been plunged in this manner to the water's edge, every man got down as well as he could. The ferryman then took hold of the most steady of the horses by a rope, and led him into the water, paddling the canoe a little from the brink ; upon which a general attack was commenced upon the other horses, who, finding themselves pelted and kicked on all sides, unanimously plunged into the river, and followed their companion. A few boys swam in after them ; and by laving water upon them when they attempted to return, urged them onwards ; and we had the satisfaction, in about fifteen minutes, to see them all safe on the other side.

It was a matter of great difficulty to manage the asses ; their natural stubbornness of disposition made them endure a great deal of pelting and shoving before they would venture into the water; and when they had reached the middle of the stream four of them turned back, in spite of every exertion to get them forwards. Two hours were spent in getting the whole of them over; an hour more was employed in transporting the baggage; and it was near sunset before the canoe returned, when Demba Sego and myself embarked in this dangerous passage-boat, which the least motion was like to overset. The king's nephew thought this a proper time to have a peep into a tin box of mine that stood in the forepart of the canoe; and in stretching out his hand for it he unfortunately destroyed the equilibrium, and overset the canoe. Luckily we were not far advanced, and got back to the shore without much difficulty; from whence, after wringing the water from our clothes, we took a fresh departure, and were soon afterwards safely landed in Kasson.

CHAPTER VI.

Arrival at Teesee—Interview with Tiggity Sego, the King's Brother—
Detention at Teesee—Incidents at Teesee—Rapacity of Tiggity
Sego—Start for Kooniakary, the Capital of the Kingdom.

WE no sooner found ourselves safe in Kasson, than Demba
Sego told me that we were now in his uncle's
dominions, and he hoped I would consider, being now out of
danger, the obligation I owed to him, and make him a suitable
return for the trouble he had taken on my account, by a
handsome present. This, as he knew how much had been
pilfered from me at Joag, was rather an unexpected proposition ; and I began to fear that I had not much improved
my condition by crossing the water ; but as it would have
been folly to complain, I made no observation upon his conduct, and gave him seven bars of amber and some tobacco,
with which he seemed to be content.

After a long day's journey, in the course of which I
observed a number of large loose nodules of white granite,
we arrived at Teesee on the evening of December 29, and were
accommodated in Demba Sego's hut. The next morning he
introduced me to his father, Tiggity Sego, brother to the king
of Kasson, chief of Teesee. The old man viewed me with
great earnestness, having never, he said, beheld but one white
man before, whom by his description I immediately knew to be

Major Houghton. I related to him, in answer to his inquiries, the motives that induced me to explore the country. But he seemed to doubt the truth of what I asserted, thinking, I believe, that I secretly meditated some project which I was afraid to avow. He told me it would be necessary I should go to Kooniakary, the residence of the king, to pay my respects to that prince, but desired me to come to him again before I left Teesee.

In the afternoon one of his slaves eloped; and a general alarm being given, every person that had a horse rode into the woods in the hopes of apprehending him; and Demba Sego begged the use of my horse for the same purpose. I readily consented; and in about an hour they all returned with the slave, who was severely flogged, and afterwards put in irons. On the day following (Dec. 31), Demba Sego was ordered to go, with twenty horsemen, to a town in Gedumah, to adjust some dispute with the Moors, a party of whom were supposed to have stolen three horses from Teesee. Demba begged, a second time, the use of my horse; adding that the sight of my bridle and saddle would give him consequence among the Moors. This request also I readily granted, and he promised to return at the end of three days. During his absence I amused myself with walking about the town, and conversing with the natives, who attended me everywhere with great kindness and curiosity, and supplied me with milk, eggs, and what other provisions I wanted, on very easy terms.

Teesee is a large unwalled town, having no security against the attack of an enemy, except a sort of citadel, in which Tiggity and his family constantly reside. This town, according to the report of the natives, was formerly inhabited only by

a few Foulah shepherds, who lived in considerable affluence
by means of the excellent meadows in the neighbourhood, in
which they reared great herds of cattle. But their prosperity
attracting the envy of some Mandingoes, the latter drove out
the shepherds and took possession of their lands.

The present inhabitants, though they possess both cattle
and corn in abundance, are not over nice in articles of diet ;
rats, moles, squirrels, snakes, locusts, etc., are eaten without
scruple by the highest and lowest. My people were one
evening invited to a feast given by some of the townsmen,
where, after making a hearty meal of what they thought fish and
kouskous, one of them found a piece of hard skin in the dish,
and brought it along with him to show me what sort of fish
they had been eating. On examining the skin, I found they
had been feasting on a large snake. Another custom still
more extraordinary is, that no woman is allowed to *eat an egg*.
This prohibition, whether arising from ancient superstition, or
from the craftiness of some old Bushreen who loved eggs
himself, is rigidly adhered to, and nothing will more affront
a woman of Teesee than to offer her an egg. The custom is
the more singular, as the men eat eggs without scruple in the
presence of their wives, and I never observed the same prohibition in any other of the Mandingo countries.

The third day after his son's departure, Tiggity Sego held
a palaver on a very extraordinary occasion, which I attended ;
and the debates on both sides of the question displayed much
ingenuity. The case was this : A young man, a Kafir, of considerable affluence, who had recently married a young and
handsome wife, applied to a very devout Bushreen, or Mussulman priest, of his acquaintance, to procure him saphies for his

protection during the approaching war. The Bushreen complied with the request; and in order, as he pretended, to render the saphies more efficacious, enjoined the young man to avoid any nuptial intercourse with his bride for the space of six weeks. Severe as the injunction was, the Kafir strictly obeyed; and without telling his wife the real cause, absented himself from her company. In the meantime it began to be whispered at Teesee, that the Bushreen, who always performed his evening devotions at the door of the Kafir's hut, was more intimate with the young wife than he ought to be. At first, the good husband was unwilling to suspect the honour of his sanctified friend, and one whole month elapsed before any jealousy rose in his mind; but hearing the charge repeated, he at last interrogated his wife on the subject, who frankly confessed that the Bushreen had seduced her. Hereupon the Kafir put her into confinement, and called a palaver upon the Bushreen's conduct. The fact was clearly proved against him; and he was sentenced to be sold into slavery, or to find two slaves for his redemption, according to the pleasure of the complainant. The injured husband, however, was unwilling to proceed against his friend to such extremity, and desired rather to have him publicly flogged before Tiggity Sego's gate. This was agreed to, and the sentence was immediately executed. The culprit was tied by the hands to a strong stake; and a long black rod being brought forth, the executioner, after flourishing it round his head for some time, applied it with such force and dexterity to the Bushreen's back as to make him roar until the woods resounded with his screams. The surrounding multitude, by their hooting and laughing, manifested how much they enjoyed the punishment of this old gallant ; and it is worthy of remark, that the number of stripes was precisely the same as are enjoined by the Mosaic law— *forty, save one.*

As there appeared great probability that Teesee, from its being a frontier town, would be much exposed during the war to the predatory excursions of the Moors of Gadumah, Tiggity Sego had, before my arrival, sent round to the neighbouring villages, to beg or to purchase as much provisions as would afford subsistence to the inhabitants for one whole year, independently of the crop on the ground, which the Moors might destroy.   This project was well received by the country people, and they fixed a day on which to bring all the provisions they could spare to Teesee ; and as my horse was not yet returned, I went in the afternoon of January 4th, 1796, to meet the escort with the provisions.

It was composed of about four hundred men, marching in good order, with corn and ground-nuts in large calabashes upon their heads.   They were preceded by a strong guard of bowmen, and followed by eight musicians or singing-men. As soon as they approached the town, the latter began a song, every verse of which was answered by the company, and succeeded by a few strokes on the large drums.   In this manner they proceeded, amidst the acclamations of the populace, till they reached the house of Tiggity Sego, where the loads   deposited ; and in the evening they all assembled under the Bentang tree, and spent the night in dancing and merriment.   Many of these strangers remained at Teesee for three days, during which time I was constantly attended by as many of them as could conveniently see me ; one party giving way to another as soon as curiosity was gratified.

On the 5th of January an embassy of ten people belonging to Almami Abdulkader, king of Foota Torra, a country to the west of Bondou, arrived at Teesee, and desiring Tiggity Sego to call an assembly of the inhabitants, announced publicly their king's determination to this effect :—" That unless all the people of Kasson would embrace the Mahomedan religion, and evince their conversion by saying eleven public prayers, he (the king of Foota Torra) could not possibly stand neuter in the present contest, but would certainly join his arms to those of Kajaaga." A message of this nature, from so powerful a prince, could not fail to create great alarm ; and the inhabitants of Teesee, after a long consultation, agreed to conform to his good pleasure, humiliating as it was to them. Accordingly, one and all publicly offered up eleven prayers, which were considered a sufficient testimony of their having renounced paganism, and embraced the doctrines of the Prophet.

It was the 8th of January before Demba Sego returned with my horse ; and being quite wearied out with the delay, I went immediately to inform his father that I should set out for Kooniakary early the next day. The old man made many frivolous objections ; and at length gave me to understand that I must not think of departing without first paying him the same duties he was entitled to receive from all travellers ; besides which he expected, he said, some acknowledgment for his kindness towards me. Accordingly, on the morning of the 9th, my friend Demba, with a number of people, came to me, and said that they were sent by Tiggity Sego for my present, and wished to see what goods I had appropriated for that purpose. I knew that resistance was hopeless, and com-

plaint unavailing ; and being in some measure prepared by
the intimation I had received the night before, I quietly offered
him seven bars of amber and five of tobacco.   After surveying
these articles for some time very coolly, Demba laid them
down, and told me this was not a present for a man of Tiggity
Sego's consequence, who had it in his own power to take whatever he pleased from me.   He added, that if I did not consent
to make him a larger offering, he would carry all my baggage
to his father, and let him choose for himself.   I had not time
for reply, for Demba and his attendants immediately began to
open my bundles, and spread the different articles upon the
floor, where they underwent a more strict examination than
they had done at Joag.   Everything that pleased them they
took without scruple; and amongst other things Demba seized
the tin box which had so much attracted his attention in
crossing the river.   Upon collecting the scattered remains of
my little fortune after these people had left me, I found that
as at Joag I had been plundered of half, so here, without
even the shadow of accusation, I was deprived of half the remainder.   The blacksmith himself, though a native of Kasson,
had also been compelled to open his bundles, and take an oath
that the different articles they contained were his own exclusive property.   There was, however, no remedy ; and having
been under some obligation to Demba Sego for his attention
towards me in the journey from Joag, I did not reproach him
for his rapacity, but determined to quit Teesee at all events
the next morning.   In the meanwhile, in order to raise the
drooping spirits of my attendants, I purchased a fat sheep, and
had it dressed for our dinner.

Early in the morning of January 10th, therefore, I left

Teesee, and about midday ascended a ridge, from whence we had a distant view of the hills round Kooniakary. In the evening we reached a small village, where we slept; and, departing from thence, the next morning crossed in a few hours a narrow but deep stream called Krieko, a branch of the Senegal. About two miles farther to the eastward we passed a large town called Madina, and at two o'clock came in sight of Jumbo, the blacksmith's native town, from whence he had been absent more than four years. Soon after this his brother, who had by some means been apprised of his coming, came out to meet him, accompanied by a singing-man; he brought a horse for the blacksmith, that he might enter his native town in a dignified manner; and he desired each of us to put a good charge of powder into our guns. The singing-man now led the way, followed by the two brothers; and we were presently joined by a number of people from the town, all of whom demonstrated great joy at seeing their old acquaintance the blacksmith, by the most extravagant jumping and singing. On entering the town, the singing-man began an extempore song in praise of the blacksmith, extolling his courage in having overcome so many difficulties, and concluding with a strict injunction to his friends to dress him plenty of victuals.

When we arrived at the blacksmith's place of residence we dismounted and fired our muskets. The meeting between him and his relations was very tender; for these rude children of nature, free from restraint, display their emotions in the strongest and most expressive manner. Amidst these transports, the blacksmith's aged mother was led forth, leaning upon a staff. Every one made way for her; and she stretched out her hand to bid her son welcome. Being totally blind, she stroked his hands, arms, and face, with great care, and seemed highly delighted that her latter days were blessed by his return, and that her ears once more heard the music of his voice. From this interview I was fully convinced that, whatever difference there is between the Negro and European in the conformation of the nose and the colour of the skin, there is none in the genuine sympathies and characteristic feelings of our common nature.

During the tumult of these congratulations I had seated myself apart by the side of one of the huts, being unwilling to interrupt the flow of filial and parental tenderness; and the attention of the company was so entirely taken up with the blacksmith that I believe none of his friends had observed me. When all the people present had seated themselves, the blacksmith was desired by his father to give them some account of his adventures; and silence being commanded, he began, and after repeatedly thanking God for the success that had attended them, related every material occurrence that had happened to him from his leaving Kasson to his arrival at the Gambia, his employment and success in those parts, and the dangers he had escaped in returning to his native country. In the latter part of his narration he had frequently occasion to mention me; and after many strong expressions concerning my kindness to him, he pointed to the place where I sat, and exclaimed, *Affille ibi siring,* "See him sitting there." In a moment all eyes were turned upon me. I appeared like a being dropped from the clouds; every one was surprised that they had not observed me before; and a few women and children expressed great uneasiness at being so near a man of such an uncommon appearance. By degrees, however, their apprehensions subsided ; and when the black-smith assured them that I was perfectly inoffensive, and would hurt nobody, some of them ventured so far as to examine the texture of my clothes, but many of them were still very suspicious ; and when by accident I happened to move myself, or look at the young children, their mothers would scamper off with them with the greatest precipita-tion. In a few hours, however, they all became reconciled to me.

With these worthy people I spent the remainder of that, and the whole of the ensuing day, in feasting and merriment ; and the blacksmith declared he would not quit me during my stay at Kooniakary, for which place we set out early on the morning of the 14th of January, and arrived about the middle of the day at Soolo, a small village three miles to the south of it.

As this place was somewhat out of the direct road, it is necessary to observe that I went thither to visit a Slatee, or Gambia trader, of great note and reputation, named Salim Daucari. He was well known to Dr. Laidley, who had trusted him with effects to the value of five slaves, and had given me an order for the whole of the debt. We luckily found him at home, and he received me with great kindness and attention.

It is remarkable, however, that the king of Kasson was by some means immediately apprised of my motions ; for I had been at Soolo but a few hours before Sambo Sego, his second son, came thither with a party of horse to inquire what had prevented me from proceeding to Kooniakary, and waiting immediately upon the king, who, he said, was impatient to see me. Salim Daucari made my apology, and promised to accompany me to Kooniakary the same evening; we accordingly departed from Soolo at sunset, and in about an hour entered Kooniakary. But as the king had gone to sleep, we deferred the interview till next morning, and slept at the hut of Sambo Sego.

CHAPTER VII.

Interview with the King of Kasson—Incidents which occurred in the Kingdoms of Kasson and Kaarta.

ABOUT eight o'clock in the morning of January 15, 1796, we went to have an audience of the king (Demba Sego Jalla); but the crowd of people to see me was so great, that I could scarcely get admittance. When a passage was at length obtained, I made my bow to the monarch, whom we found sitting upon a mat, in a large hut: he appeared to be a man of about sixty years of age; his success in war, and the mildness of his behaviour in time of peace, had much endeared him to all his subjects. He surveyed me with great attention; and when Salim Daucari explained to him the object of my journey, and my reasons for passing through his country, the good old king appeared not only perfectly satisfied, but promised me every assistance in his power. He informed me that he had seen Major Houghton and presented him with a white horse; but that, after crossing the kingdom of Kaarta, he had lost his life among the Moors; in what manner he could not inform me. When this audience was ended we returned to our lodging, and I made up a small present out of the few effects that were left me; for I had not yet received anything from Salim Daucari. This present, though inconsiderable in itself, was well received by the king, who sent me in return a large white bullock. The sight of this

animal quite delighted my attendants; not so much on
account of its bulk, as from its being of a white colour, which
is considered as a particular mark of favour. But although
the king himself was well disposed towards me, and readily
granted me permission to pass through his territories, I soon
discovered that very great and unexpected obstacles were
likely to impede my progress. Besides the war which was on
the point of breaking out between Kasson and Kajaaga, I was
told that the next kingdom of Kaarta, through which my
route lay, was involved in the issue, and was furthermore
threatened with hostilities on the part of Bambarra. The
king himself informed me of these circumstances, and advised
me to stay in the neighbourhood of Kooniakary till such
time as he could procure proper information respecting Bambarra, which he expected to do in the course of four or five
days, as he had already, he said, sent four messengers into
Kaarta for that purpose. I readily submitted to this proposal,
and went to Soolo, to stay there till the return of one of those
messengers. This afforded me a favourable opportunity of
receiving what money Salim Daucari could spare me on Dr.
Laidley's account. I succeeded in receiving the value of three
slaves, chiefly in gold-dust; and being anxious to proceed as
quickly as possible, I begged Daucari to use his interest with
the king to allow me a guide by the way of Fooladoo, as I
was informed that the war had already commenced between
the kings of Bambarra and Kaarta. Daucari accordingly set
out for Kooniakary on the morning of the 20th, and the same
evening returned with the king's answer, which was to this
purpose: that the king had many years ago made an agreement with Daisy, king of Kaarta, to send all merchants and

travellers through his dominions ; but that if I wished to take the route through Fooladoo, I had his permission so to do ; though he could not, consistently with his agreement, lend me a guide. Having felt the want of regal protection in a former part of my journey, I was unwilling to hazard a repetition of the hardships I had then experienced, especially as the money I had received was probably the last supply that I should obtain ; I therefore determined to wait for the return of the messengers from Kaarta.

In the interim it began to be whispered abroad that I had received plenty of gold from Salim Daucari ; and on the morning of the 23d Sambo Sego paid me a visit with a party of horsemen. He insisted upon knowing the exact amount of the money I had obtained, declaring, that whatever the sum was, one-half of it must go to the king ; besides which, he intimated that he expected a handsome present for himself as being the king's son, and for his attendants as being the king's relations. The reader will easily perceive, that if all these demands had been satisfied, I should not have been overburdened with money ; but though it was very mortifying to me to comply with the demands of injustice, and so arbitrary an exaction, yet, thinking it was highly dangerous to make a foolish resistance, and irritate the lion when within the reach of his paw, I prepared to submit ; and if Salim Daucari had not interposed, all my endeavours to mitigate this oppressive claim would have been of no avail. Salim at last prevailed upon Sambo to accept sixteen bars of European merchandise, and some powder and ball, as a complete payment of every demand that could be made upon me in the kingdom of Kasson.

In the forenoon (January 26th) I went to the top of a high hill to the southward of Soolo, where I had a most enchanting prospect of the country. The number of towns and villages, and the extensive cultivation around them, surpassed everything I had yet seen in Africa. A gross calculation may be formed of the number of inhabitants in this delightful plain by considering that the king of Kasson can raise four thousand fighting men by the sound of his war-drum. In traversing the rocky eminences of this hill, which are almost destitute of vegetation, I observed a number of large holes in the crevices and fissures of the rocks where the wolves and hyænas take refuge during the day. Some of these animals paid us a visit on the evening of the 27th ; their approach was discovered by the dogs of the village ; and on this occasion it is remarkable that the dogs did not bark, but howl in the most dismal manner. The inhabitants of the village no sooner heard them, than, knowing the cause, they armed themselves ; and providing bunches of dry grass, went in a body to the inclosure in the middle of the village where the cattle were kept. Here they lighted the bunches of grass, and waving them to and fro, ran whooping and hallooing towards the hills. This manœuvre had the desired effect of frightening the wolves away from the village ; but, on examination, we found that they had killed five of the cattle, and torn and wounded many others.   Limits

The messengers arrived from Kaarta (Feb. 1st) and brought intelligence that the war had not yet commenced between Bambarra and Kaarta, and that I might probably pass through Kaarta before the Bambarra army invaded that country. Early in the morning (Feb. 3d) two guides on horseback came from Kooniakary to conduct me to the frontiers of Kaarta. I accordingly took leave of Salim Daucari, and parted, for the last time, from my fellow-traveller the blacksmith, whose kind solicitude for my welfare had been so conspicuous; and about ten o'clock departed from Soolo. We travelled this day through a rocky and hilly country, along the banks of the river Krieko, and at sunset came to the village of Soomo, where we slept.

We departed from Soomo (Feb. 4th) and continued our route along the banks of the Krieko, which are everywhere well cultivated, and swarm with inhabitants. At this time they were increased by the number of people that had flown thither from Kaarta on account of the Bambarra war. In the afternoon we reached Kimo, a large village, the residence of Madi Konko, governor of the hilly country of Kasson, which is called Sorroma. From hence the guides appointed by the king of Kasson returned to join in the expedition against Kajaaga; and I waited until the 6th before I could prevail on Madi Konko to appoint me a guide to Kaarta.

Departing from Kimo (Feb. 7th), with Madi Konko's son as a guide, we continued our course along the banks of the Krieko until the afternoon, when we arrived at Kangee, a considerable town. The Krieko is here but a small rivulet. This beautiful stream takes its rise a little to the eastward of this town, and descends with a rapid and noisy current until it reaches the bottom of the high hill called Tappa, where it becomes more placid, and winds gently through the lovely plains of Kooniakary; after which, having received an additional branch from the north, it is lost in the Senegal, somewhere near the falls of Felow.

Our route lay now over a rough stony country. We

passed Seimpo and a number of other villages and arrived in
the afternoon at Lackerago, a small village which stands upon
the ridge of hills that separates the kingdoms of Kasson and
Kaarta. In the course of the day (Feb. 8th) we passed many
hundreds of people flying from Kaarta, with their families
and effects.

Early the next morning we departed from Lackerago, and
a little to the eastward came to the brow of a hill, from whence
we had an extensive view of the country. Towards the south-
east were perceived some very distant hills, which our guide
told us were the mountains of Fooladoo. We travelled with
great difficulty down a stony and abrupt precipice, and continued
our way in the bed of a dry river-course ; where the trees, meeting overhead, made the place dark and cool. In a little time
we reached the bottom of this romantic glen, and about ten
o'clock emerged from between two rocky hills, and found ourselves on the level and sandy plains of Kaarta. At noon we
arrived at a Korree, or watering-place, where, for a few strings
of beads, I purchased as much milk and corn-meal as we could
consume ; indeed, provisions are here so cheap, and the shepherds live in such affluence, that they seldom ask any return
for what refreshments a traveller receives from them. From
this Korree we reached Feesurah at sunset, where we took up
our lodging for the night.

For this our landlord (taking advantage of the unsettled
state of the country) demanded so extravagant a sum that I
suspected he wished for an opportunity to quarrel with us. I
refused to submit to his exorbitant demand ; but my attendants were so much frightened at the reports of approaching
war, that they refused to proceed any further unless I could

settle matters with him, and induce him to accompany us to Kemmoo, for our protection on the road. This I accomplished with some difficulty; and by a present of a blanket which I had brought with me to sleep in, and for which our landlord had conceived a very great liking, matters were at length amicably adjusted, and he mounted his horse and led the way. He was one of those Negroes who, together with the ceremonial part of the Mahomedan religion, retain all their ancient superstitions, and even drink strong liquors. They are called Johars, or Jowers,[14] and in this kingdom form a very numerous and powerful tribe. We had no sooner got into a dark and lonely part of the first wood than he made a sign for us to stop, and taking hold of a hollow piece of bamboo that hung as an amulet round his neck, whistled very loud three times. I confess I was somewhat startled, thinking it was a signal for some of his companions to come and attack us; but he assured me that it was done merely with a view to ascertain what success we were likely to meet with on our present journey. He then dismounted, laid his spear across the road, and having said a number of short prayers, concluded with three loud whistles; after which he listened for some time, as if in expectation of an answer, and receiving none, told us we might proceed without fear, for there was no danger. About noon we passed a number of large villages quite deserted, the inhabitants having fled into Kasson to avoid the horrors of war. We reached Karankalla at sunset; this formerly was a large town, but having been plundered by the Bambarrans about four years ago, nearly one-half of it is still in ruins.

At daylight we departed from Karankalla, and as it was but a short day's journey to Kemmoo, we travelled slower than usual, and amused ourselves by collecting such eatable fruits as grew near the road-side. In this pursuit I had wandered a little from my people, and being uncertain whether they were before or behind me, I hastened to a rising ground to look about me. As I was proceeding towards this eminence two Negro horsemen, armed with muskets, came galloping from among the bushes. On seeing them I made a full stop ; the horsemen did the same ; and all three of us seemed equally surprised and confounded at this interview. As I approached them their fears increased, and one of them, after casting upon me a look of horror, rode off at full speed ; the other in a panic of fear put his hands over his eyes, and continued muttering prayers, until his horse, seemingly without the rider's knowledge, conveyed him slowly after his companion. About a mile to the westward they fell in with my attendants, to whom they related a frightful story. It seems their fears had dressed me in the flowing robes of a tremendous spirit ; and one of them affirmed, that when I made my appearance a cold blast of wind came pouring down upon him from the sky, like so much cold water. About noon we saw at a distance Kemmoo, the capital of Kaarta, situated in the middle of an open plain, the country for two miles round being cleared of wood by the great consumption of that article for building and fuel, and we entered the town about two o'clock in the afternoon.

We proceeded, without stopping, to the court before the king's residence ; but I was so completely surrounded by the gazing multitude that I did not attempt to dismount, but sent in the landlord and Madi Konko's son to acquaint the king of my arrival. In a little time they returned, accompanied by a messenger from the king, signifying that he would see me in

the evening; and in the meantime, the messenger had orders
to procure me a lodging, and see that the crowd did not molest
me. He conducted me into a court, at the door of which he
stationed a man, with a stick in his hand to keep off the
mob, and then showed me a large hut in which I was to
lodge. I had scarcely seated myself in this spacious apart-
ment when the mob entered; it was found impossible to
keep them out, and I was surrounded by as many as the hut
could contain. When the first party, however, had seen me,
and asked a few questions, they retired to make room for
another company; and in this manner the hut was filled and
emptied thirteen different times.

A little before sunset the king sent to inform me that
he was at leisure, and wished to see me. I followed the
messenger through a number of courts surrounded with high
walls, where I observed plenty of dry grass, bundled up like
hay, to fodder the horses in case the town should be invested.
On entering the court in which the king was sitting, I was
astonished at the number of his attendants, and at the good
order that seemed to prevail among them. They were all
seated—the fighting men on the king's right hand, and the
women and children on the left, leaving a space between
them for my passage. The king, whose name was Daisy
Koorabarri,[15] was not to be distinguished from his subjects by
any superiority in point of dress; a bank of earth about two
feet high, upon which was spread a leopard's skin, constituted
the only mark of royal dignity. When I had seated myself
upon the ground before him, and related the various circumstances that had induced me to pass through his country, and
my reasons for soliciting his protection, he appeared perfectly

satisfied; but said it was not in his power at present to afford me much assistance, for that all sort of communication between Kaarta and Bambarra had been interrupted for some time past; and as Mansong, the king of Bambarra, with his army, had entered Fooladoo in his way to Kaarta, there was but little hope of my reaching Bambarra by any of the usual routes, inasmuch as, coming from an enemy's country, I should certainly be plundered, or taken for a spy. If his country had been at peace, he said, I might have remained with him until a more favourable opportunity offered; but, as matters stood at present, he did not wish me to continue in Kaarta, for fear some accident should befall me, in which case my countrymen might say that he had murdered a white man. He would therefore advise me to return into Kasson, and remain there until the war should terminate, which would probably happen in the course of three or four months; after which, if he was alive, he said he would be glad to see me, and if he was dead his sons would take care of me.

This advice was certainly well meant on the part of the king, and perhaps I was to blame in not following it; but I reflected that the hot months were approaching, and I dreaded the thoughts of spending the rainy season in the interior of Africa. These considerations, and the aversion I felt at the idea of returning without having made a greater progress in discovery, made me determine to go forwards; and though the king could not give me a guide to Bambarra, I begged that he would allow a man to accompany me as near the frontiers of his kingdom as was consistent with safety. Finding that I was determined to proceed, the king told me that one route still remained, but that, he said, was by no

means free from danger; which was to go from Kaarta into
the Moorish kingdom of Ludamar, from whence I might pass,
by a circuitous route, into Bambarra. If I wished to follow
this route, he would appoint people to conduct me to Jarra,
the frontier town of Ludamar.   He then inquired very
particularly how I had been treated since I had left the
Gambia, and asked in a jocular way how many slaves I
expected to carry home with me on my return. He was
about to proceed, when a man, mounted on a fine Moorish
horse which was covered with sweat and foam, entered the
court, and signifying that he had something of importance to
communicate, the king immediately took up his sandals,
which is the signal to strangers to retire. I accordingly took
leave, but desired my boy to stay about the place, in order to
learn something of the intelligence that this messenger had
brought. In about an hour the boy returned, and informed
me that the Bambarra army had left Fooladoo, and was on its
march towards Kaarta; that the man I had seen, who had
brought this intelligence, was one of the scouts or watchmen
employed by the king, each of whom has his particular station
(commonly on some rising ground), from whence he has the
best view of the country, and watches the motions of the
enemy.

In the evening the king sent me a fine sheep, which was
very acceptable, as none of us had tasted victuals during the
day. Whilst we were employed in dressing supper, evening
prayers were announced; not by the call of the priest, as
usual, but by beating on drums and blowing through large
elephants' teeth hollowed out in such a manner as to resemble
bugle-horns; the sound is melodious, and, in my opinion,

comes nearer to the human voice than any other artificial sound. As the main body of Daisy's army was at this juncture at Kemmoo, the mosques were very much crowded; and I observed that the disciples of Mahomet composed nearly one-half of the army of Kaarta.

At daylight I sent my horse-pistols and holsters as a present to the king, and being very desirous to get away from a place which was likely soon to become the seat of war, I begged the messenger to inform the king that I wished to depart from Kemmoo as soon as he should find it convenient to appoint me a guide. In about an hour the king sent his messenger to thank me for the present, and eight horsemen to conduct me to Jarra. They told me that the king wished me to proceed to Jarra with all possible expedition, that they might return before anything decisive should happen between the armies of Bambarra and Kaarta. We accordingly departed forthwith from Kemmoo, accompanied by three of Daisy's sons, and about two hundred horsemen, who kindly undertook to see me a little way on my journey.

CHAPTER VIII.

Journey from Kemmoo to Funingkedy—Inroad of the Moors—Interest-
ing Death-scene—Fate of Major Houghton—Reach Jarra—
Account of the War between Kaarta and Bambarra.

ON the evening of the day of our departure from Kemmoo
(the king's eldest son and great part of the horsemen
having returned) we reached a village called Marina, where
we slept. During the night some thieves broke into the hut
where I had deposited my baggage, and having cut open one
of my bundles, stole a quantity of beads, part of my clothes,
and some amber and gold, which happened to be in one of the
pockets. I complained to my protectors, but without effect.
The next day (Feb. 14th) was far advanced before we departed
from Marina, and we travelled slowly on account of the
excessive heat until four o'clock in the afternoon, when two
Negroes were observed sitting among some thorny bushes at
a little distance from the road. The king's people, taking it
for granted that they were runaway slaves, cocked their
muskets and rode at full speed in different directions through
the bushes, in order to surround them, and prevent their
escaping. The Negroes, however, waited with great composure
until we came within bowshot of them, when each of them
took from his quiver a handful of arrows, and putting two
between his teeth and one in his bow, waved to us with his

hand to keep at a distance; upon which one of the king's
people called out to the strangers to give some account of
themselves. They said that they were natives of Toorda, a
neighbouring village, and had come to that place to gather
tomberongs. These are small farinaceous berries, of a yellow
colour and delicious taste, which I knew to be the fruit of the
Rhamnus lotus[16] of Linnæus. The Negroes showed us two large
basketfuls which they had collected in the course of the day.
These berries are much esteemed by the natives, who convert
them into a sort of bread, by exposing them for some days to
the sun, and afterwards pounding them gently in a wooden
mortar, until the farinaceous part of the berry is separated
from the stone. This meal is then mixed with a little water
and formed into cakes, which, when dried in the sun, resemble
in colour and flavour the sweetest gingerbread. The stones
are afterwards put into a vessel of water, and shaken about
so as to separate the meal which may still adhere to them.
This communicates a sweet and agreeable taste to the water,
and with the addition of a little pounded millet forms a
pleasant gruel called *fondi*, which is the common breakfast in
many parts of Ludamar during the months of February and
March. The fruit is collected by spreading a cloth upon the
ground, and beating the branches with a stick.

The lotus is very common in all the kingdoms which I
visited, but is found in the greatest plenty on the sandy soil
of Kaarta, Ludamar, and the northern parts of Bambarra,
where it is one of the most common shrubs of the country.
I had observed the same species at Gambia. The leaves of
the desert shrub are, however, much smaller, and more
resembling, in that particular, those represented in the engrav-

ing given by Desfontaines[17] in the *Mémoires de l'Académie Royal des Sciences.*

As this shrub is found in Tunis, and also in the Negro kingdoms, and as it furnishes the natives of the latter with a food resembling bread, and also with a sweet liquor which is much relished by them, there can be little doubt of its being the lotus mentioned by Pliny[18] as the food of the Lybian Lotophagi.[19] An army may very well have been fed with the bread I have tasted, made of the meal of the fruit, as is said by Pliny to have been done in Lybia; and as the taste of the bread is sweet and agreeable, it is not likely that the soldiers would complain of it.

We arrived in the evening at the village of Toorda, when all the rest of the king's people turned back except two, who remained with me as guides to Jarra.

I departed from Toorda (Feb. 15th), and about two o'clock came to a considerable town called Funingkedy. As we approached the town the inhabitants were much alarmed; for as one of my guides wore a turban, they mistook us for some Moorish banditti. This misapprehension was soon cleared up, and we were well received by a Gambia Slatee who resides at this town, and at whose house we lodged.

We were informed that a number of people were about to go from this town to Jarra; and as the road was much infested by the Moors we resolved to stay and accompany the travellers. In the meantime, we were told, that a few days before our arrival most of the Bushreens and people of property in Funingkedy had gone to Jarra, to consult about removing their families and effects to that town, for fear of the approaching war; and that the Moors, in their absence, had stolen some of their cattle.

About two o'clock, as I was lying asleep upon a bullock's hide behind the door of the hut, I was awakened by the screams of women, and a general clamour and confusion among the inhabitants. At first I suspected that the Bambarrans had actually entered the town; but observing my boy upon the top of one of the huts, I called to him to know what was the matter. He informed me that the Moors were come a second time to steal the cattle, and that they were now close to the town. I mounted the roof of the hut, and observed a large herd of bullocks coming towards the town, followed by five Moors on horseback, who drove the cattle forward with their muskets. When they had reached the wells, which are close to the town, the Moors selected from the herd sixteen of the finest beasts, and drove them off at full gallop.

During this transaction the townspeople, to the number of five hundred, stood collected close to the walls of the town; and when the Moors drove the cattle away, though they passed within pistol-shot of them, the inhabitants scarcely made a show of resistance. I only saw four muskets fired, which, being loaded with gunpowder of the Negroes' own manufacture, did no execution. Shortly after this I observed a number of people supporting a young man upon horseback, and conducting him slowly towards the town. This was one of the herdsmen, who, attempting to throw his spear, had been wounded by a shot from one of the Moors. His mother walked on before, quite frantic with grief, clapping her hands, and enumerating the good qualities of her son. *Ee maffo fonio* (he never told a lie), said the disconsolate mother, as her wounded son was carried in at the gate;—*Ee maffo fonio abada* (he never told a lie ; no, never). When they had conveyed him to his hut, and laid him upon a mat, all the spectators joined in lamenting his fate, by screaming and howling in the most piteous manner.

After their grief had subsided a little I was desired to examine the wound. I found that the ball had passed quite through his leg, having fractured both bones a little below the knee ; the poor boy was faint from the loss of blood, and his situation withal so very precarious, that I could not console his relations with any great hopes of his recovery. However, to give him a possible chance, I observed to them that it was necessary to cut off his leg above the knee. This proposal made every one start with horror ; they had never heard of such a method of cure, and would by no means give their consent to it ; indeed, they evidently considered me as a sort of cannibal for proposing so cruel and unheard-of an operation, which, in their opinion, would be attended with more pain and danger than the wound itself. The patient was therefore committed to the care of some old Bushreens, who endeavoured to secure him a passage into paradise, by whispering in his ear some Arabic sentences, and desiring him to repeat them. After many unsuccessful attempts, the poor heathen at last pronounced, *La illah el allah, Mahomet rasowl allahi* (there is but one God, and Mahomet is his Prophet), and the disciples of the Prophet assured his mother that her son had given sufficient evidence of his faith, and would be happy in a future state. He died the same evening.

My guides informed me that in order to avoid the Moorish banditti, it was necessary to travel in the night ; we accordingly departed from Funingkedy (Feb. 17th) in the afternoon, accompanied by about thirty people, carrying their effects

[handwritten marginal note:] Do not take his doctors advice

with them into Ludamar, for fear of the war. We travelled
with great silence and expedition until midnight, when we
stopped in a sort of inclosure near a small village; but the
thermometer being so low as 68°, none of the Negroes could
sleep on account of the cold

At daybreak on the 18th we resumed our journey, and at
eight o'clock passed *Simbing*, the frontier village of Ludamar,
situated in a narrow pass between two rocky hills, and surrounded with a high wall. From this village Major Houghton
(deserted by his Negro servants, who refused to follow him
into the Moorish country) wrote his last letter with a pencil
to Dr. Laidley. This brave but unfortunate man, having surmounted many difficulties, had taken a northerly direction,
and endeavoured to pass through the kingdom of Ludamar,
where I afterwards learned the following particulars concerning his melancholy fate :—On his arrival at Jarra he got
acquainted with certain Moorish merchants who were travelling to Tisheet (a place near the salt-pits in the Great Desert,
ten days' journey to the northward) to purchase salt; and the
Major, at the expense of a musket and some tobacco, engaged
them to convey him thither. It is impossible to form any
other opinion on this determination, than that the Moors in-
tentionally deceived him either with regard to the route that
he wished to pursue, or the state of the intermediate country
between Jarra and Timbuctoo. Their intention probably was
to rob and leave him in the desert. At the end of two days
he suspected their treachery, and insisted on returning to
Jarra. Finding him persist in this determination, the Moors
robbed him of everything he possessed, and went off with
their camels; the poor Major being thus deserted, returned

on foot to a watering-place in possession of the Moors called Tarra. He had been some days without food, and the unfeeling Moors refusing to give him any, he sank at last under his distresses. Whether he actually perished of hunger, or was murdered outright by the savage Mahomedans, is not certainly known; his body was dragged into the woods, and I was shown, at a distance, the spot where his remains were left to perish.

About four miles to the north of Simbing we came to a small stream of water, where we observed a number of wild horses; they were all of one colour, and galloped away from us at an easy rate, frequently stopping and looking back. The Negroes hunt them for food, and their flesh is much esteemed.

About noon we arrived at Jarra, a large town situated at the bottom of some rocky hills. But before I proceed to describe the place itself, and relate the various occurrences which befell me there, it will not be improper to give my readers a brief recital of the origin of the war which induced me to take this route—an unfortunate determination, the immediate cause of all the misfortunes and calamities which afterward befell me. The recital which I propose to give in this place will prevent interruptions hereafter.

This war, which desolated Kaarta soon after I had left that kingdom, and spread terror into many of the neighbouring states, arose in the following manner:—A few bullocks belonging to a frontier village of Bambarra having been stolen by a party of Moors, were sold to the Dooty or chief man of a town in Kaarta. The villagers claimed their cattle, and being refused satisfaction, complained of the Dooty to their sovereign, Mansong, king of Bambarra, who probably beheld with an eye of jealousy the growing prosperity of Kaarta, and availed himself of this incident to declare hostilities against that kingdom.

With this view, he sent a messenger and a party of horsemen to Daisy, king of Kaarta, to inform him that the king of Bambarra, with nine thousand men, would visit Kemmoo in the course of the dry season; and to desire that he (Daisy) would direct his slaves to sweep the houses, and have everything ready for their accommodation. The messenger concluded this insulting notification by presenting the king with a pair of *iron sandals;* at the same time adding, that "until such time as Daisy had worn out these sandals in his flight, he should never be secure from the arrows of Bambarra."

Daisy, having consulted with his chief men about the best means of repelling so formidable an enemy, returned an answer of defiance, and made a Bushreen write in Arabic, upon a piece of thin board, a sort of proclamation, which was suspended to a tree in the public square; and a number of aged men were sent to different places to explain it to the common people. This proclamation called upon all the friends of Daisy to join him immediately; but to such as had no arms, or were afraid to enter into the war, permission was given to retire into any of the neighbouring kingdoms; and it was added, that provided they observed a strict neutrality, they should always be welcome to return to their former habitations. If, however, they took any active part against Kaarta, they had then "broken the key of their huts, and could never afterwards enter the door." Such was the expression

This proclamation was very generally applauded ; but many of the Kaartans, and amongst others the powerful tribes of Jower and Kakaroo, availing themselves of the indulgent clause, retired from Daisy's dominions, and took refuge in Ludamar and Kasson.   By means of these desertions Daisy's army was not so numerous as might have been expected ; and when I was at Kemmoo, the whole number of effective men, according to report, did not exceed four thousand ; but they were men of spirit and enterprise, and could be depended on.

On the 22d of February (four days after my arrival at Jarra) Mansong with his army advanced towards Kemmoo ; and Daisy, without hazarding a battle, retired to Joko, a town to the north-west of Kemmoo, where he remained three days, and then took refuge in a strong town called Gedingooma, situated in the hilly country and surrounded with high walls of stone.   When Daisy departed from Joko, his sons refused to follow him, alleging that "the singing-men would publish their disgrace, as soon as it should be known that Daisy and his family had fled from Joko without firing a gun."   They were therefore left behind with a number of horsemen to defend Joko ; but after many skirmishes, they were totally defeated and one of Daisy's sons taken prisoner ; the remainder fled to Gedingooma, which Daisy had stored with provisions, and where he determined to make his final stand.

Mansong, finding that Daisy was determined to avoid a pitched battle, placed a strong force at Joko to watch his motions ; and separating the remainder of his army into small detachments, ordered them to overrun the country and seize upon the inhabitants before they had time to escape.   These orders were executed with such promptitude, that in a few days the whole kingdom of Kaarta became a scene of desolation. Most of the poor inhabitants of the different towns and villages, being surprised in the night, fell an easy prey; and their corn, and everything which could be useful to Daisy, was burnt and destroyed. During these transactions Daisy was employed in fortifying Gedingooma. This town is built in a narrow pass between two high hills, having only two gates, one towards Kaarta and the other towards Jaffnoo. The gate towards Kaarta was defended by Daisy in person, and that towards Jaffnoo was committed to the charge of his sons. When the army of Bambarra approached the town, they made some attempts to storm it, but were always driven back with great loss; and Mansong, finding Daisy more formidable than he expected, resolved to cut off his supplies, and starve him into submission. He accordingly sent all the prisoners he had taken into Bambarra, and having collected a considerable quantity of provisions, remained with his army two whole months in the vicinity of Gedingooma without doing anything decisive. During this time he was much harassed by sallies from the besieged; and his stock of provisions being nearly exhausted, he sent to Ali, the Moorish king of Ludamar, for two hundred horsemen, to enable him to make an attack upon the north gate of the town, and give the Bambarrans an opportunity of storming the place. Ali, though he had made an agreement with Mansong at the commencement of the war to afford him assistance, now refused to fulfil his engagement, which so enraged Mansong, that he marched part of his army to Funingkedy, with a view to surprise the camp of Benowm; but the Moors having received intelligence of his design fled to the northward, and Mansong, without attempting anything farther, returned to Sego. This happened while I was myself in captivity in Ali's camp, as will hereafter be seen.

As the king of Kaarta had now got quit of his most formidable antagonist, it might have been hoped that peace would have been restored to his dominions ; but an extraordinary incident involved him, immediately afterwards, in hostilities with Kasson, the king of which country dying about that time, the succession was disputed by his two sons. The younger (Sambo Sego, my old acquaintance) prevailed, and drove his brother from the country. He fled to Gedingooma ; and being pursued thither, Daisy, who had lived in constant friendship with both the brothers, refused to deliver him up—at the same time declaring that he would not support his claim, nor any way interfere in the quarrel. Sambo Sego, elated with success, and proud of the homage that was paid him as sovereign of Kasson, was much displeased with Daisy's conduct, and joined with some disaffected fugitive Kaartans in a plundering expedition against him. Daisy, who little expected such a visit, had sent a number of people to Joko to plant corn, and collect together such cattle as they might find straying in the woods, in order to supply his army. All these people fell into the hands of Sambo Sego, who carried them to Kooniakary, and afterwards sent them in caravans to be sold to the French at Fort Louis, on the river Senegal.

This attack was soon retaliated ; for Daisy, who was now in distress for want of provisions, thought he was justified in supplying himself from the plunder of Kasson. He accordingly took with him eight hundred of his best men, and marching secretly through the woods, surprised in the night three large villages near Kooniakary, in which many of his traitorous subjects who were in Sambo's expedition had taken up their residence. All these, and indeed all the able men that fell into Daisy's hands, were immediately put to death.

After this expedition, Daisy began to indulge the hopes of peace. Many of his discontented subjects had returned to their allegiance, and were repairing the towns which had been desolated by the war. The rainy season was approaching, and everything wore a favourable appearance, when he was suddenly attacked from a different quarter.

The Jowers, Kakaroos, and some other Kaartans, who had deserted from him at the commencement of the war, and had shown a decided preference to Mansong and his army during the whole campaign, were now afraid or ashamed to ask forgiveness of Daisy, and being very powerful in themselves, joined together to make war upon him. They solicited the Moors to assist them in their rebellion (as will appear hereafter), and having collected a considerable army they plundered a large village belonging to Daisy, and carried off a number of prisoners.

Daisy immediately prepared to revenge this insult; but the Jowers, and indeed almost all the Negro inhabitants of Ludamar, deserted their towns, and fled to the eastward; and the rainy season put an end to the war of Kaarta, which had enriched a few individuals, but destroyed the happiness of thousands.

Such was the state of affairs among the nations in the neighbourhood of Jarra, soon after the period of my arrival there. I shall now proceed, after giving some description of that place, with the detail of events as they occurred.

CHAPTER IX.

Jarra and its Moorish Inhabitants—Arrival at Deena—Cruel Treat-
ment of the Moors—Sampaka—Negro Gunpowder—Samee—
Seized by Moors—Carried a Prisoner to the Moorish Camp at
Benowm, on the borders of the Great Desert.

THE town of Jarra is of considerable extent. The houses are
built of clay and stone intermixed, the clay answering
the purpose of mortar. It is situated in the Moorish kingdom
of Ludamar; but the major part of the inhabitants are Negroes
from the borders of the southern states, who prefer a precarious
protection under the Moors, which they purchase by a tribute,
rather than continue exposed to their predatory hostilities.
The tribute they pay is considerable ; and they manifest
towards their Moorish superiors the most unlimited obedience
and submission, and are treated by them with the utmost in-
dignity and contempt. The Moors of this and the other states
adjoining the country of the Negroes resemble in their persons
the Mulattoes of the West Indies to so great a degree as not
easily to be distinguished from them; and in truth, the present
generation seem to be a mixed race between the Moors (properly so called) of the north and the Negroes of the south,
possessing many of the worst qualities of both nations.

Of the origin of these Moorish tribes, as distinguished
from the inhabitants of Barbary, from whom they are divided

by the Great Desert, nothing further seems to be known than what is related by John Leo,[20] the African, whose account may be abridged as follows :—

Before the Arabian conquest, about the middle of the seventh century, all the inhabitants of Africa, whether they were descended from Numidians, Phœnicians, Carthaginians, Romans, Vandals, or Goths, were comprehended under the general name of *Mauri*, or Moors. All these nations were converted to the religion of Mahomet, during the Arabian empire under the Caliphs. About this time many of the Numidian tribes, who led a wandering life in the Desert, and supported themselves upon the produce of their cattle, retired southward across the Great Desert, to avoid the fury of the Arabians ; and one of those tribes, says Leo (that of Zanhaga), was discovered and conquered by the Negro nations on the Niger. By the Niger is here undoubtedly meant the river Senegal, which in the Mandingo language is called *Bafing*, or the Black River.

To what extent these people are now spread over the African continent it is difficult to ascertain. There is reason to believe that their dominion stretches from west to east, in a narrow line or belt, from the mouth of the Senegal (on the northern side of that river) to the confines of Abyssinia. They are a subtle and treacherous race of people, and take every opportunity of cheating and plundering the credulous and unsuspecting Negroes. But their manners and general habits of life will be best explained as incidents occur in the course of my narrative.] Shows written for the reader

On my arrival at Jarra I obtained a lodging at the house of Daman Jumma, a Gambia Slatee. This man had formerly

Shows Moors to be horrible
Negroes as innocent or childlike

borrowed goods from Dr. Laidley, who had given me an order for the money, to the amount of six slaves ; and though the debt was of five years' standing he readily acknowledged it, and promised me what money he could raise. He was afraid, he said, in his present situation, he could not pay more than two slaves' value. He gave me his assistance, however, in exchanging my beads and amber for gold, which was a more portable article, and more easily concealed from the Moors.

The difficulties we had already encountered, the unsettled state of the country, and above all, the savage and overbearing deportment of the Moors, had so completely frightened my attendants, that they declared they would rather relinquish every claim to reward than proceed one step farther to the eastward. Indeed the danger they incurred of being seized by the Moors and sold into slavery became every day more apparent ; and I could not condemn their apprehensions. In this situation, deserted by my attendants, and reflecting that my retreat was cut off by the war behind me, and that a Moorish country of ten days' journey lay before me, I applied to Daman to obtain permission from Ali, the chief or sovereign of Ludamar, that I might pass through his country unmolested into Bambarra ; and I hired one of Daman's slaves to accompany me thither, as soon as such permission should be obtained. A messenger was despatched to Ali, who at this time was encamped near Benowm ; and as a present was necessary in order to insure success, I sent him five garments of cotton cloth, which I purchased of Daman for one of my fowling-pieces. Fourteen days elapsed in settling this affair ; but on the evening of the 26th of February, one of Ali's slaves arrived with directions, as he pretended, to conduct me in safety as

far as Goomba, and told me I was to pay him one garment
of blue cotton cloth for his attendance. My faithful boy,
observing that I was about to proceed without him, resolved
to accompany me ; and told me that though he wished me to
turn back, he never had entertained any serious thoughts of
deserting me, but had been advised to it by Johnson, with a
view to induce me to return immediately for Gambia.

I delivered most of my papers to Johnson, to convey them
to Gambia as soon as possible, reserving a duplicate for myself in case of accidents. I likewise left in Daman's possession
a bundle of clothes and other things that were not absolutely
necessary ; for I wished to diminish my baggage as much as
possible, that the Moors might have fewer inducements to
plunder us.

Things being thus adjusted, we departed from Jarra in the
forenoon, and slept at Troomgoomba, a small walled village
inhabited by a mixture of Negroes and Moors. On the day
following (Feb. 28th) we reached Quira ; and on the 29th,
after a toilsome journey over a sandy country, we came to
Compe, a watering-place belonging to the Moors ; from
whence, on the morning following, we proceeded to Deena,
a large town, and like Jarra, built of stone and clay. The
Moors are here in greater proportion to the Negroes than at
Jarra. They assembled round the hut of the Negro where I
lodged, and treated me with the greatest insolence. They
hissed, shouted, and abused me ; they even spat in my face
with a view to irritate me and afford them a pretext for seizing
my baggage. But finding such insults had not the desired
effect, they had recourse to the final and decisive argument
that I was a Christian, and of course that my property was

lawful plunder to the followers of Mahomet. They accordingly opened my bundles and robbed me of everything they fancied. My attendants, finding that everybody could rob me with impunity, insisted on returning to Jarra.

The day following (March 2d) I endeavoured by all means in my power to prevail upon my people to go on, but they still continued obstinate, and having reason to fear some further insult from the fanatic Moors, I resolved to proceed alone. Accordingly the next morning about two o'clock I departed from Deena. It was moonlight, but the roaring of the wild beasts made it necessary to proceed with caution.

When I had reached a piece of rising ground about half-a-mile from the town I heard somebody halloo, and looking back, saw my faithful boy running after me. He informed me that Ali's man had gone back to Benowm, and that Daman's Negro was about to depart for Jarra; but he said he had no doubt if I would stop a little that he could persuade the latter to accompany us. I waited accordingly, and in about an hour the boy returned with the Negro; and we continued travelling over a sandy country, covered chiefly with the *Asclepias giganteo*,[21] until mid-day, when we came to a number of deserted huts, and seeing some appearances of water at a little distance, I sent the boy to fill a soofroo; but as he was examining the place for water, the roaring of a lion, that was probably on the same pursuit, induced the frightened boy to return in haste, and we submitted patiently to the disappointment. In the afternoon we reached a town inhabited chiefly by Foulahs, called Samamingkoos.

Next morning (March 4th) we set out for Sampaka, which place we reached about two o'clock. On the road we observed immense quantities of locusts; the trees were quite black with them. These insects devour every vegetable that comes in their way, and in a short time completely strip a tree of its leaves. The noise of their excrement falling upon the leaves and withered grass very much resembles a shower of rain. When a tree is shaken or struck, it is astonishing to see what a cloud of them will fly off. In their flight they yield to the current of the wind, which at this season of the year is always from the north-east. Should the wind shift, it is difficult to conceive where they could collect food, as the whole of their course was marked with desolation.

Sampaka is a large town, and when the Moors and Bambarrans were at war was thrice attacked by the former; but they were driven off with great loss, though the king of Bambarra was afterwards obliged to give up this, and all the other towns as far as Goomba, in order to obtain a peace. Here I lodged at the house of a Negro who practised the art of making gunpowder. He showed me a bag of nitre, very white, but the crystals were much smaller than common. They procure it in considerable quantities from the ponds, which are filled in the rainy season, and to which the cattle resort for coolness during the heat of the day. When the water is evaporated, a white efflorescence is observed on the mud, which the natives collect and purify in such a manner as to answer their purpose. The Moors supply them with sulphur from the Mediterranean; and the process is completed by pounding the different articles together in a wooden mortar. The grains are very unequal, and the sound of its explosion is by no means so sharp as that produced by European gunpowder.

We departed from Sampaka (March 5th) at daylight.

About noon we stopped a little at a village called Dangali; and in the evening arrived at Dalli. We saw upon the road two large herds of camels feeding. When the Moors turn their camels to feed they tie up one of their fore-legs to prevent them straying. This happened to be a feast-day at Dalli, and the people were dancing before the Dooty's house. But when they were informed that a white man was come into the town, they left off dancing and came to the place where I lodged, walking in regular order, two and two, with the music before them. They play upon a sort of flute; but instead of blowing into a hole in the side, they blow obliquely over the end, which is half-shut by a thin piece of wood; they govern the holes on the side with their fingers, and play some simple and very plaintive airs. They continued to dance and sing until midnight; during which time I was surrounded by so great a crowd as made it necessary for me to satisfy their curiosity by sitting still.

We stopped here this day (March 6th) because some of the townspeople, who were going to Goomba on the day following, wished to accompany us; but in order to avoid the crowd of people which usually assembled in the evening, we went to a Negro village to the east of Dalli called Samee, where we were kindly received by the hospitable Dooty, who on this occasion killed two fine sheep, and invited his friends to come and feast with him. And so proud was our landlord of the honour of entertaining a white man, that he insisted on my staying with him and his friends until the cool of the evening of the next day, when he said he would conduct me to the next village. As I was now within two days' journey of Goomba, I had no apprehensions from the Moors, and readily accepted the invitation. I spent the forenoon very pleasantly with these poor Negroes ; their company was the more acceptable, as the gentleness of their manners presented a striking contrast to the rudeness and barbarity of the Moors. They enlivened their conversation by drinking a fermented liquor made from corn—the same sort of beer that I have described in a former chapter—and better I never tasted in Great Britain.

In the midst of this harmless festivity I flattered myself that all danger from the Moors was over. Fancy had already placed me on the banks of the Niger, and presented to my imagination a thousand delightful scenes in my future progress, when a party of Moors unexpectedly entered the hut and dispelled the golden dream. They came, they said, by Ali's orders, to convey me to his camp at Benowm. If I went peaceably they told me I had nothing to fear; but if I refused, they had orders to bring me by force. I was struck dumb by surprise and terror, which the Moors observing, endeavoured to calm my apprehensions by repeating the assurance that I had nothing to fear. Their visit, they added, was occasioned by the curiosity of Ali's wife, Fatima, who had heard so much about Christians that she was very anxious to see one. As soon as her curiosity should be satisfied, they had no doubt, they said, that Ali would give me a handsome present, and send a person to conduct me to Bambarra. Finding entreaty and resistance equally fruitless, I prepared to follow the messengers, and took leave of my landlord and his company with great reluctance. Accompanied by my faithful boy (for Daman's slave made his escape on seeing the Moors), we reached Dalli in the evening, where we were strictly watched by the Moors during the night.

We were conducted by a circuitous path through the woods to Dangali, where we slept, and in the afternoon arrived at Sampaka. On the road we saw a party of Moors, well armed, who told us that they were hunting for a runaway slave; but the townspeople informed us that a party of Moors had attempted to steal some cattle from the town in the morning, but were repulsed; and on their describing the persons, we were satisfied that they were the same banditti that we had seen in the woods.

Next morning (March 10th) we set out for Samamingkoos. On the road we overtook a woman and two boys, with an ass; she informed us that she was going to Bambarra, but had been stopped on the road by a party of Moors, who had taken most of her clothes and some gold from her; and that she would be under the necessity of returning to Deena till the fast moon was over. The same evening the new moon was seen, which ushered in the month Rhamadan. Large fires were made in different parts of the town, and a greater quantity of victuals than usual dressed upon the occasion.

By daylight the Moors were in readiness; but as I had suffered much from thirst on the road, I made my boy fill a soofroo of water for my own use; for the Moors assured me that they should not taste either meat or drink until sunset. However I found that the excessive heat of the sun, and the dust we raised in travelling, overcame their scruples, and made my soofroo a very useful part of our baggage. On our arrival at Deena I went to pay my respects to one of Ali's sons. I found him sitting in a low hut, with five or six more of his companions, washing their hands and feet, and frequently taking water into their mouths, gargling, and spitting it out again. I was no sooner seated than he handed me a double-barrelled gun, and told me to dye the stock of a blue colour and repair one of the locks. I found great difficulty in persuading him that I knew nothing about the matter. However, says he, if you cannot repair the gun, you shall give me some knives and scissors immediately ; and when my boy, who acted as interpreter, assured him that I had no such articles, he hastily snatched up a musket that stood by him, cocked it, and putting the muzzle close to the boy's ear would certainly have shot him dead upon the spot, had not the Moors wrested the musket from him, and made signs for us to retreat. The boy being terrified at this treatment attempted to make his escape in the night, but was prevented by the vigilance of the Moors, who guarded us with strict attention, and at night always went to sleep by the door of the hut in such a situation that it was almost impossible to pass without stepping upon them.

March 12th.—We departed from Deena towards Benowm, and about nine o'clock came to a Korree, whence the Moors were preparing to depart to the southward, on account of the scarcity of water ; here we filled our soofroo, and continued our journey over a hot sandy country covered with small stunted shrubs, until about one o'clock, when the heat of the sun obliged us to stop. But our water being expended, we could not prudently remain longer than a few minutes to collect a little gum, which is an excellent succedaneum[22]for water, as it keeps the mouth moist, and allays for a time the pain in the throat.

About five o'clock we came in sight of Benowm, the residence of Ali. It presented to the eye a great number of dirty-looking tents, scattered without order over a large space of ground ; and among the tents appeared large herds of camels, cattle, and goats. We reached the skirts of the camp a little before sunset, and, with much entreaty, procured a little water. My arrival was no sooner observed, than the people who drew water at the wells threw down their buckets, those in the tents mounted their horses, and men, women, and children, came running or galloping towards me. I soon found myself sur- rounded by such a crowd that I could scarcely move ; one pulled my clothes, another took off my hat, a third stopped me to examine my waistcoat-buttons, and a fourth called out, *La illah el allah Mahomet rasowl allahi* (There is but one God, and Mahomet is his Prophet), and signified, in a threatening manner, that I must repeat those words. We reached at length the king's tent, where we found a great number of people, men and women, assembled. Ali was sitting upon a black leather cushion, clipping a few hairs from his upper lip ; a female attendant holding up a looking-glass before him. He appeared to be an old man, of the Arab cast, with a long white beard ; and he had a sullen and indignant aspect. He surveyed me with attention, and inquired of the Moors if I could speak Arabic ; being answered in the negative, he appeared much surprised, and continued silent. The surrounding attendants, and especially the ladies, were abundantly more inquisitive : they asked a thousand questions, inspected every part of my apparel, searched my pockets, and obliged me to unbutton my waistcoat, and display the whiteness of my skin ; they even counted my toes and fingers, as if they doubted whether I was in truth a human being. In a little time the priest announced evening prayers ; but before the people departed, the Moor,

who had acted as interpreter, informed me that Ali was about
to present me with something to eat; and looking round I
observed some boys bringing a wild hog, which they tied to one
of the tent-strings, and Ali made signs to me to kill and dress
it for supper.   Though I was very hungry I did not think it
prudent to eat any part of an animal so much detested by the
Moors, and therefore told him that I never ate such food.   They
then untied the hog, in hopes that it would run immediately
at me—for they believe that a great enmity subsists between
hogs and Christians; but in this they were disappointed, for
the animal no sooner regained his liberty, than he began to
attack indiscriminately every person that came in his way, and
at last took shelter under the couch upon which the king was
sitting.   The assembly being thus dissolved, I was conducted
to the tent of Ali's chief slave, but was not permitted to enter,
nor allowed to touch anything belonging to it. I requested
something to eat, and a little boiled corn, with salt and water,
was at length sent me in a wooden bowl; and a mat was spread
upon the sand before the tent, on which I passed the night,
surrounded by the curious multitude.

At sunrise, Ali, with a few attendants, came on horseback
to visit me, and signified that he had provided a hut for me,
where I would be sheltered from the sun.   I was accordingly
conducted thither, and found the hut comparatively cool and
pleasant.   It was constructed of corn-stalks set up on end in
the form of a square, with a flat roof of the same materials
supported by forked sticks, to one of which was tied the wild
hog before mentioned.   This animal had certainly been placed
there by Ali's order, out of derision to a Christian; and I found
it a very disagreeable inmate, as it drew together a number of

boys, who amused themselves by beating it with sticks, until they had so irritated the hog that it ran and bit at every person within its reach.

I was no sooner seated in this my new habitation than the Moors assembled in crowds to behold me; but I found it rather a troublesome levee, for I was obliged to take off one of my stockings and show them my foot, and even to take off my jacket and waistcoat to show them how my clothes were put on and off; they were much delighted with the curious contrivance of buttons. All this was to be repeated to every succeeding visitor, for such as had already seen these wonders insisted on their friends seeing the same, and in this manner I was employed, dressing and undressing, buttoning and unbuttoning, from noon to night. About eight o'clock Ali sent me for supper some kouskous and salt and water, which was very acceptable, being the only victuals I had tasted since morning.

I observed that in the night the Moors kept regular watch, and frequently looked into the hut to see if I was asleep; and if it was quite dark they would light a wisp of grass. About two o'clock in the morning a Moor entered the hut, probably with a view to steal something, or perhaps to murder me; and groping about he laid his hand upon my shoulder. As night visitors were at best but suspicious characters I sprang up the moment he laid his hand upon me : and the Moor in his haste to get off, stumbled over my boy, and fell with his face upon the wild hog, which returned the attack by biting the Moor's arm. The screams of this man alarmed the people in the king's tent, who immediately conjectured that I had made my escape, and a number of them mounted their horses and prepared to

Moors

pursue me. I observed upon this occasion that Ali did not sleep in his own tent, but came galloping upon a white horse from a small tent at a considerable distance : indeed, the tyrannical and cruel behaviour of this man made him so jealous of every person around him, that even his own slaves and domestics knew not where he slept. When the Moors had explained to him the cause of this outcry they all went away, and I was permitted to sleep quietly until morning.

With the returning day commenced the same round of insult and irritation : the boys assembled to beat the hog, and the men and women to plague the Christian. It is impossible for me to describe the behaviour of a people who study mischief as a science, and exult in the miseries and misfortunes of their fellow-creatures. It is sufficient to observe that the rudeness, ferocity, and fanaticism, which distinguish the Moors from the rest of mankind, found here a proper subject whereon to exercise their propensities. I was a *stranger*, I was *unprotected*, and I was a *Christian ;* each of these circumstances is sufficient to drive every spark of humanity from the heart of a Moor ; but when all of them, as in my case, were combined in the same person, and a suspicion prevailed withal that I had come as a *spy* into the country, the reader will easily imagine that in such a situation I had every thing to fear. Anxious, however, to conciliate favour, and if possible to afford the Moors no pretence for ill-treating me, I readily complied with every command, and patiently bore every insult ; but never did any period of my life pass away so heavily : from sunrise to sunset was I obliged to suffer, with an unruffled countenance, the insults of the rudest savages on earth.

CHAPTER X.

Confinement at Benowm—Robbed by the Moors—Story of the Compass—Persecution—A Funeral and Wedding—Female Curiosity—Whirlwind—Wedding Ceremony.

THE Moors, though very indolent themselves, are rigid task-masters, and keep every person under them in full employment. My boy Demba was sent to the woods to collect withered grass for Ali's horses; and after a variety of projects concerning myself, they at last found out an employment for me; this was no other than the respectable office of *barber*. I was to make my first exhibition in this capacity in the royal presence, and to be honoured with the task of shaving the head of the young prince of Ludamar. I accordingly seated myself upon the sand, and the boy with some hesitation sat down beside me. A small razor, about three inches long, was put into my hand, and I was ordered to proceed; but whether from my own want of skill, or the improper shape of the instrument, I unfortunately made a slight incision in the boy's head, at the very commencement of the operation; and the king observing the awkward manner in which I held the razor, concluded that his son's head was in very improper hands, and ordered me to resign the razor and walk out of the tent. This I considered as a very fortunate circumstance; for I had laid it down as a rule, to make myself as useless and insignificant as possible, as the only means of recovering my liberty.

Subsequent to this four Moors arrived from Jarra with Johnson my interpreter, having seized him before he had received intimation of my confinement: and bringing with them a bundle of clothes that I had left at Daman Jumma's house, for my use, in case I should return by the way of Jarra. Johnson was led into Ali's tent and examined ; the bundle was opened, and I was sent for to explain the use of the different articles. I was happy however to find that Johnson had committed my papers to the charge of one of Daman's wives. When I had satisfied Ali's curiosity respecting the different articles of apparel, the bundle was again tied up and put into a large cowskin bag that stood in a corner of the tent. The same evening Ali sent three of his people to inform me that there were many thieves in the neighbourhood, and that to prevent the rest of my things from being stolen, it was necessary to convey them all into his tent. My clothes, instruments, and everything that belonged to me were accordingly carried away, and though the heat and dust made clean linen very necessary and refreshing, I could not procure a single shirt out of the small stock I had brought along with me. Ali was however disappointed by not finding among my effects the quantity of gold and amber that he expected ; but to make sure of everything, he sent the same people on the morning following, to examine whether I had any thing concealed about my person. They, with their usual rudeness, searched every part of my apparel, and stripped me of all my gold, amber, my watch, and one of my pocket-compasses. I had, fortunately, in the night buried the other compass in the sand ; and this, with the clothes I had on, was all that the tyranny of Ali had now left me.

The gold and amber were highly gratifying to Moorish avarice, but the pocket-compass soon became an object of superstitious curiosity. Ali was very desirous to be informed why that small piece of iron, the needle, always pointed to the Great Desert, and I found myself somewhat puzzled to answer the question. To have pleaded my ignorance would have created a suspicion that I wished to conceal the real truth from him ; I therefore told him that my mother resided far beyond the sands of Sahara, and that whilst she was alive the piece of iron would always point that way and serve as a guide to conduct me to her, and that if she was dead it would point to her grave. Ali now looked at the compass with redoubled amazement, turned it round and round repeatedly ; but observing that it always pointed the same way he took it up with great caution and returned it to me, manifesting that he thought there was something of magic in it, and that he was afraid of keeping so dangerous an instrument in his possession.

March 20th.—This morning a council of chief men was held in Ali's tent respecting me ; their decisions, though they were all unfavourable to me, were differently related by different persons. Some said that they intended to put me to death, others that I was only to lose my right hand ; but the most probable account was that which I received from Ali's own son, a boy about nine years of age, who came to me in the evening, and with much concern, informed me that his uncle had persuaded his father to put out my eyes which they said resembled those of a cat, and that all the Bushreens had

approved of this measure. His father however, he said, would
not put the sentence into execution until Fatima the queen,
who was at present in the north, had seen me.

Anxious to know my destiny I went to the king early in
the morning (March 21st), and as a number of Bushreens
were assembled I thought this a favourable opportunity of
discovering their intentions. I therefore began by begging
his permission to return to Jarra ; which was flatly refused
his wife he said had not yet seen me, and I must stay until
she came to Benowm, after which I should be at liberty to
depart ; and that my horse, which had been taken away from
me the day after I arrived, should be again restored to me.
Unsatisfactory as this answer was, I was forced to appear
pleased, and as there was little hopes of making my escape at
this season of the year, on account of the excessive heat and
the total want of water in the woods, I resolved to wait
patiently until the rains had set in, or until some more favourable opportunity should present itself ;—but *hope deferred
maketh the heart sick.*[23] This tedious procrastination from day
to day, and the thoughts of travelling through the Negro
kingdoms in the rainy season which was now fast approaching,
made me very melancholy, and having passed a restless night
I found myself attacked in the morning by a smart fever. I
had wrapped myself close up in my cloak with a view to
induce perspiration, and was asleep ; when a party of Moors
entered the hut, and with their usual rudeness, pulled the cloak
from me. I made signs to them that I was sick and wished
much to sleep, but I solicited in vain, my distress was matter
of sport to them, and they endeavoured to heighten it by
every means in their power. This studied and degraded

insolence to which I was constantly exposed was one of the bitterest ingredients in the cup of captivity, and often made life itself a burden to me. In these distressing moments I have frequently envied the situation of the slave, who amidst all his calamities could still possess the enjoyment of his own thoughts; the happiness to which I had for some time been a stranger. Wearied out with such continual insults, and perhaps a little peevish from the fever, I trembled lest my passion might unawares overleap the bounds of prudence, and spur me to some sudden act of resentment when death must be the inevitable consequence. In this perplexity I left my hut and walked to some shady trees at a little distance from the camp, where I lay down. But even here persecution followed me, and solitude was thought too great an indulgence for a distressed Christian. Ali's son, with a number of horsemen, came galloping to the place and ordered me to rise and follow them. I begged they would allow me to remain where I was, if it was only for a few hours; but they paid little attention to what I said, and after a few threatening words, one of them pulled out a pistol from a leather bag that was fastened to the pummel of his saddle, and presenting it towards me snapped it twice. He did this with so much indifference, that I really doubted whether the pistol was loaded. He cocked it a third time, and was striking the flint with a piece of steel, when I begged them to desist, and returned with them to the camp. When we entered Ali's tent we found him much out of humour. He called for the Moor's pistol, and amused himself for some time with opening and shutting the pan; at length taking up his powder-horn he fresh primed it, and turning round to me with a menacing look said something in Arabic which I did not understand. I desired my boy who was sitting before the tent, to inquire what offence I had committed ; when I was informed that having gone out of the camp without Ali's permission, they suspected that I had some design of making my escape, and that in future if I was seen without the skirts of the camp, orders had been given that I should be shot by the first person that observed me.

In the afternoon the horizon, to the eastward, was thick and hazy, and the Moors prognosticated a sand-wind ; which accordingly commenced on the morning following and lasted, with slight intermissions, for two days. The force of the wind was not in itself very great, it was what a seaman would have denominated a *stiff breeze*, but the quantity of sand and dust carried before it was such as to darken the whole atmosphere. It swept along from east to west in a thick and constant stream, and the air was at times so dark and full of sand that it was difficult to discern the neighbouring tents. As the Moors always dress their victuals in the open air, this sand fell in great plenty among the kouskous ; it readily adhered to the skin when moistened by perspiration, and formed a cheap and universal hair-powder. The Moors wrap a cloth round their face to prevent them from inhaling the sand, and always turn their backs to the wind when they look up, to prevent the sand falling into their eyes.

About this time all the women of the camp had their feet and the ends of their fingers stained of a dark saffron colour. I could never ascertain whether this was done from motives of religion or by way of ornament. The curiosity of the Moorish ladies had been very troublesome to me ever since my arrival at Benowm ; and on the evening of the 25th

Reaprocity

(whether from the instigation of others, or impelled by their
own ungovernable curiosity, or merely out of frolic, I cannot
affirm), a party of them came into my hut, and gave me
plainly to understand that the object of their visit was to
ascertain, by actual inspection, whether the rite of circumcision extended to the Nazarenes (Christians) as well as to the
followers of Mahomet. The reader will easily judge of my
surprise at this unexpected declaration, and in order to avoid
the proposed scrutiny I thought it best to treat the business
jocularly. I observed to them that it was not customary in
my country to give ocular demonstration in such cases before
so many beautiful women; but that if all of them would
retire except the young lady to whom I pointed (selecting the
youngest and handsomest) I would satisfy her curiosity. The
ladies enjoyed the jest, and went away laughing heartily; and
the young damsel herself, to whom I had given the preference
(though she did not avail herself of the privilege of inspection),
seemed no way displeased at the compliment, for she soon
afterwards sent me some meal and milk for my supper.

March 28th.—This morning a large herd of cattle arrived
from the eastward; and one of the drivers, to whom Ali had
lent my horse, came into my hut with the leg of an antelope
as a present, and told me that my horse was standing before
Ali's tent. In a little time Ali sent one of his slaves to inform me, that in the afternoon I must be in readiness to ride
out with him, as he intended to show me to some of his
women. About four o'clock, Ali with six of his courtiers,
came riding to my hut and told me to follow them. I readily
complied. But here a new difficulty occurred. The Moors,
accustomed to a loose and easy dress, could not reconcile

themselves to the appearance of my *nankeen breeches*, which
they said were not only inelegant, but, on account of their
tightness, very indecent; and as this was a visit to ladies, Ali
ordered my boy to bring out the loose cloak which I had
always worn since my arrival at Benowm, and told me to
wrap it close round me. We visited the tents of four different
ladies, at every one of which I was presented with a bowl of
milk and water. All these ladies were remarkably corpulent,
which is considered here as the highest mark of beauty. They
were very inquisitive, and examined my hair and skin with
great attention, but affected to consider me as a sort of inferior
being to themselves, and would knit their brows, and seemed
to shudder when they looked at the whiteness of my skin.
In the course of this evening's excursion, my dress and appearance afforded infinite mirth to the company, who galloped
round me as if they were baiting a wild animal, twirling
their muskets round their heads, and exhibiting various feats
of activity and horsemanship, seemingly to display their
superior prowess over a miserable captive.

The Moors are certainly very good horsemen. They ride
without fear. Their saddles being high before and behind afford
them a very secure seat, and if they chance to fall, the whole
country is so soft and sandy, that they are very seldom hurt.
Their greatest pride, and one of their principal amusements, is
to put the horse to his full speed and then stop him with a
sudden jerk, so as frequently to bring him down upon his
haunches. Ali always rode upon a milk-white horse, with its
tail dyed red. He never walked unless when he went to say
his prayers; and even in the night two or three horses were
always kept ready saddled, at a little distance from his own

tent. The Moors set a very high value upon their horses, for it is by their superior fleetness that they are enabled to make so many predatory excursions into the Negro countries. They feed them three or four times a day, and generally give them a large quantity of sweet milk in the evening, which the horses appear to relish very much.

April 3d.—This forenoon a child, which had been some time sickly, died in the next tent, and the mother and relations immediately began the death howl. They were joined by a number of female visitors who came on purpose to assist at this melancholy concert. I had no opportunity of seeing the burial, which is generally performed secretly in the dusk of the evening, and frequently at only a few yards' distance from the tent. Over the grave they plant one particular shrub; and no stranger is allowed to pluck a leaf, or even to touch it, so great a veneration have they for the dead.

April 7th.—About four o'clock in the afternoon a whirlwind passed through the camp with such violence that it overturned three tents and blew down one side of my hut. These whirlwinds come from the Great Desert, and at this season of the year are so common that I have seen five or six of them at one time. They carry up quantities of sand to an amazing height, which resemble at a distance so many moving pillars of smoke.

The scorching heat of the sun upon a dry and sandy country makes the air insufferably hot. Ali having robbed me of my thermometer I had no means of forming a comparative judgment; but in the middle of the day, when the beams of the vertical sun are seconded by the scorching wind from the Desert, the ground is frequently heated to such a degree as not to be borne by the naked foot—even the Negro slaves will not run from one tent to another without their sandals. At this time of the day the Moors lie stretched at length in their tents, either asleep or unwilling to move, and I have often felt the wind so hot that I could not hold my hand in the current of air, which came through the crevices of my hut, without feeling sensible pain.

In the evening (April 10th) the tabala, or large drum, was beat to announce a wedding, which was held at one of the neighbouring tents. A great number of people of both sexes assembled, but without that mirth and hilarity which take place at a Negro wedding : here was neither singing nor dancing, nor any other amusement that I could perceive. A woman was beating the drum, and the other women joining at times like a chorus, by setting up a shrill scream, and at the same time moving their tongues from one side of their mouth to the other with great celerity. I was soon tired, and had returned into my hut, where I was sitting almost asleep, when an old woman entered, with a wooden bowl in her hand, and signified that she had brought me a present from the bride. Before I could recover from the surprise which this message created, the woman discharged the contents of the bowl full in my face. Finding that it was the same sort of holy water with which, among the Hottentots, a priest is said to sprinkle a new married couple, I began to suspect that the old lady was actuated by mischief or malice ; but she gave me seriously to understand that it was a nuptial bene-diction from the bride's own person, and which, on such occasions, is always received by the young unmarried Moors as a mark of distinguished favour. This being the case, I wiped my face, and sent my acknowledgments to the lady. The wedding-drum continued to beat, and the women to sing, or rather whistle, all night. About nine in the morning the bride was brought in state from her mother's tent, attended by a number of women who carried her tent (a present from the husband), some bearing up the poles, others holding by the strings; and in this manner they marched, whistling as formerly, until they came to the place appointed for her residence, where they pitched the tent. The husband followed, with a number of men leading four bullocks, which they tied to the tent strings; and having killed another, and distributed the beef among the people, the ceremony was concluded.

CHAPTER XI.

Captivity at the Camp of Benowm continued—Information collected concerning Houssa and Timbuctoo — the Route described from Morocco to Benowm—Distress from Hunger—Ali removes his Camp to the northward — Park carried Prisoner to the new Encampment, and presented to Queen Fatima—Great Distress from the Want of Water.

ONE whole month had now elapsed since I was led into captivity, during which time each returning day brought me fresh distresses. I watched the lingering course of the sun with anxiety, and blessed his evening beams as they shed a yellow lustre along the sandy floor of my hut; for it was then that my oppressors left me, and allowed me to pass the sultry night in solitude and reflection.

About midnight a bowl of kouskous, with some salt and water, was brought for me and my two attendants; this was our common fare, and it was all that was allowed us to allay the cravings of hunger and support nature for the whole of the following day; for it is to be observed that this was the Mahomedan Lent,[24] and as the Moors keep the fast with a religious strictness, they thought it proper to compel me, though a Christian, to a similar observance. Time, however, somewhat reconciled me to my situation. I found that I could bear hunger and thirst better than I expected; and at length I endeavoured to beguile the tedious hours by learning to write Arabic. The people who came to see me soon made me acquainted with the characters; and I discovered, that by engaging their attention in this way they were not so troublesome as otherwise they would have been. Indeed, when I observed any person whose countenance I thought bore malice towards me, I made it a rule to ask him either to write in the sand himself, or to decipher what I had already written, and the pride of showing his superior attainments generally induced him to comply with my request.

As Queen Fatima had not yet arrived, Ali proposed to go to the north and bring her back with him; but as the place was two days' journey from Benowm it was necessary to have some refreshment on the road, and Ali, suspicious of those about him, was so afraid of being poisoned that he never ate anything but what was dressed under his own immediate inspection. A fine bullock was therefore killed, and the flesh being cut up into thin slices was dried in the sun; and this, with two bags of dry kouskous, formed his travelling provisions.

Previous to his departure the black people of the town of Benowm came, according to their annual custom, to show their arms, and bring their stipulated tribute of corn and cloth. They were but badly armed; twenty-two with muskets, forty or fifty with bows and arrows, and nearly the same number of men and boys with spears only. They arranged themselves before the tent, where they waited until their arms were examined and some little disputes settled.

About midnight on the 16th April Ali departed quietly from Benowm, accompanied by a few attendants. He was expected to return in the course of nine or ten days.

Two days after the departure of Ali, a Shereef [25] arrived with salt and some other articles from Walet, [26] the capital of the kingdom of Biroo. As there was no tent appropriated for him he took up his abode in the same hut with me. He seemed to be a well-informed man, and his acquaintance both with the Arabic and Bambarra tongues enabled him to travel with ease and safety through a number of kingdoms; for though his place of residence was Walet he had visited Houssa, and had lived some years at Timbuctoo. Upon my inquiring so particularly about the distance from Walet to Timbuctoo, he asked me if I intended to travel that way; and being answered in the affirmative, he shook his head and said *it would not do;* for that Christians were looked upon there as the devil's children, and enemies to the Prophet. From him I learned the following particulars :—That Houssa was the largest town he had ever seen; that Walet was larger that Timbuctoo; but being remote from the Niger, and its trade consisting chiefly of salt, it was not so much resorted to by strangers; that between Benowm and Walet was ten days' journey, but the road did not lead through any remarkable towns, and travellers supported themselves by purchasing milk from the Arabs who keep their herds by the watering-places; two of the days' journeys were over a sandy country without water. From Walet to Timbuctoo was eleven days more, but water was more plentiful, and the journey was usually performed upon bullocks. He said there were many Jews at Timbuctoo, but they all spoke Arabic, and used the same prayers as the Moors. He frequently pointed his hand to the south-east quarter, or rather the east by south, observing that Timbuctoo was situated in that direction; and though I made him repeat this information again and again, I never found him to vary more than half a point, which was to the southward.

April 24th.—This morning Shereef Sidi Mahomed Moora Abdalla, a native of Morocco, arrived with five bullocks loaded with salt. He had formerly resided some months at Gibraltar, where he had picked up as much English as enabled him to make himself understood. He informed me that he had been five months in coming from Santa Cruz; but that great part of the time had been spent in trading. When I requested him to enumerate the days employed in travelling from Morocco to Benowm, he gave them as follows:—To Swera, three days; to Agadier, three; to Jiniken, ten; to Wadenoon, four; to Lakeneigh, five; to Zeeriwin-zeriman, five; to Tisheet, ten; to Benowm ten: in all, fifty days—but travellers usually rest a long while at Jiniken and Tisheet, at the latter of which places they dig the rock salt, which is so great an article of commerce with the Negroes.

In conversing with these Shereefs, and the different strangers that resorted to the camp, I passed my time with rather less uneasiness than formerly. On the other hand, as the dressing of my victuals was now left entirely to the care of Ali's slaves, over whom I had not the smallest control, I found myself but ill supplied, worse even than in the fast month. For two successive nights they neglected to send us our accustomed meal; and though my boy went to a small Negro town near the camp and begged with great diligence from hut to hut, he could only procure a few handfuls of ground nuts, which he readily shared with me. Hunger at first is certainly a very painful sensation, but when it has continued for some time this pain is succeeded by languor and debility; in which case, a draught of water, by keeping the stomach distended, will greatly exhilarate the spirits, and remove for a short time every sort of uneasiness. Johnson and Demba were very much dejected. They lay stretched upon the sand in a sort of torpid slumber, and even when the kouskous arrived I found some difficulty in awakening them. I felt no inclination to sleep, but was affected with a deep convulsive respiration, like constant sighing, and what alarmed me still more, a dimness of sight and a tendency to faint when I attempted to sit up. These symptoms did not go off until some time after I had received nourishment.

We had been for some days in daily expectation of Ali's return from Saheel (or the north country) with his wife Fatima. In the meanwhile Mansong, king of Bambarra (as I have related in Chapter VIII) had sent to Ali for a party of horse to assist in storming Gedingooma. With this demand Ali had not only refused to comply, but had treated the messengers with great haughtiness and contempt; upon which Mansong gave up all thoughts of taking the town, and prepared to chastise Ali for his contumacy.

Things were in this situation when, on the 29th of April, a messenger arrived at Benowm with the disagreeable intelligence that the Bambarra army was approaching the frontiers of Ludamar. This threw the whole country into confusion; and in the afternoon, Ali's son, with about twenty horsemen, arrived at Benowm. He ordered all the cattle to be driven away immediately, all the tents to be struck, and the people to hold themselves in readiness to depart at daylight the next morning.

At daybreak the whole camp was in motion. The baggage was carried upon bullocks, the two tent poles being placed one on each side, and the different wooden articles of the tent distributed in like manner; the tent cloth was thrown over all, and upon this was commonly placed one or two women— for the Moorish women are very bad walkers. The king's favourite concubines rode upon camels, with a saddle of a particular construction and a canopy to shelter them from the sun. We proceeded to the northward until noon, when the king's son ordered the whole company, except two tents, to enter a thick low wood which was upon our right. I was sent along with the two tents, and arrived in the evening at a Negro town called Farani; here we pitched the tents in an open place at no great distance from the town.

The hurry and confusion which attended this decampment prevented the slaves from dressing the usual quantity of victuals; and lest their dry provisions should be exhausted before they reached their place of destination (for as yet none but Ali and the chief men knew whither we were going), they thought proper to make me observe this day as a day of fasting.

As I had some reason to suspect that the succeeding day was also to be considered as a fast, I went in the morning to the Negro town of Farani and begged some provisions from the Dooty, who readily supplied my wants, and desired me to come to his house every day during my stay in the neighbourhood. These hospitable people are looked upon by the Moors as an abject race of slaves, and are treated accordingly. Two of Ali's household slaves, a man and a woman, who had come along with the two tents, went this morning to water the cattle from the town wells, at which there began to be a great scarcity. When the Negro women observed the cattle approaching, they took up their pitchers and ran with all

possible haste towards the town ; but before they could enter
the gate they were stopped by the slaves, who compelled
them to bring back the water they had drawn for their own
families, and empty it into the troughs for the cattle. When
this was exhausted, they were ordered to draw water until
such time as the cattle had all drank ; and the woman slave
actually broke two wooden bowls over the heads of the black
girls, because they were somewhat dilatory in obeying her
commands.

We departed from the vicinity of Farani (May 3d) and
after a circuitous route through the woods arrived at Ali's
camp in the afternoon. This encampment was larger than
that of Benowm, and was situated in the middle of a thick
wood about two miles distant from a Negro town, called
Bubaker. I immediately waited upon Ali, in order to pay
my respects to Queen Fatima, who had come with him
from Saheel. He seemed much pleased with my coming ;
shook hands with me, and informed his wife that I was the
Christian. She was a woman of the Arab cast, with long
black hair, and remarkably corpulent. She appeared at first
rather shocked at the thought of having a Christian so near
her ; but when I had (by means of a Negro boy who spoke
the Mandingo and Arabic tongues) answered a great many
questions, which her curiosity suggested, respecting the country
of the Christians, she seemed more at ease, and presented me
with a bowl of milk, which I considered as a very favourable
omen.

The heat was now almost insufferable ; all nature seemed
sinking under it. The distant country presented to the eye a
dreary expanse of sand, with a few stunted trees and prickly

bushes, in the shade of which the hungry cattle licked up the withered grass, while the camels and goats picked off the scanty foliage. The scarcity of water was greater here than at Benowm. Day and night the wells were crowded with cattle, lowing and fighting with each other to come at the troughs ; excessive thirst made many of them furious ; others, being too weak to contend for the water, endeavoured to quench their thirst by devouring the black mud from the gutters near the wells ; which they did with great avidity, though it was commonly fatal to them.

This great scarcity of water was felt severely by all the people of the camp, and by none more than myself ; for though Ali allowed me a skin for containing water, and Fatima once or twice gave me a small supply when I was in distress, yet such was the barbarous disposition of the Moors at the wells, that when my boy attempted to fill the skin, he commonly received a sound drubbing for his presumption. Every one was astonished that the slave of a Christian should attempt to draw water from wells which had been dug by the followers of the Prophet. This treatment at length so frightened the boy, that I believe he would sooner have perished with thirst than attempted again to fill the skin. He therefore contented himself with begging water from the Negro slaves who attended the camp, and I followed his example, but with very indifferent success, for though I let no opportunity slip, and was very urgent in my solicitations, both to the Moors and the Negroes, I was but ill supplied, and frequently passed the night in the situation of Tantalus. No sooner had I shut my eyes than fancy would convey me to the streams and rivers of my native land ; there, as I wandered along the verdant brink, I surveyed

the clear stream with transport and hastened to swallow the delightful draught ;—but alas ! disappointment awakened me, and I found myself a lonely captive perishing of thirst amidst the wilds of Africa.

One night, having solicited in vain for water at the camp, and being quite feverish, I resolved to try my fortune at the wells, which were about half a-mile distant from the camp. Accordingly I set out about midnight, and being guided by the lowing of the cattle soon arrived at the place, where I found the Moors very busy drawing water. I requested permission to drink, but was driven away with outrageous abuse. Passing, however, from one well to another, I came at last to one where there was only an old man and two boys. I made the same request to this man, and he immediately drew me up a bucket of water ; but as I was about to take hold of it he recollected that I was a Christian, and fearing that his bucket might be polluted by my lips, he dashed the water into the trough and told me to drink from thence. Though this trough was none of the largest, and three cows were already drinking in it, I resolved to come in for my share ; and kneeling down thrust my head between two of the cows and drank with great pleasure until the water was nearly exhausted and the cows began to contend with each other for the last mouthful.

In adventures of this nature I passed the sultry month of May, during which no material change took place in my situation. Ali still considered me as a lawful prisoner; and Fatima, though she allowed me a larger quantity of victuals than I had been accustomed to receive at Benowm, had as yet said nothing on the subject of my release. In the meantime the frequent changes of the wind, the gathering clouds, and distant lightning, with other appearances of approaching rain, indicated that the wet season was at hand ; when the Moors annually evacuate the country of the Negroes, and return to the skirts of the Great Desert. This made me consider that my fate was drawing towards a crisis, and I resolved to wait for the event without any seeming uneasiness ; but circumstances occurred which produced a change in my favour more suddenly than I had foreseen or had reason to expect. The case was this : The fugitive Kaartans, who had taken refuge in Ludamar, as I have related in Chapter VIII., finding that the Moors were about to leave them, and dreading the resentment of their own sovereign whom they had so basely deserted, offered to treat with Ali for two hundred Moorish horsemen to co-operate with them in an effort to expel Daisy from Gedingooma ; for until Daisy should be vanquished or humbled they considered that they could neither return to their native towns, nor live in security in any of the neighbouring kingdoms. With a view to extort money from these people by means of this treaty, Ali despatched his son to Jarra, and prepared to follow him in the course of a few days. This was an opportunity of too great consequence to me to be neglected. I immediately applied to Fatima (who, I found, had the chief direction in all affairs of state), and begged her interest with Ali to give me permission to accompany him to Jarra. This request after some hesitation was favourably received. Fatima looked kindly on me, and I believe was at length moved with compassion towards me. My bundles were brought from the large cowskin-bag that stood in the corner of Ali's tent, and I was ordered to explain the use of the different articles, and show the method of putting on the boots, stockings, etc., **with** all which I cheerfully complied, and was told that in the course of a few days I should be at liberty to depart.

Believing, therefore, that I should certainly find the means of escaping from Jarra, if I should once get thither, I now freely indulged the pleasing hope that my captivity would soon terminate.

CHAPTER XII.

Character of the Moors—Religion—Education—Idea of Beauty—
Employments—Dress—The King—Subjects—Great Desert, its
wild and domestic animals.

THE Moors of this part of Africa are divided into many separate tribes, of which the most formidable, according to what was reported to me, are those of Trasart and Il Braken, which inhabit the northern bank of the Senegal river. The tribes of Gedumah, Jafnoo, and Ludamar, though not so numerous as the former, are nevertheless very powerful and warlike, and are each governed by a chief, or king, who exercises absolute jurisdiction over his own horde, without acknowledging allegiance to a common sovereign. In time of peace the employment of the people is pasturage. The Moors, indeed, subsist chiefly on the flesh of their cattle, and are always in the extreme of either gluttony or abstinence. In consequence of the frequent and severe fasts which their religion enjoins, and the toilsome journeys which they sometimes undertake across the Desert, they are enabled to bear both hunger and thirst with surprising fortitude; but whenever opportunities occur of satisfying their appetite, they generally devour more at one meal than would serve a European for three. They pay but little attention to agriculture, purchasing their corn, cotton, cloth, and other necessaries, from the Negroes, in exchange for salt, which they dig from the pits in the Great Desert.

The natural barrenness of the country is such that it furnishes but few materials for manufacture. The Moors, however, contrive to weave a strong cloth with which they cover their tents ; the thread is spun by their women from the hair of goats, and they prepare the hides of their cattle so as to furnish saddles, bridles, pouches, and other articles of leather. They are likewise sufficiently skilful to convert the native iron, which they procure from the Negroes, into spears and knives, and also into pots for boiling their food ; but their sabres and other weapons, as well as their fire-arms and ammunition, they purchase from the Europeans in exchange for the Negro slaves which they obtain in their predatory excursions. Their chief commerce of this kind is with the French traders on the Senegal river.

The Moors are rigid Mahomedans, and possess, with the bigotry and superstition, all the intolerance of their sect. They have no mosques at Benowm, but perform their devotions in a sort of open shed, or inclosure made of mats. The priest is at the same time schoolmaster to the juniors. His pupils assemble every evening before his tent, where by the light of a large fire made of brushwood and cow's dung, they are taught a few sentences from the Koran, and are initiated into the principles of their creed. Their alphabet differs but little from that in Richardson's Arabic Grammar. They always write with the vowel points. Their priests even affect to know something of foreign literature. The priest of Benowm assured me that he could read the writings of the Christians. He showed me a number of barbarous characters, which he asserted were the Roman Alphabet ; and he produced another specimen, equally unintelligible, which he declared to be the

Kallam il Indi, or Persian. His library consisted of nine volumes in quarto ; most of them, I believe, were books of religion, for the name of Mahomet appeared in red letters in almost every page of each. His scholars wrote their lessons upon thin boards, paper being too expensive for general use. The boys were diligent enough, and appeared to possess a considerable share of emulation, carrying their boards slung over their shoulders when about their common employments. When a boy has committed to memory a few of their prayers, and can read and write certain parts of the Koran, he is reckoned sufficiently instructed, and with this slender stock of learning commences his career of life. Proud of his acquirements, he surveys with contempt the unlettered Negro, and embraces every opportunity of displaying his superiority over such of his countrymen as are not distinguished by the same accomplishments.

The education of the girls is neglected altogether ; mental accomplishments are but little attended to by the women, nor is the want of them considered by the men as a defect in the female character. They are regarded, I believe, as an inferior species of animals, and seem to be brought up for no other purpose than that of administering to the sensual pleasures of their imperious masters. Voluptuousness is therefore considered as their chief accomplishment, and slavish submission as their indispensable duty.

The Moors have singular ideas of feminine perfection. The gracefulness of figure and motion and a countenance enlivened by expression, are by no means essential points in their standard ; with them corpulence and beauty appear to be terms nearly synonymous. A woman of even moderate pretensions must be one who cannot walk without a slave under each arm to support her, and a perfect beauty is a load for a camel. In consequence of this prevalent taste for unwieldiness of bulk the Moorish ladies take great pains to acquire it early in life, and for this purpose many of the young girls are compelled by their mothers to devour a great quantity of kouskous, and drink a large bowl of camel's milk every morning. It is of no importance whether the girl has an appetite or not, the kouskous and milk must be swallowed, and obedience is frequently enforced by blows. I have seen a poor girl sit crying, with a bowl at her lips, for more than an hour, and her mother, with a stick in her hand, watching her all the while, and using the stick without mercy whenever she observed that her daughter was not swallowing. This singular practice, instead of producing indigestion and disease, soon covers the young lady with that degree of plumpness which, in the eye of a Moor, is perfection itself.

As the Moors purchase all their clothing from the Negroes, the women are forced to be very economical in the article of dress. In general they content themselves with a broad piece of cotton cloth, which is wrapped round the middle, and hangs round like a petticoat almost to the ground; to the upper part of this are sewed two square pieces, one before and the other behind, which are fastened together over the shoulders. The head-dress is commonly a bandage of cotton cloth, with some parts of it broader than others, which serve to conceal the face when they walk in the sun; frequently, however, when they walk abroad they veil themselves from head to foot.

The employment of the women varies, according to their

degrees of opulence. Queen Fatima and a few others of high
rank, like the great ladies in some parts of Europe, pass their
time chiefly in conversing with their visitors, performing their
devotions, or admiring their charms in a looking-glass. The
women of inferior class employ themselves in different
domestic duties. They are very vain and talkative, and when
anything puts them out of humour they commonly vent their
anger upon their female slaves, over whom they rule with
severe and despotic authority, which leads me to observe that
the condition of these poor captives is deplorably wretched.
At daybreak they are compelled to fetch water from the wells
in large skins called *girbas*; and as soon as they have brought
water enough to serve the family for the day, as well as the
horses (for the Moors seldom give their horses the trouble of
going to the wells), they are then employed in pounding the
corn and dressing the victuals. This being always done in
the open air, the slaves are exposed to the combined heat of
the sun, the sand, and the fire. In the intervals, it is their
business to sweep the tent, churn the milk, and perform other
domestic offices. With all this they are badly fed and oftentimes cruelly punished.

The men's dress among the Moors of Ludamar differs but
little from that of the Negroes (which has been already
described), except that they have all adopted that characteristic of the Mahomedan sect, the *turban*; which is here
universally made of white cotton cloth. Such of the Moors
as have long beards display them with a mixture of pride and
satisfaction as denoting an Arab ancestry. Of this number
was Ali himself; but among the generality of the people, the
hair is short and bushy and universally black. And here I

may be permitted to observe, that if any one circumstance excited among them favourable thoughts towards my own person it was my beard, which was now grown to an enormous length, and was always beheld with approbation or envy. I believe in my conscience they thought it too good a beard for a Christian.

The only diseases which I observed to prevail among the Moors were the intermittent fever and dysentery, for the cure of which, nostrums are sometimes administered by their old women; but, in general, nature is left to her own operations. Mention was made to me of the small-pox as being sometimes very destructive; but it had not, to my knowledge, made its appearance in Ludamar while I was in captivity. That it prevails, however, among some tribes of the Moors, and that it is frequently conveyed by them to the Negroes in the southern states, I was assured on the authority of Dr. Laidley, who also informed me that the Negroes on the Gambia practise innoculation.

The administration of criminal justice, as far as I had opportunities of observing, was prompt and decisive. For although civil rights were but little regarded in Ludamar, it was necessary when crimes were committed that examples should sometimes be made. On such occasions the offender was brought before Ali, who pronounced, of his sole authority, what judgment he thought proper. But I understood that capital punishment was seldom or never inflicted except on the Negroes.

Although the wealth of the Moors consist chiefly in their numerous herds of cattle, yet, as the pastoral life does not afford full employment, the majority of the people are perfectly idle, and spend the day in trifling conversation about their horses, or in laying schemes of depredation on the Negro villages.

The usual place of rendezvous for the indolent is the king's tent, where great liberty of speech seems to be exercised by the company towards each other, while in speaking of their chief they express but one opinion. In praise of their sovereign they are unanimous. Songs are composed in his honour, which the company frequently sing in concert; but they are so loaded with gross adulations, that no man but a Moorish despot could hear them without blushing.

The king is distinguished by the fineness of his dress, which is composed of blue cotton cloth brought from Timbuctoo, or white linen or muslin from Morocco. He has likewise a larger tent than any other person, with a white cloth over it; but in his usual intercourse with his subjects, all distinctions of rank are frequently forgotten. He sometimes eats out of the same bowl with his camel-driver, and reposes himself during the heat of the day upon the same bed. The expenses of his government and household are defrayed by a tax upon his Negro subjects, which is paid by every householder, either in corn, cloth, or gold dust; a tax upon the different Moorish korrees, or watering-places, which is commonly levied in cattle; and a tax upon all merchandise which passes through the kingdom, and is generally collected in kind. But a considerable part of the king's revenue arises from the plunder of individuals. The Negro inhabitants of Ludamar and the travelling merchants are afraid of appearing rich; for Ali, who has spies stationed in the different towns to give him information concerning the wealth of his subjects, frequently invents some frivolous plea for seizing their property, and reducing the opulent to a level with their fellow-citizens.

Of the number of Ali's Moorish subjects I had no means of forming a correct estimate. The military strength of Ludamar consists in cavalry. They are well mounted, and appear to be very expert in skirmishing and attacking by surprise. Every soldier furnishes his own horse, and finds his accoutrements, consisting of a large sabre, a double-barrelled gun, a small red leather bag for holding his balls, and a powder-horn slung over the shoulder. He has no pay, nor any remuneration but what arises from plunder. This body is not very numerous; for when Ali made war upon Bambarra, I was informed that his whole force did not exceed two thousand cavalry. They constitute, however, by what I could learn, but a very small proportion of his Moorish subjects. The horses are very beautiful, and so highly esteemed that the Negro princes will sometimes give from twelve to fourteen slaves for one horse.

Ludamar has for its northern boundary the Great Desert of Sahara. From the best inquiries I could make, this vast ocean of sand, which occupies so large a space in Northern Africa, may be pronounced almost destitute of inhabitants, except where the scanty vegetation which appears in certain spots affords pasturage for the flocks of a few miserable Arabs, who wander from one well to another. In other places, where the supply of water and pasturage is more abundant, small parties of the Moors have taken up their residence. Here they live in independent poverty, secure from the tyrannical government of Barbary. But the greater part of the Desert, being totally destitute of water, is seldom visited by any human being, unless where the trading caravans trace out their toilsome and dangerous route across it. In some parts of this extensive waste, the ground is covered with low stunted shrubs, which serve as landmarks for the caravans, and furnish the camels with a scanty forage. In other parts the disconsolate wanderer, wherever he turns, sees nothing around him but a vast interminable expanse of sand and sky —a gloomy and barren void, where the eye finds no particular object to rest upon, and the mind is filled with painful apprehensions of perishing with thirst. "Surrounded by this dreary solitude, the traveller sees the dead bodies of birds which the violence of the wind has brought from happier regions ; and as he ruminates on the fearful length of his remaining passage, listens with horror to the voice of the driving blast, the only sound that interrupts the awful repose of the Desert."*

The few wild animals which inhabit these melancholy regions are the antelope and the ostrich, their swiftness of foot enabling them to reach the distant watering-places. On the skirts of the desert, where water is more plentiful, are found lions, panthers, elephants, and wild boars.

Of domestic animals, the only one that can endure the fatigue of crossing the desert is the camel. By the particular conformation of the stomach he is enabled to carry a supply of water sufficient for ten or twelve days; his broad and yielding foot is well adapted for a sandy country, and by a singular motion of his upper lip, he picks the smallest leaves from the thorny shrubs of the desert as he passes along. The

* Proceedings of the African Association, Part I.

Paragraph on Moors

camel is, therefore, the only beast of burthen employed by the trading caravans which traverse the desert in different directions from Barbary to Nigritia. As this useful and docile creature has been sufficiently described by systematical writers, it is unnecessary for me to enlarge upon his properties. I shall only add that his flesh, though to my own taste dry and unsavoury, is preferred by the Moors to any other, and that the milk of the female is in universal esteem, and is indeed sweet, pleasant, and nutritive.

I have observed that the Moors in their complexion resemble the Mulattoes of the West Indies, but they have something unpleasant in their aspect which the Mulattoes have not. I fancied that I discovered in the features of most of them a disposition towards cruelty and low cunning; and I could never contemplate their physiognomy without feeling sensible uneasiness. From the staring wildness of their eyes a stranger would immediately set them down as a nation of lunatics. The treachery and malevolence of their character are manifested in their plundering excursions against the Negro villages. Oftentimes, without the smallest provocation, and sometimes under the fairest professions of friendship, they will suddenly seize upon the Negroes' cattle, and even on the inhabitants themselves. The Negroes very seldom retaliate. The enterprising boldness of the Moors, their knowledge of the country, and, above all, the superior fleetness of their horses, make them such formidable enemies that the petty Negro states which border upon the desert are in continual terror while the Moorish tribes are in the vicinity, and are too much awed to think of resistance.

Like the roving Arabs, the Moors frequently remove from

one place to another, according to the season of the year or the convenience of pasturage. In the month of February, when the heat of the sun scorches up every sort of vegetation in the desert, they strike their tents and approach the Negro country to the south, where they reside until the rains commence in the month of July. At this time, having purchased corn and other necessaries from the Negroes in exchange for salt, they again depart to the northward, and continue in the desert until the rains are over, and that part of the country becomes burnt up and barren.

This wandering and restless way of life, while it inures them to hardships, strengthens, at the same time, the bonds of their little society, and creates in them an aversion towards strangers, which is almost insurmountable. Cut off from all intercourse with civilised nations, and boasting an advantage over the Negroes, by possessing, though in a very limited degree, the knowledge of letters, they are at once the vainest and proudest, and perhaps the most bigoted, ferocious, and intolerant of all the nations on the earth—combining in their character the blind superstition of the Negro with the savage cruelty and treachery of the Arab.

It is probable that many of them had never beheld a white man before my arrival at Benowm ; but they had all been taught to regard the Christian name with inconceivable abhorrence, and to consider it nearly as lawful to murder a European as it would be to kill a dog. The melancholy fate of Major Houghton, and the treatment I experienced during my confinement among them, will, I trust, serve as a warning to future travellers to avoid this inhospitable district.

CHAPTER XIII.

*Departure for Jarra—Demba seized and sent back into Slavery—Life
at Jarra—Approach of Daisy King of Kaarta's army towards
Jarra—Desertion of the town—Park's Flight—Overtaken by a
party of Moors and robbed—Eventual Escape.*

HAVING, as has been related, obtained permission to accompany Ali to Jarra, I took leave of Queen Fatima,
who, with much grace and civility, returned me part of my
apparel ; and the evening before my departure, my horse, with
the saddle and bridle, were sent me by Ali's order.

Early on the morning of the 26th of May I departed from
the camp of Bubaker, accompanied by my two attendants,
Johnson and Demba, and a number of Moors on horseback ;
Ali, with about fifty horsemen, having gone privately from the
camp during the night. We stopped about noon at Farani,
and were there joined by twelve Moors riding upon camels,
and with them we proceeded to a watering-place in the woods,
where we overtook Ali and his fifty horsemen. They were
lodged in some low shepherds' tents near the wells. As the
company was numerous, the tents could scarcely accommodate
us all ; and I was ordered to sleep in the open space in the
centre of the tents, where every one might observe my motions.
During the night there was much lightning from the north-
east ; and about day-break a very heavy sand-wind commenced,

which continued with great violence until four in the afternoon. The quantity of sand which passed to the westward, in
the course of this day, must have been prodigiously great. At
times it was impossible to look up; and the cattle were so
tormented by the particles lodging in their ears and eyes that
they ran about like mad creatures, and I was in continual
danger of being trampled to death by them.

Early in the succeeding morning the Moors saddled their
horses, and Ali's chief slave ordered me to get in readiness. In
a little time the same messenger returned, and taking my boy
by the shoulders, told him, in the Mandingo language, that
"Ali was to be his master in future;" and then turning to me,
"The business is settled at last (said he); the boy, and everything but your horse, goes back to Bubaker; but you may take
the old fool (meaning Johnson, the interpreter) with you to
Jarra." I made him no answer; but being shocked beyond
description at the idea of losing the poor boy, I hastened to Ali,
who was at breakfast before his tent, surrounded by many of
his courtiers. I told him (perhaps in rather too passionate a
strain) that whatever imprudence I had been guilty of in
coming into his country, I thought I had already been sufficiently punished for it by being so long detained, and then
plundered of all my little property, which, however, gave me
no uneasiness, when compared with what he had just now done
to me. I observed that the boy he had now seized upon was
not a slave, and had been accused of no offence; he was indeed
one of my attendants, and his faithful services in that station
had procured him his freedom; his fidelity and attachment
had made him follow me into my present situation; and as he
looked up to me for protection, I could not see him deprived

of his liberty without remonstrating against such an act. as the height of cruelty and injustice. Ali made no reply, but with a haughty air and malignant smile, told his interpreter that if I did not mount my horse immediately, he would send me back likewise. There is something in the frown of a tyrant which rouses the most secret emotions of the heart; I could not suppress my feelings, and for once entertained an indignant wish to rid the world of such a monster.

Poor Demba was not less affected than myself; he had formed a strong attachment towards me, and had a cheerfulness of disposition which often beguiled the tedious hours of captivity; he was likewise a proficient in the Bambarra tongue, and promised on that account to be of great utility to me in future. But it was in vain to expect anything favourable to humanity from people who were strangers to its dictates. So, having shaken hands with this unfortunate boy, and blended my tears with his, assuring him, however, that I would do my utmost to redeem him, I saw him led off by three of Ali's slaves towards the camp at Bubaker.

When the Moors had mounted their horses I was ordered to follow them; and after a toilsome journey through the woods in a very sultry day, we arrived in the afternoon at a walled village, called Doombani; where we remained two days, waiting for the arrival of some horsemen from the northward.

On the 1st of June we departed from Doombani towards Jarra. Our company now amounted to two hundred men, all on horseback; for the Moors never use infantry in their wars. They appeared capable of enduring great fatigue; but from their total want of discipline, our journey to Jarra was more like a fox-chace than the march of an army.

At Jarra I took up my lodging at the house of my old acquaintance Daman Jumma, and informed him of everything that had befallen me. I particularly requested him to use his interest with Ali to redeem my boy, and promised him a bill upon Dr. Laidley for the value of two slaves, the moment he brought him to Jarra. Daman very readily undertook to negotiate the business, but found that Ali considered the boy as my principal interpreter, and was unwilling to part with him, lest he should fall a second time into my hands, and be instrumental in conducting me to Bambarra. Ali therefore put off the matter from day to day, but withal told Daman that if he wished to purchase the boy for himself he should have him thereafter at the common price of a slave ; which Daman agreed to pay for him whenever Ali should send him to Jarra.

The chief object of Ali in this journey to Jarra, as I have already related, was to procure money from such of the Kaartans as had taken refuge in his country. Some of these had solicited his protection to avoid the horrors of war ; but by far the greatest number of them were dissatisfied men, who wished the ruin of their own sovereign. These people no sooner heard that the Bambarran army had returned to Sego without subduing Daisy, as was generally expected, than they resolved to make a sudden attack themselves upon him before he could recruit his forces, which were now known to be much diminished by a bloody campaign and in great want of provisions. With this view they solicited the Moors to join them, and offered to hire of Ali two hundred horsemen, which Ali, with the warmest professions of friendship, agreed to furnish, upon condition that they should previously supply him with four hundred head of cattle, two hundred garments of blue cloth, and a considerable quantity of beads and ornaments. The raising this impost somewhat perplexed them; and in order to procure the cattle, they persuaded the king to demand one-half the stipulated number from the people of Jarra, promising to replace them in a short time. Ali agreed to this proposal; and the same evening (June 2d) the drum was sent through the town, and the crier announced that if any person suffered his cattle to go into the woods the next morning, before the king had chosen his quota of them, his house should be plundered and his slaves taken from him. The people dared not disobey the proclamation, and next morning about two hundred of their best cattle were selected and delivered to the Moors; the full complement was made up afterwards by means equally unjust and arbitrary.

Some days after, Ali sent his chief slave to inform me that he was about to return to Bubaker; but as he would only stay there a few days to keep the approaching festival (*Banna Salee*), and then return to Jarra, I had permission to remain with Daman until his return. This was joyful news to me; but I had experienced so many disappointments that I was unwilling to indulge the hope of its being true until Johnson came and told me that Ali, with part of the horsemen, were actually gone from the town, and that the rest were to follow him in the morning.

Early next morning the remainder of the Moors departed from the town. They had, during their stay, committed many acts of robbery; and this morning, with the most unparalleled audacity, they seized upon three girls who were bringing water from the wells, and carried them away into slavery.

The anniversary of *Banna Salee*, at Jarra, very well deserved to be called a festival. The slaves were all finely clad on this occasion, and the householders vied with each other in providing large quantities of victuals, which they distributed to all their neighbours with the greatest profusion ; hunger was literally banished from the town—man, woman, and child, bond and free, all had as much as they could eat.

At this time (June 12th) two people were discovered dreadfully wounded, at a watering-place in the woods ; one of them had just breathed his last, but the other was brought alive to Jarra. On recovering a little he informed the people that he had fled through the woods from Kasson, that Daisy had made war upon Sambo the king of that country, had surprised three of his towns, and put all the inhabitants to the sword. He enumerated by name many of the friends of the Jarra people who had been murdered in Kasson. This intelligence made the death-howl universal in Jarra for the space of two days.

This piece of bad news was followed by another not less distressing. A number of runaway slaves arrived from Kaarta on the 14th, and reported that Daisy, having received information concerning the intended attack upon him, was about to visit Jarra. This made the Negroes call upon Ali for the two hundred horsemen which he was to furnish them, according to engagement. But Ali paid very little attention to their remonstrances, and at last plainly told them that his cavalry were otherwise employed. The Negroes, thus deserted by the Moors, and fully apprised that the king of Kaarta would show them as little clemency as he had shown the inhabitants of Kasson, resolved to collect all their forces and hazard a battle, before the king, who was now in great distress for want of provisions, should become too powerful for them. They therefore assembled about eight hundred effective men on the whole ; and with these they entered Kaarta, on the evening of the 18th of June.

Every attempt to redeem my boy had hitherto been unsuccessful, and in all probability would continue to prove so whilst I remained in the country. It was therefore necessary to come to some determination concerning my own safety before the rains should be fully set in, for my landlord, seeing no likelihood of being paid for his trouble, began to wish me away, and Johnson my interpreter refusing to proceed, my situation became very perplexing. If I continued where I was, I foresaw that I must soon fall a victim to the barbarity of the Moors, and yet, if I went forward singly it was evident that I must sustain great difficulties, both from the want of means to purchase the necessaries of life, and of an interpreter to make myself understood. On the other hand, to return to England without accomplishing the object of my mission, was worse than either. I therefore determined to avail myself of the first opportunity of escaping, and to proceed directly for Bambarra, as soon as the rains had set in for a few days, so as to afford me the certainty of finding water in the woods.

Such was my situation when, on the evening of the 24th of June, I was startled by the report of some muskets close to the town, and inquiring the reason, was informed that the Jarra army had returned from fighting Daisy, and that this firing was by way of rejoicing. However, when the chief men of the town had assembled, and heard a full detail of the expedition, they were by no means relieved from their uneasiness on Daisy's account. The deceitful Moors having drawn back from the confederacy, after being hired by the Negroes, greatly dispirited the insurgents ; who instead of finding Daisy with a few friends concealed in the strong fortress of Gedingooma, had found him at a town near Joka, in the open country, surrounded by so numerous an army, that every attempt to attack him was at once given up : and the confederates only thought of enriching themselves by the plunder of the small towns in the neighbourhood. They accordingly fell upon one of Daisy's towns and carried off the whole of the inhabitants ; but lest intelligence of this might reach Daisy, and induce him to cut off their retreat, they returned through the woods by night, bringing with them the slaves and cattle which they had captured.

Shortly after this a spy from Kaarta brought the alarming intelligence that Daisy had taken Simbing, and would be in Jarra some time in the course of the ensuing day. A number of people were immediately stationed on the tops of the rocks, and in the different passages leading into the town, to give early intelligence of Daisy's motions, and the women set about making the necessary preparations for quitting the town as soon as possible. They continued beating corn and packing up different articles during the night, and early in the morning nearly one-half of the townspeople took the road for Bambarra, by the way of Deena.

Their departure was very affecting; the women and children crying ; the men sullen and dejected ; and all of them looking back with regret on their native town, and on the wells and rocks, beyond which their ambition had never tempted them to stray, and where they had laid all their plans of future happiness ; all of which they were now forced to abandon, and to seek shelter among strangers.

The next day (June 27th) the sentinels brought information that Daisy was on his march towards Jarra, and that the confederate army had fled before him without firing a gun. The terror of the townspeople was now not easily to be described. Indeed, the screams of the women and children, and the great hurry and confusion that everywhere prevailed, made me suspect that the Kaartans had already entered the town ; and although I had every reason to be pleased with Daisy's behaviour to me when I was at Kemmoo, I had no wish to expose myself to the mercy of his army, who might, in the general confusion, mistake me for a Moor. I therefore mounted my horse, and taking a large bag of corn before me, rode slowly along with the townspeople, until we reached the foot of a rocky hill, where I dismounted, and drove my horse up before me. When I had reached the summit I sat down, and having a full view of the town and the neighbouring country, could not help lamenting the situation of the poor inhabitants, who were thronging after me, driving their sheep, cows, goats, etc., and carrying a scanty portion of provisions, and a few clothes. There was a great noise and crying everywhere upon the road ; for many aged people and children were unable to walk, and these, with the sick, were obliged to be carried ; otherwise they must have been left to certain destruction.

About five o'clock we arrived at a small farm belonging to the Jarra people, called Kadeeja ; and here I found Daman and Johnson employed in filling large bags of corn to be carried upon bullocks, to serve as provisions for Daman's family on the road.

At daybreak we departed from Kadeeja, and having passed Troongoomba without stopping, arrived in the afternoon at Queira. I remained here two days in order to recruit my horse, which the Moors had reduced to a perfect Rosinante, and to wait for the arrival of some Mandingo Negroes, who were going to Bambarra in the course of a few days.

On the afternoon of the 1st of July, as I was tending my horse in the fields, Ali's chief slave and four Moors arrived at Queira, and took up their lodging at the Dooty's house. My interpreter, Johnson, who suspected the nature of this visit, sent two boys to overhear their conversation, from which he learnt that they were sent to convey me back to Bubaker. The same evening two of the Moors came privately to look at my horse, and one of them proposed taking it to the Dooty's hut, but the other observed that such a precaution was unnecessary, as I could never escape upon such an animal. They then inquired where I slept, and returned to their companions.

All this was like a stroke of thunder to me, for I dreaded nothing so much as confinement again among the Moors, from whose barbarity I had nothing but death to expect. I therefore determined to set off immediately for Bambarra, a measure which I thought offered almost the only chance of saving my life and gaining the object of my mission. I communicated the design to Johnson, who, although he applauded my resolution, was so far from showing any inclination to accompany me, that he solemnly protested he would rather forfeit his wages than go any farther. He told me that Daman had agreed to give him half the price of a slave for his service, to assist in conducting a coffle of slaves to Gambia, and that he was determined to embrace the opportunity of returning to his wife and family.

Having no hopes, therefore, of persuading him to accompany me, I resolved to proceed by myself. About midnight I got my clothes in readiness, which consisted of two shirts, two pair of trousers, two pocket handkerchiefs, an upper and under waistcoat, a hat, and a pair of half-boots; these, with a cloak, constituted my whole wardrobe. And I had not one single bead, nor any other article of value in my possession, to purchase victuals for myself, or corn for my horse.

About daybreak, Johnson, who had been listening to the Moors all night, came and whispered to me that they were asleep. The awful crisis was now arrived when I was again either to taste the blessing of freedom, or languish out my days in captivity. A cold sweat moistened my forehead as I thought on the dreadful alternative, and reflected that, one way or the other, my fate must be decided in the course of the ensuing day. But to deliberate was to lose the only chance of escaping. So taking up my bundle, I stepped gently over the Negroes who were sleeping in the open air, and having mounted my horse, bade Johnson farewell, desiring him to take particular care of the papers I had intrusted him with, and inform my friends in Gambia that he had left me in good health on my way to Bambarra.

I proceeded with great caution, surveying each bush and frequently listening and looking behind me for the Moorish horsemen, until I was about a mile from the town, when I was surprised to find myself in the neighbourhood of a korree belonging to the Moors. The shepherds followed me for

about a mile hooting and throwing stones after me. When I
was out of their reach and had began to indulge the pleasing
hopes of escaping, I was again greatly alarmed to hear somebody halloo behind me, and looking back I saw three Moors
on horseback coming after me at full speed, whooping and
brandishing their double-barrelled guns. I knew it was in
vain to think of escaping, and therefore turned back and met
them, when two of them caught hold of my bridle, one on
each side, and the third, presenting his musket, told me I
must go back to Ali.

When the human mind has for some time been fluctuating
between hope and despair, tortured with anxiety, and hurried
from one extreme to another, it affords a sort of gloomy relief
to know the worst that can possibly happen—such was my
situation. An indifference about life and all its enjoyments
had completely benumbed my faculties, and I rode back with
the Moors with apparent unconcern. But a change took place
much sooner than I had any reason to expect. In passing
through some thick bushes one of the Moors ordered me to
untie my bundle and show them the contents. Having
examined the different articles, they found nothing worth
taking except my cloak, which they considered as a very
valuable acquisition; and one of them pulling it from me
wrapped it about himself. This cloak had been of great use
to me, it served to cover me from the rains in the day and to
protect me from the mosquitoes in the night; I therefore
earnestly begged him to return it, and followed him some
little way to obtain it, but without paying any attention to
my request, he and one of his companions rode off with the
prize. When I attempted to follow them, the third, who had

remained with me, struck my horse over the head, and presenting his musket, told me I should proceed no further.

I now perceived that these men had not been sent by any
authority to apprehend me, but had pursued me solely in the
view to rob and plunder me. Turning my horse's head,
therefore, once more towards the east, and observing the Moor
follow the track of his confederates, I congratulated myself on
having escaped with my life, though in great distress, from
such a horde of barbarians.

I was no sooner out of sight of the Moor than I struck
into the woods to prevent being pursued, and kept pushing on
with all possible speed, until I found myself near some high
rocks which I remembered to have seen in my former route
from Queira to Deena ; and directing my course a little to the
northward, I fortunately fell in with the path.

CHAPTER XIV.

Journey through the Wilderness—Deplorable situation—Suffering from thirst—Faints on the sand—Recovery and renewed effort to push forward—Providential Relief by a Fall of Rain—Arrival at a Foulah village—Refused Relief by the Dooty, but obtains Food from a Poor Woman—Journey through the Wilderness—Is hospitably received by a Shepherd—Arrival at Wawra.

IT is impossible to describe the joy that arose in my mind when I looked around and concluded that I was out of danger. I felt like one recovered from sickness ; I breathed freer ; I found unusual lightness in my limbs ; even the desert looked pleasant, and I dreaded nothing so much as falling in with some wandering parties of Moors, who might convey me back to the land of thieves and murderers from which I had just escaped.

I soon became sensible, however, that my situation was very deplorable, for I had no means of procuring food, nor prospect of finding water. About ten o'clock, perceiving a herd of goats feeding close to the road, I took a circuitous route to avoid being seen, and continued travelling through the wilderness, directing my course by compass, nearly east-south-east, in order to reach as soon as possible some town or village of the kingdom of Bambarra.

A little after noon, when the burning heat of the sun was

reflected with double violence from the hot sand, and the distant ridges of the hills, seen through the ascending vapour, seemed to wave and fluctuate like the unsettled sea, I became faint with thirst, and climbed a tree in hopes of seeing distant smoke or some other appearance of a human habitation, but in vain ; nothing appeared all around but thick underwood and hillocks of white sand.

About four o'clock I came suddenly upon a large herd of goats, and pulling my horse into a bush, I watched to observe if the keepers were Moors or Negroes. In a little time I perceived two Moorish boys, and with some difficulty per-suaded them to approach me. They informed me that the herd belonged to Ali, and that they were going to Deena where the water was more plentiful, and where they intended to stay until the rain had filled the pools in the Desert. They showed me their empty water-skins, and told me that they had seen no water in the woods. This account afforded me but little consolation ; however, it was in vain to repine, and I pushed on as fast as possible, in hopes of reaching some watering-place in the course of the night. My thirst was by this time become insufferable ; my mouth was parched and inflamed ; a sudden dimness would frequently come over my eyes, with other symptoms of fainting ; and my horse being very much fatigued, I began seriously to apprehend that I should perish of thirst. To relieve the burning pain in my mouth and throat, I chewed the leaves of different shrubs, but found them all bitter, and of no service.

A little before sunset, having reached the top of a gentle rising, I climbed a high tree, from the topmost branches of which I cast a melancholy look over the barren wilderness, but without discovering the most distant trace of a human dwelling. The same dismal uniformity of shrubs and sand everywhere presented itself, and the horizon was as level and uninterrupted as that of the sea.

Descending from the tree, I found my horse devouring the stubble and brushwood with great avidity; and as I was now too faint to attempt walking, and my horse too much fatigued to carry me, I thought it but an act of humanity, and perhaps the last I should ever have it in my power to perform, to take off his bridle and let him shift for himself; in doing which I was suddenly affected with sickness and giddiness, and falling upon the sand felt as if the hour of death was fast approaching.

> "*Here then (thought I), after a short but ineffectual struggle, terminate all my hopes of being useful in my day and generation; here must the short span of my life come to an end.*"

Glorification or Peart

I cast (as I believed) a last look on the surrounding scene, and whilst I reflected on the awful change that was about to take place, this world with its enjoyments seemed to vanish from my recollection. Nature however at length resumed its functions, and on recovering my senses I found myself stretched upon the sand with the bridle still in my hand, and the sun just sinking behind the trees. I now summoned all my resolution, and determined to make another effort to prolong my existence. And as the evening was somewhat cool I resolved to travel as far as my limbs would carry me, in hopes of reaching (my only resource) a watering-place. With this view I put the bridle on my horse, and driving him before me went slowly along for about an hour, when I perceived some lightning from the north-east, a most delightful sight, for it promised rain. The darkness and lightning increased very rapidly, and in less than an hour I heard the wind roaring among the bushes. I had already opened my mouth to receive the refreshing drops which I expected ; but I was instantly covered with a cloud of sand, driven with such force by the wind as to give a very disagreeable sensation to my face and arms, and I was obliged to mount my horse and stop under a bush to prevent being suffocated. The sand continued to fly in amazing quantities for near an hour, after which I again set forward and travelled with difficulty until ten o'clock. About this time I was agreeably surprised by some very vivid flashes of lightning, followed by a few heavy drops of rain. In a little time the sand ceased to fly, and I alighted and spread out all my clean clothes to collect the rain which at length I saw would certainly fall. For more than an hour it rained plentifully, and I quenched my thirst by wringing and sucking my clothes.

There being no moon it was remarkably dark, so that I was obliged to lead my horse, and direct my way by the compass, which the lightning enabled me to observe. In this manner I travelled with tolerable expedition until past midnight ; when the lightning becoming more distant I was under the necessity of groping along, to the no small danger of my hands and eyes. About two o'clock my horse started at something, and looking round I was not a little surprised to see a light at a short distance among the trees ; and supposing it to be a town, I groped along the sand in hopes of finding corn-stacks, cotton, or other appearances of cultivation, but found none. As I approached, I perceived a number of other lights in different places, and began to suspect that I had fallen upon a party of Moors. However, in my present situation I was resolved to see who they were, if I could do it with safety. I accordingly led my horse cautiously towards the light, and heard, by the lowing of the cattle and the clamorous tongues of the herdsmen, that it was a watering-place and most likely belonged to the Moors. Delightful as the sound of the human voice was to me, I resolved once more to strike into the woods, and rather run the risk of perishing of hunger than trust myself again in their hands; but being still thirsty, and dreading the approach of the burning day, I thought it prudent to search for the wells, which I expected to find at no great distance. In this pursuit I inadvertently approached so near to one of the tents as to be perceived by a woman, who immediately screamed out. Two people came running to her assistance from some of the neighbouring tents, and passed so very near to me that I thought I was discovered, and hastened again into the woods.

About a mile from this place, I heard a loud and confused noise somewhere to the right of my course, and in a short time was happy to find it was the croaking of frogs, which was heavenly music to my ears. I followed the sound, and at daybreak arrived at some shallow muddy pools, so full of frogs that it was difficult to discern the water. The noise they made frightened my horse, and I was obliged to keep them quiet by beating the water with a branch until he had drank. Having here quenched my thirst I ascended a tree, and the morning being calm, I soon perceived the smoke of the watering-place which I had passed in the night; and observed another pillar of smoke east-south-east, distant twelve or fourteen miles. Towards this I directed my route, and reached the cultivated ground a little before eleven o'clock, where, seeing a number of Negroes at work planting corn, I inquired the name of the town, and was informed that it was a Foulah village, belonging to Ali, called Shrilla. I had now some doubts about entering it; but my horse being very much fatigued, and the day growing hot, not to mention the pangs of hunger which began to assail me, I resolved to venture, and accordingly rode up to the Dooty's house, where I was unfortunately denied admittance, and could not obtain even a handful of corn either for myself or horse. Turning from this inhospitable door I rode slowly out of the town, and perceiving some low scattered huts without the walls I directed my route towards them; knowing that in Africa, as well as in Europe, hospitality does not always prefer the highest dwellings. At the door of one of these huts an old motherly-looking woman sat spinning cotton. I made signs to her that I was hungry, and inquired if she had any victuals with her in the hut. She immediately laid down her distaff, and desired me, in Arabic, to come in. When I had seated myself upon the floor, she set before me a dish of kouskous that had been left the preceding night, of which I made a tolerable meal; and in return for this kindness I gave her one of my pocket-handkerchiefs; begging, at the same time, a little corn for my horse, which she readily brought me.

Overcome with joy at so unexpected a deliverance I lifted up my eyes to heaven, and whilst my heart swelled with gratitude, I returned thanks to that gracious and bountiful Being, whose power had supported me under so many dangers, and had now spread for me a table in the wilderness.

Romantic Writing.

Whilst my horse was feeding, the people began to assemble, and one of them whispered something to my hostess which very much excited her surprise. Though I was not well acquainted with the Foulah language, I soon discovered that some of the men wished to apprehend and carry me back to Ali, in hopes, I suppose, of receiving a reward. I therefore tied up the corn ; and lest any one should suspect I had ran away from the Moors, I took a northerly direction, and went cheerfully along, driving my horse before me, followed by all the boys and girls of the town. When I had travelled about two miles, and got quit of all my troublesome attendants, I struck again into the woods, and took shelter under a large tree, where I found it necessary to rest myself ; a bundle of twigs serving me for a bed, and my saddle for a pillow.

Here I lay until I was awakened by three Foulahs, who, taking me for a Moor, pointed to the sun, and told me it was time to pray, it being about two o'clock. Without entering into conversation with them, I saddled my horse and continued my journey. I travelled over a level, but more fertile country than I had seen for some time, until sunset, when, coming to a path that took a southerly direction, I followed it until midnight, at which time I arrived at a small pool of rain-water, and the wood being open, I determined to rest by it for the night. Having given my horse the remainder of the corn I made my bed as formerly ; but the mosquitoes and flies from the pool prevented sleep for some time, and I was twice disturbed in the night by wild beasts, which came very near, and whose howlings kept the horse in continual terror.

At daybreak on the 4th of July I pursued my course through the woods as formerly ; saw numbers of antelopes, wild hogs, and ostriches; but the soil was more hilly, and not so fertile as I had found it the preceding day. Ascending an eminence where I climbed a tree, I discovered, at about eight miles' distance, an open part of the country, with several red spots, which I concluded were cultivated land; and directing my course that way, came to the precincts of a watering-place.

From the appearance of the place I judged it to belong to the Foulahs, and was hopeful that I should meet a better reception than I had experienced at Shrilla. In this I was not deceived, for one of the shepherds invited me to come into his tent and partake of some dates. This was one of those low Foulah tents in which there is room just sufficient to sit upright, and in which the family, furniture, etc., seem huddled together like so many articles in a chest. When I had crept upon my hands and knees into this humble habitation, I found that it contained a woman and three children, who, together with the shepherd and myself, completely occupied the floor. A dish of boiled corn and dates was produced, and the master of the family, as is customary in this part of the country, first tasted himself, and then desired me to follow his example. Whilst I was eating, the children kept their eyes fixed upon me; and no sooner did the shepherd pronounce the word *Nazarani* than they began to cry, and their mother crept slowly towards the door, out of which she sprang like a greyhound, and was instantly followed by her children; so frightened were they at the very name of a Christian that no entreaties could induce them to approach the tent. Here I purchased some corn for my horse in exchange for some brass buttons; and having thanked the shepherd for his hospitality, struck again into the woods. At sunset I came to a road that took the direction for Bambarra, and resolved to follow it for the night; but about eight o'clock, hearing some people coming from the southward, I thought it prudent to hide myself among some thick bushes near the road. As these thickets are generally full of wild beasts, I found my situation rather unpleasant, sitting in the dark, holding my horse by the nose with both hands to prevent him from neighing, and equally afraid of the natives without, and the wild beasts within. My fears, however, were soon dissipated, for the people, after looking round the thicket and perceiving nothing, went away; and I hastened to the more open parts of the wood, where I pursued my journey E.S.E. until midnight. The joyful cry of frogs induced me once more to deviate a little from my route, in order to quench my thirst, which I accomplished at a large pool of rainwater. I then sought for an open place, with a single tree in the midst, under which I made my bed for the night. Here I was disturbed by some wolves towards morning, which induced me to set forward a little before day; and having passed a small village called Wassalita, I came about ten o'clock (July 5th) to a Negro town called Wawra, which properly belongs to Kaarta, but was at this time tributary to Mansong, king of Bambarra.

CHAPTER XV.

*Discovery of the Niger—Sego, the Capital of Bambarra—Mansong,
the King—Refused Admittance to the Town—Subsequent Bounty
of the King—Compassionate Treatment of a Negro Woman.*

A.D. 1796.

WAWRA is a small town surrounded with high walls, and
inhabited by a mixture of Mandingoes and Foulahs.
The inhabitants employ themselves chiefly in cultivating corn,
which they exchange with the Moors for salt. Here, being in
security from the Moors and very much fatigued, I resolved
to rest myself, and meeting with a hearty welcome from the
Dooty, whose name was Flancharee, I laid myself down upon
a bullock's hide and slept soundly for about two hours. The
curiosity of the people would not allow me to sleep any
longer. They had seen my saddle and bridle, and were
assembled in great number to learn who I was and whence I
came. Some were of opinion that I was an Arab, others
insisted that I was some Moorish Sultan ; and they continued
to debate the matter with such warmth that the noise awoke
me. The Dooty (who had formerly been at Gambia) at last
interposed in my behalf, and assured them that I was
certainly a white man, but he was convinced from my
appearance that I was a very poor one.

In the course of the day several women, hearing that I was

going to Sego, came and begged me to inquire of Mansong, the king, what was become of their children. One woman in particular told me that her son's name was Mamadee : that he was no heathen, but prayed to God morning and evening, and had been taken from her about three years ago by Mansong's army, since which she had never heard of him. She said she often dreamed about him, and begged me if I should see him, either in Bambarra or in my own country, to tell him that his mother and sister were still alive. In the afternoon the Dooty examined the contents of the leather bag in which I had packed up my clothes, but finding nothing that was worth taking he returned it and told me to depart in the morning.

At daylight then I departed, in company with a Negro who was going to a town called Dingyee for corn ; but we had not proceeded above a mile before the ass upon which he rode kicked him off, and he returned, leaving me to prosecute the journey by myself.

I reached Dingyee about noon, but the Dooty and most of the inhabitants had gone into the fields to cultivate corn. An old Foulah, observing me wandering about the town, desired me to come to his hut, where I was well entertained ; and the Dooty, when he returned, sent me some victuals for myself and corn for my horse.

In the morning when I was about to leave, my landlord, with a great deal of diffidence, begged me to give him a lock of my hair. He had been told, he said, that white men's hair made a saphie that would give to the possessor all the knowledge of white men. I had never before heard of so simple a mode of education, but instantly complied with the request ; and my landlord's thirst for learning was such that, with cutting and pulling, he cropped one side of my head pretty closely, and would have done the same with the other had I not signified my disapprobation by putting on my hat, and assuring him that I wished to reserve some of this precious merchandise for a future occasion.

I reached a small town called Wassiboo, about twelve o'clock, where I was obliged to stop until an opportunity should offer of procuring a guide to Satilé, which is distant a very long day's journey through woods without any beaten path. I accordingly took up my residence at the Dooty's house, where I staid four days, during which time I amused myself by going to the fields with the family to plant corn. Cultivation is carried on here on a very extensive scale ; and, as the natives themselves express it, "hunger is never known." In cultivating the soil the men and women work together. They use a large sharp hoe, much superior to that used in Gambia, but they are obliged, for fear of the Moors, to carry their arms with them to the field. The master with the handle of his spear marks the field into regular plats, one of which is assigned to every three slaves.

One evening eight of the fugitive Kaartans arrived at Wassiboo. They had found it impossible to live under the tyrannical government of the Moors, and were now going to transfer their allegiance to the king of Bambarra. They offered to take me along with them as far as Satilé, and I accepted the offer.

At daybreak (July 12th) we set out, and travelled with uncommon expedition until sunset : we stopped only twice in the course of the day, once at a watering-place in the woods, and another time at the ruins of a town, formerly belonging to

Daisy, called *Illa-Compe* (the corn town). When we arrived
in the neighbourhood of Satilé, the people who were employed
in the corn-fields seeing so many horsemen took us for a party
of Moors, and ran screaming away from us. The whole town
was instantly alarmed, and the slaves were seen in every
direction driving the cattle and horses towards the town. It
was in vain that one of our company galloped up to un-
deceive them : it only frightened them the more, and when
we arrived at the town we found the gates shut and the
people all under arms. After a long parley we were permitted
to enter, and as there was every appearance of a heavy
tornado, the Dooty allowed us to sleep in his baloon, and gave
us each a bullock's hide for a bed.

Early next morning we again set forward. The roads were
wet and slippery ; but the country was very beautiful, abounding with rivulets, which were increased by the rain into rapid
streams. About ten o'clock we came to the ruins of a village
which had been destroyed by war about six months before ;
and in order to prevent any town from being built there in
future the large Bentang tree, under which the natives spent
the day, had been burned down, the wells filled up, and everything that could make the spot desirable completely destroyed.

About noon my horse was so much fatigued that I could
not keep up with my companions ; I therefore dismounted,
and desired them to ride on, telling them that I would follow as
soon as my horse had rested a little. But I found them unwilling to leave me. The lions, they said, were very numerous
in those parts, and though they might not so readily attack a
body of people, they would soon find out an individual. It
was therefore agreed that one of the company should stay

with me to assist in driving my horse, while the others passed
on to Galloo to procure lodgings and collect grass for the
horses before night. Accompanied by this worthy Negro, I
drove my horse before me until about four o'clock, when we
came in sight of Galloo, a considerable town, standing in a
fertile and beautiful valley surrounded with high rocks.

As my companions had thoughts of settling in this neighbourhood, they had a fine sheep given them by the Dooty ;
and I was fortunate enough to procure plenty of corn for my
horse. Here they blow upon elephants' teeth when they
announce evening prayers, in the same manner as at Kemmoo.

Early next morning (July 14th), having first returned
many thanks to our landlord for his hospitality, while my
fellow-travellers offered up their prayers that he might never
want, we set forward, and about three o'clock arrived at
Moorja, a large town famous for its trade in salt, which the
Moors bring here in great quantities to exchange for corn and
cotton cloth. As most of the people here are Mahomedans, it
is not allowed to the Kafirs to drink beer, which they call
Neo-dollo (corn spirit), except in certain houses. In one of
these I saw about twenty people sitting round large vessels of
this beer with the greatest conviviality, many of them in a
state of intoxication. As corn is plentiful, the inhabitants
are very liberal to strangers. I believe we had as much corn
and milk sent us by different people as would have been
sufficient for three times our number ; and though we
remained here two days, we experienced no diminution of
their hospitality.

We again set forward, accompanied by a coffle of fourteen
asses, loaded with salt, bound for Sansanding. The road was

particularly romantic, between two rocky hills; but the
Moors sometimes lie in wait here to plunder strangers. As
soon as we had reached the open country, the master of the
salt coffle thanked us for having staid with him so long, and
now desired us to ride on. The sun was almost set before we
reached Datliboo. In the evening we had a most tremendous
tornado. The house in which we lodged, being flat-roofed,
admitted the rain in streams. The floor was soon ankle deep,
the fire extinguished, and we were left to pass the night upon
some bundles of firewood that happened to lie in a corner.

Departing from Datliboo, we passed a large coffle returning
from Sego with corn hoes, mats, and other household utensils,
and came to a large village where we intended to pass the
night, but the Dooty would not receive us. When we departed
from this place my horse was so much fatigued that I was
under the necessity of driving him, and it was dark before we
reached Fanimboo, a small village; the Dooty of which no
sooner heard that I was a white man than he brought out three
old muskets, and was much disappointed when he was told
that I could not repair them.

Next day we continued our journey, and owing to a light
supper endeavoured to procure some corn at a village, but
without success. The towns were now more numerous, and
the land, not employed in cultivation, affords excellent pasturage for large herds of cattle ; but owing to the great con-
course of people daily going to and returning from Sego,[27] the
inhabitants are less hospitable to strangers.

My horse became weaker and weaker every day, and was
now of very little service to me. I was therefore obliged to
drive him before me for the greater part of the day, and did not

reach Geosorro until eight o'clock in the evening. I found
my companions wrangling with the Dooty, who had absolutely
refused to give or sell them any provisions; and as none of
us had tasted victuals for the last twenty-four hours, we were
by no means disposed to fast another day if we could help it.
But finding our entreaties without effect, and being very much
fatigued, I fell asleep, from which I was awakened about midnight, with the joyful information, "*kinnenata*" (the victuals
are come). This made the remainder of the night pass away
pleasantly; and at daybreak we resumed our journey, proposing to stop at a village called Doolinkeaboo for the night
following. My fellow-travellers, having better horses than
myself, soon left me, and I was walking barefoot, driving my
horse, when I was met by a coffle of slaves, about seventy in
number, coming from Sego. They were tied together by their
necks with thongs of a bullock's hide twisted like a rope;
seven slaves upon a thong, and a man with a musket between
every seven. Many of the slaves were ill-conditioned, and a
great number of them women. In the rear came Sidi
Mahomed's servant, whom I remembered to have seen at the
camp of Benowm; he presently knew me, and told me that
these slaves were going to Morocco by the way of Ludamar
and the Great Desert.

When I arrived at Doolinkeaboo, I was informed that my
fellow-travellers had gone on, but my horse was so much
fatigued that I could not possibly proceed after them. The
Dooty of the town, at my request, gave me a draught of water,
which is generally looked upon as an earnest of greater hospitality, and I had no doubt of making up for the toils of the
day by a good supper and a sound sleep; unfortunately I had

neither one nor the other. The night was rainy and tempestuous, and the Dooty limited his hospitality to the draught of water.

Next morning (July 20) I endeavoured, both by entreaties and threats, to procure some victuals from the Dooty, but in vain. I even begged some corn from one of his female slaves as she was washing it at the well, and had the mortification to be refused. However, when the Dooty was gone to the fields, his wife sent me a handful of meal, which I mixed with water and drank for breakfast. About eight o'clock I departed from Doolinkeaboo, and at noon stopped a few minutes at a large korree, where I had some milk given me by the Foulahs; and hearing that two Negroes were going from thence to Sego, I was happy to have their company, and we set out immediately. About four o'clock we stopped at a small village, where one of the Negroes met with an acquaintance who invited us to a sort of public entertainment, which was conducted with more than common propriety. A dish, made of sour milk and meal, called *Sinkatoo*, and beer made from their corn, was distributed with great liberality, and the women were admitted into the society—a circumstance I had never before observed in Africa. There was no compulsion, every one was at liberty to drink as he pleased; they nodded to each other when about to drink, and on setting down the calabash commonly said *Berka* (thank you). Both men and women appeared to be somewhat intoxicated, but they were far from being quarrelsome.

Departing from thence, we passed several large villages, where I was constantly taken for a Moor, and became the subject of much merriment to the Bambarrans; who, seeing me drive my horse before me, laughed heartily at my appearance. "He has been at Mecca," says one, "you may see that by his clothes;" another asked "if my horse was sick;" a third wished to purchase it; so that I believe the very slaves were ashamed to be seen in my company. Just before it was dark we took up our lodging for the night at a small village, where I procured some victuals for myself and some corn for my horse, at the moderate price of a button, and was told that I should see the Niger (which the Negroes called Jolliba, or *the great water*) early the next day. The lions are here very numerous; the gates are shut a little after sunset, and nobody allowed to go out. The thoughts of seeing the Niger in the morning, and the troublesome buzzing of mosquitoes, prevented me from shutting my eyes during the night, and I had saddled my horse and was in readiness before daylight; but on account of the wild beasts we were obliged to wait until the people were stirring and the gates opened. This happened to be a market-day at Sego, and the roads were everywhere filled with people carrying different articles to sell. We passed four large villages, and at eight o'clock saw the smoke over Sego.

As we approached the town, I was fortunate enough to overtake the fugitive Kaartans to whose kindness I had been so much indebted in my journey through Bambarra. They readily agreed to introduce me to the king; and we rode together through some marshy ground where, as I was anxiously looking around for the river, one of them called out, *geo affili* (see the water), and looking forwards, I saw with infinite pleasure the great object of my mission—the long sought for majestic Niger, glittering to the morning sun, as broad as the Thames at Westminster, and flowing slowly *to the eastward.* I hastened to the brink, and having drank of the water, lifted up my fervent thanks in prayer to the Great Ruler of all things, for having thus far crowned my endeavours with success.

The circumstance of the Niger's flowing towards the east, and its collateral points, did not, however, excite my surprise; for although I had left Europe in great hesitation on this subject, and rather believed that it ran in the contrary direction, I had made such frequent inquiries during my progress concerning this river, and received from Negroes of different nations such clear and decisive assurances that its general course was *towards the rising sun,* as scarce left any doubt on my mind; and more especially as I knew that Major Houghton had collected similar information in the same manner.

Sego, the capital of Bambarra, at which I had now arrived, consists, properly speaking, of four distinct towns ; two on the northern bank of the Niger, called Sego Korro and Sego Boo ; and two on the southern bank, called Sego Soo Korro and Sego See Korro. They are all surrounded with high mud walls ; the houses are built of clay, of a square form, with flat roofs ; some of them have two storeys, and many of them are whitewashed. Besides these buildings, Moorish mosques are seen in every quarter ; and the streets, though narrow, are broad enough for every useful purpose, in a country where wheel-carriages are entirely unknown. From the best inquiries I could make, I have reason to believe that Sego contains altogether about thirty thousand inhabitants. The king of Bambarra constantly resides at Sego See Korro ; he employs a great many slaves in conveying people over the river, and the money they receive (though the fare is only ten cowrie shells for each individual) furnishes a considerable revenue to the king in the course of a year. The canoes are of a singular construction, each of them being formed of the trunks of two large trees rendered concave, and joined together, not side by side, but end-ways, the junction being exactly across the middle of the canoe ; they are therefore very long and disproportionably narrow, and have neither decks nor masts ; they are however very roomy, for I observed in one of them four horses and several people crossing over the river. When we arrived at this ferry, with a view to pass over to that part of the town in which the king resides, we found a great number waiting for a passage ; they looked at me with silent wonder, and I distinguished, with concern, many Moors among them. There were three different places of embarkation, and the ferrymen were very diligent and expeditious ; but from the crowd of people I could not immediately obtain a passage, and sat down upon the bank of the river to wait for a more favourable opportunity. The view of this extensive city, the numerous canoes upon the river, the crowded population and the cultivated state of the surrounding country, formed altogether a prospect of civilisation and magnificence which I little expected to find in the bosom of Africa.

I waited more than two hours without having an opportunity of crossing the river ; during which time, the people who had crossed carried information to Mansong, the king, that a white man was waiting for a passage, and was coming to see him. He immediately sent over one of his chief men, who informed me that the king could not possibly see me, until he knew what had brought me into his country ; and that I must not presume to cross the river without the king's permission.

He therefore advised me to lodge at a distant village, to which he pointed, for the night ; and said that in the morning he would give me further instructions how to conduct myself. This was very discouraging.   However, as there was no remedy, I set off for the village ; where I found, to my great mortification, that no person would admit me into his house.   I was regarded with astonishment and fear, and was obliged to sit all day without victuals in the shade of a tree ; and the night threatened to be very uncomfortable, for the wind rose, and there was great appearance of a heavy rain ; and the wild beasts are so very numerous in the neighbourhood that I should have been under the necessity of climbing up the tree, and resting among the branches.   About sunset, however, as I was preparing to pass the night in this manner, and had turned my horse loose that he might graze at liberty, a woman, returning from the labours of the field, stopped to observe me, and perceiving that I was weary and dejected, inquired into my situation, which I briefly explained to her ; whereupon, with looks of great compassion, she took up my saddle and bridle and told me to follow her.   Having conducted me into her hut, she lighted up a lamp, spread a mat on the floor, and told me I might remain there for the night.   Finding that I was very hungry she said she would procure me something to eat.   She accordingly went out, and returned in a short time with a very fine fish ; which having caused to be half broiled upon some embers, she gave me for supper.   The rites of hospitality being thus performed towards a stranger in distress, my worthy benefactress (pointing to the mat, and telling me I might sleep there without apprehension) called to the female part of her family, who had stood gazing on me all the while in fixed astonishment, to resume their task of spinning cotton ; in which they continued to employ themselves great part of the night. They lightened their labour by songs, one of which was composed extempore ; for I was myself the subject of it. It was sung by one of the young women, the rest joining in a sort of chorus. The air was sweet and plain-tive, and the words, literally translated, were these :—" The winds roared and the rains fell. The poor white man, faint and weary, came and sat under our tree. He has no mother to bring him milk, no wife to grind his corn." *Chorus.*— " Let us pity the white man; no mother has he," etc. etc. Trifling as this recital may appear to the reader, to a person in my situation the circumstance was affecting in the highest degree. I was oppressed by such unexpected kindness, and sleep fled from my eyes. In the morning I presented my compassionate landlady with two of the four brass buttons which remained on my waistcoat ; the only recompense I could make her.

I continued in the village all this day (July 21) in con-versation with the natives, who came in crowds to see me ; but was rather uneasy towards evening to find that no message had arrived from the king ; the more so as the people began to whisper that Mansong had received some very unfavourable accounts of me from the Moors and Slatees residing at Sego who, it seems, were exceedingly suspicious concerning the motives of my journey. I learnt that many consultations had been held with the king concerning my reception and disposal; and some of the villagers frankly told me that I had many enemies and must expect no favour.

About eleven o'clock next day a messenger arrived from

I was oppressed by such unexpected kindness; and sleep fled from my eyes.—Page 182.

the king, but he gave me very little satisfaction. He inquired particularly if I had brought any present, and seemed much disappointed when he was told that I had been robbed of everything by the Moors. When I proposed to go along with him, he told me to stop until the afternoon, when the king would send for me.

In the afternoon another messenger arrived from Mansong, with a bag in his hands. He told me it was the king's pleasure that I should depart forthwith from the vicinage of Sego ; but that Mansong, wishing to relieve a white man in distress, had sent me five thousand cowries,* to enable me to purchase provisions in the course of my journey ; the messenger added, that if my intentions were really to proceed to Jenné, he had orders to accompany me as a guide to Sansanding. I was at first puzzled to account for this behaviour of the king ; but from the conversation I had with the guide, I had afterwards reason to believe that Mansong would willingly have admitted me into his presence at Sego, but was apprehensive he might not be able to protect me against the blind and inveterate malice of the Moorish inhabitants. His conduct, therefore, was at once prudent and liberal. The circumstances under which I made my appearance at Sego were undoubtedly such as might create in the mind of the king a well-warranted suspicion that I wished to conceal the true object of my journey. He argued probably, as my guide argued : who, when he was

* Mention has already been made of these little shells (p. 22.) which pass current as money in many parts of the East Indies, as well as Africa. In Bambarra, and the adjacent countries, where the necessaries of life are very cheap, one hundred of them would commonly purchase a day's provisions for myself and corn for my horse. I reckoned about two hundred and fifty cowries equal to one shilling.

told that I had come from a great distance, and through many
dangers, to behold the Jolliba river, naturally inquired, if there
were no rivers in my own country, and whether one river was
not like another.   Notwithstanding this, and in spite of the
jealous machinations of the Moors, this benevolent prince
thought it sufficient that a white man was found in his dominions in a condition of extreme wretchedness, and that no
other plea was necessary to entitle the sufferer to his bounty.

CHAPTER XVI.

*Departure from Sego and Arrival at Kabba—Description of the Shea,
or Vegetable Butter-tree—Park and his Guide arrive at Sansanding—Behaviour of the Moors at that place—Park pursues
his journey to the Eastward—Incidents on the Road—Park
arrives at Modiboo, and proceeds to Kea; obliged to leave his
Horse by the way—Embarks at Kea in a fisherman's canoe for
Moorzan; conveyed from thence across the Niger to Silla—
Determines to proceed no further Eastward—Some Account of
the further Course of the Niger.*

A.D. 1796.

BEING, in the manner that has been related, compelled to
leave Sego, I was conducted the same evening to a village
about seven miles to the eastward, with some of the inhabitants
of which my guide was acquainted, and by whom we were
well received.* He was very friendly and communicative, and
spoke highly of the hospitality of his countrymen ; but withal
told me, that if Jenné was the place of my destination, which
he seemed to have hitherto doubted, I had undertaken an enterprise of greater danger than probably I was apprised of ; for
although the town of Jenné was nominally a part of the king
of Bambarra's dominions, it was in fact, he said, a city of the

---

* I should have before observed, that I found the language of Bambarra a
sort of corrupted Mandingo. After a little practice, I understood and spoke it
without difficulty.

Moors; the leading part of the inhabitants being Bushreens, and even the governor himself, though appointed by Mansong, of the same sect. Thus was I in danger of falling a second time into the hands of men who would consider it not only justifiable, but meritorious, to destroy me; and this reflection was aggravated by the circumstance, that the danger increased as I advanced in my journey; for I learned that the places beyond Jenné were under the Moorish influence in a still greater degree than Jenné itself; and Timbuctoo, the great object of my search, altogether in possession of that savage and merciless people, who allow no Christian to live there. But I had now advanced too far to think of returning to the westward on such vague and uncertain information, and determined to proceed; and being accompanied by the guide, I departed from the village on the morning of the 24th July. About eight o'clock we passed a large town called Kabba, situated in the midst of a beautiful and highly-cultivated country; bearing a greater resemblance to the centre of England than to what I should have supposed had been the middle of Africa. The people were everywhere employed in collecting the fruit of the shea trees, from which they prepare the vegetable butter mentioned in former parts of this work. These trees grow in great abundance all over this part of Bambarra. They are not planted by the natives, but are found growing naturally in the woods; and in clearing woodland for cultivation, every tree is cut down but the shea. The tree itself very much resembles the American oak; and the fruit—from the kernel of which being first dried in the sun, the butter is prepared by boiling the kernel in water—has somewhat the appearance of a Spanish olive. The kernel is enveloped in a sweet pulp, under a thin green rind;

and the butter produced from it, besides the advantage of its
keeping the whole year without salt, is whiter, firmer, and to
my palate, of a richer flavour than the best butter I ever tasted
made from cow's milk. The growth and preparation of this
commodity seem to be among the first objects of African industry in this and the neighbouring states ; and it constitutes
a main article of their inland commerce.

We passed in the course of the day a great many villages
inhabited chiefly by fishermen, and in the evening about five
o'clock arrived at Sansanding, a very large town, containing, as
I was told, from eight to ten thousand inhabitants. This
place is much resorted to by the Moors, who bring salt from
Beeroo, and beads and coral from the Mediterranean, to exchange here for gold dust and cotton cloth. This cloth they
sell to great advantage in Beeroo and other Moorish countries,
where, on account of the want of rain, no cotton is cultivated.

I desired my guide to conduct me to the house in which
we were to lodge by the most private way possible. We
accordingly rode along between the town and the river, passing by a creek or harbour in which I observed twenty large
canoes, most of them fully loaded and covered with mats to
prevent the rain from injuring the goods. As we proceeded,
three other canoes arrived, two with passengers and one with
goods. I was happy to find that all the Negro inhabitants
took me for a Moor ; under which character I should probably
have passed unmolested, had not a Moor who was sitting by
the river side discovered the mistake, and setting up a loud
exclamation brought together a number of his countrymen.

When I arrived at the house of Counti Mamadi, the Dooty
of the town, I was surrounded with hundreds of people speak-

ing a variety of different dialects, all equally unintelligible to
me. At length, by the assistance of my guide, who acted as
interpreter, I understood that one of the spectators pretended
to have seen me at one place, and another at some other place,
and a Moorish woman absolutely swore that she had kept my
house three years at Gallam on the river Senegal. It was
plain that they mistook me for some other person, and I
desired two of the most confident to point towards the place
where they had seen me. They pointed due south; hence I
think it probable that they came from Cape coast, where they
might have seen many white men. Their language was
different from any I had yet heard. The Moors now assembled
in great numbers; with their usual arrogance compelling the
Negroes to stand at a distance. They immediately began
to question me concerning my religion; but finding that I
was not master of the Arabic, they sent for two men whom
they call *Ilhuidi* (Jews), in hopes that they might be able to
converse with me. These Jews, in dress and appearance, very
much resemble the Arabs; but though they so far conform to
the religion of Mahomet as to recite in public, prayers from the
Koran, they are but little respected by the Negroes; and even
the Moors themselves allowed, that though I was a Christian
I was a better man than a Jew. They however insisted that,
like the Jews, I must conform so far as to repeat the
Mahomedan prayers; and when I attempted to waive the
subject, by telling them that I could not speak Arabic, one of
them, a Shereef from Tuat in the Great Desert, started up,
and swore by the Prophet, that if I refused to go to the
mosque he would be one that would assist in carrying me
thither. And there is no doubt but this threat would have

been immediately executed had not my landlord interposed in my behalf. He told them that I was the king's stranger, and he could not see me ill-treated whilst I was under his protection. He therefore advised them to let me alone for the night; assuring them that in the morning I should be sent about my business. This somewhat appeased their clamour; but they compelled me to ascend a high seat by the door of the mosque in order that everybody might see me, for the people had assembled in such numbers as to be quite ungovernable—climbing upon the houses, and squeezing each other like the spectators at an execution. Upon this seat I remained until sunset, when I was conducted into a neat little hut, with a small court before it, the door of which Counti Mamadi shut, to prevent any person from disturbing me. But this precaution could not exclude the Moors. They climbed over the top of the mud-wall, and came in crowds into the court, in order, they said, to see me *perform my evening devotions, and eat eggs.* The former of these ceremonies I did not think proper to comply with; but I told them I had no objections to eat eggs, provided they would bring me eggs to eat. My landlord immediately brought me seven hens' eggs, and was much surprised to find that I could not eat them raw; for it seems to be a prevalent opinion among the inhabitants of the interior, that Europeans subsist almost entirely on this diet. When I had succeeded in persuading my landlord that this opinion was without foundation, and that I would gladly partake of any victuals which he might think proper to send me, he ordered a sheep to be killed and part of it to be dressed for my supper. About midnight, when the Moors had left me, he paid me a visit, and with much earnestness desired me to write him a saphie. "If a Moor's saphie is good (said this hospitable old man), a white man's must needs be better." I readily furnished him with one possessed of all the virtues I could concentrate, for it contained the Lord's prayer. The pen with which it was written was made of a reed, a little charcoal and gum-water made very tolerable ink, and a thin board answered the purpose of paper.

Early in the morning of the 25th July, before the Moors were assembled, I departed from Sansanding, and slept the ensuing night at a small town called Sibili ; from whence, on the day following, I reached Nyara, a large town at some distance from the river, where I halted the 27th to have my clothes washed and recruit my horse. The Dooty there has a very commodious house, flat roofed and two storeys high. He showed me some gunpowder of his own manufacturing ; and pointed out, as a great curiosity, a little brown monkey that was tied to a stake by the door, telling me that it came from a far distant country called Kong.

Departing from Nyara I reached Nyamee, a town inhabited chiefly by Foulahs from the kingdom of Masina. The Dooty (I know not why) would not receive me, but civilly sent his son on horseback to conduct me to Modiboo, which he assured me was at no great distance.

We rode nearly in a direct line through woods, but in general went forwards with great circumspection. I observed that my guide frequently stopped and looked under the bushes. On inquiring the reason of this caution, he told me that lions were very numerous in that part of the country, and frequently attacked people travelling through the woods. While he was speaking my horse started, and looking round I observed a large animal of the camelopard[28] kind standing at a little distance. The neck and fore-legs were very long; the head was furnished with two short black horns, turning backwards ; the tail, which reached down to the ham-joint, had a tuft of hair at the end. The animal was of a mouse colour, and it trotted away from us in a very sluggish manner, moving its head from side to side to see if we were pursuing it. Shortly after this, as we were crossing a large open plain where there were a few scattered bushes, my guide, who was a little way before me, wheeled his horse round in a moment, calling out something in the Foulah language which I did not understand. I inquired in Mandingo what he meant. *Wara billi billi* (a very large lion), said he, and made signs for me to ride away. But my horse was too much fatigued ; so we rode slowly past the bush from which the animal had given us the alarm. Not seeing anything myself, however, I thought my guide had been mistaken, when the Foulah suddenly put his hand to his mouth, exclaiming, *Soubah an alluhi* (God preserve us!), and to my great surprise I then perceived a large red lion at a short distance from the bush, with his head couched between his fore-paws. I expected he would instantly spring upon me, and instinctively pulled my feet from my stirrups to throw myself on the ground, that my horse might become the victim rather than myself. But it is probable the lion was not hungry, for he quietly suffered us to pass, though we were fairly within his reach. My eyes were so rivetted upon this sovereign of the beasts that I found it impossible to remove them until we were at a considerable distance. We now took a circuitous route, through some swampy ground, to avoid any more of these disagreeable rencontres. At sunset we arrived at Modiboo, a delightful village on the banks of the Niger, commanding a view of the river for many miles, both to the east and west. The small green islands (the peaceful retreat of some industrious Foulahs, whose cattle are here secure from the depredations of wild beasts), and the majestic breadth of the river, which is here much larger than at Sego, render the situation one of the most enchanting in the world. Here are caught great plenty of fish by means of long cotton nets which the natives make themselves, and use nearly in the same manner as nets are used in Europe. I observed the head of a crocodile lying upon one of the houses, which they told me had been killed by the shepherds in a swamp near the town. These animals are not uncommon in the Niger, but I believe they are not oftentimes found dangerous. They are of little account to the traveller when compared with the amazing swarms of mosquitoes, which rise from the swamps and creeks in such numbers as to harass even the most torpid of the natives; and as my clothes were now almost worn to rags, I was but ill-prepared to resist their attacks. I usually passed the night without shutting my eyes, walking backwards and forwards, fanning myself with my hat. Their stings raised numerous blisters on my legs and arms, which, together with the want of rest, made me very feverish and uneasy.

Early in the morning (July 29) my landlord, observing that I was sickly, hurried me away, sending a servant with me as a guide to Kea. But though I was little able to walk, my horse was still less able to carry me, and about six miles to the east of Modiboo, in crossing some rough clayey ground, he fell, and the united strength of the guide and myself could not place him again upon his legs. I sat down for some time beside this worn-out associate of my adventures ; but finding him still unable to rise, I took off the saddle and bridle, and placed a quantity of grass before him. I surveyed the poor animal, as he lay panting on the ground, with sympathetic emotion ; for I could not suppress the sad apprehension that I should myself in a short time lie down and perish in the same manner of fatigue and hunger. With this foreboding I left my poor horse, and with great reluctance followed my guide on foot along the bank of the river until about noon, when we reached Kea, which I found to be nothing more than a small fishing village. The Dooty, a surly old man, who was sitting by the gate, received me very coolly, and when I informed him of my situation, and begged his protection, told me with great indifference that he paid very little attention to fine speeches, and that I should not enter his house. My guide remonstrated in my favour, but to no purpose, for the Dooty remained inflexible in his determination. I knew not where to rest my wearied limbs, but was happily relieved by a fishing-canoe belonging to Silla, which was at that moment coming down the river. The Dooty waved to the fisherman to come near, and desired him to take charge of me as far as Moorzan. The fisherman, after some hesitation, consented to carry me, and I embarked in the canoe, in company with the fisherman, his wife, and a boy. The Negro who had conducted me from Modiboo now left me. I requested him to look to my horse on his return, and take care of him if he was still alive, which he promised to do.

Departing from Kea, we proceeded about a mile down the

river, when the fisherman paddled the canoe to the bank and
desired me to jump out.   Having tied the canoe to a stake, he
stripped off his clothes, and dived for such a length of time
that I thought he had actually drowned himself, and was surprised to see his wife behave with so much indifference upon
the occasion ; but my fears were over when he raised up his
head astern of the canoe and called for a rope.   With this
rope he dived a second time, and then got into the canoe, and
ordered the boy to assist him in pulling.   At length they
brought up a large basket, about ten feet in diameter, containing two fine fish, which the fisherman (after returning the
basket into the water) immediately carried ashore and hid in
the grass.   We then went a little farther down, and took up
another basket in which was one fish.   The fisherman now
left us to carry his prizes to some neighbouring market, and
the woman and boy proceeded with me in the canoe down
the river.

About four o'clock we arrived at Moorzan, a fishing town
on the northern bank, from which I was conveyed across the
river to Silla, a large town, where I remained until it was
quite dark under a tree, surrounded by hundreds of people.
But their language was very different from the other parts of
Bambarra ; and I was informed that in my progress eastward
the Bambarra tongue was but little understood, and that when
I reached Jenné I should find that the majority of the inhabitants spoke a different language, called *Jenné Kummo* by the
Negroes, and *Kalam Soudan* by the Moors.

With a great deal of entreaty the Dooty allowed me to
come into his baloon to avoid the rain, but the place was very
damp, and I had a smart paroxysm of fever during the night

Worn down by sickness, exhausted with hunger and fatigue, half naked, and without any article of value by which I might procure provisions, clothes, or lodging, I began to reflect seriously on my situation. I was now convinced, by painful experience, that the obstacles to my further progress were insurmountable. The tropical rains were already set in with all their violence; the rice grounds and swamps were everywhere overflowed; and in a few days more, travelling of every kind, unless by water, would be completely obstructed. The cowries which remained of the king of Bambarra's present were not sufficient to enable me to hire a canoe for any great distance, and I had but little hopes of subsisting by charity in a country where the Moors have such influence. But above all, I perceived that I was advancing more and more within the power of those merciless fanatics; and from my reception, both at Sego and Sansanding, I was apprehensive that in attempting to reach even Jenné (unless under the protection of some man of consequence amongst them, which I had no means of obtaining), I should sacrifice my life to no purpose, for my discoveries would perish with me. The prospect either way was gloomy. In returning to the Gambia, a journey on foot of many hundred miles presented itself to my contemplation, through regions and countries unknown. Nevertheless, this seemed to be the only alternative, for I saw inevitable destruction in attempting to proceed to the eastward. With this conviction on my mind, I hope my readers will acknowledge that I did right in going no farther. I had made every effort to execute my mission in its fullest extent, which prudence could justify. Had there been the most distant prospect of a successful termination, neither the unavoidable hardships of the journey, nor the dangers of a second captivity, should have forced me to desist. This, however, necessity compelled me to do ; and whatever may be the opinion of my general readers on this point, it affords me inexpressible satisfaction that my honourable employers have been pleased, since my return, to express their full approbation of my conduct.

Having thus brought my mind, after much doubt and perplexity, to a determination to return westward, I thought it incumbent on me, before I left Silla, to collect from the Moorish and Negro traders all the information I could concerning the further course of the Niger eastward, and the situation and extent of the kingdoms in its vicinage, and the following few notices I received from such various quarters as induce me to think they are authentic.

Two short days' journey to the eastward of Silla, is the town of Jenné, which is situated on a small island in the river, and is said to contain a greater number of inhabitants than Sego itself, or any other town in Bambarra. At the distance of two days more, the river spreads into a considerable lake called *Dibbie* (or the dark lake), concerning the extent of which all the information I could obtain was, that in crossing it from west to east, the canoes lose sight of land one whole day. From this lake the water issues in many different streams, which terminate in two large branches, one whereof flows towards the north-east and the other to the east ; but these branches join at Kabra, which is one day's journey to the southward of Timbuctoo, and is the port or shipping-place of that city. The tract of land which the two streams encircle is called Jinbala, and is inhabited by Negroes, and the whole distance by land from Jenné to Timbuctoo is twelve days' journey.

From Kabra, at the distance of eleven days' journey down the stream, the river passes to the southward of Houssa, which is two days' journey distant from the river. Of the further progress of this great river, and its final exit, all the natives with whom I conversed seemed to be entirely ignorant. Their commercial pursuits seldom induce them to travel further than the cities of Timbuctoo and Houssa; and as the sole object of those journeys is the acquirement of wealth, they pay but little attention to the course of rivers, or the geography of countries. It is, however, highly probable that the Niger affords a safe and easy communication between very remote nations. All my informants agreed, that many of the Negro merchants who arrive at Timbuctoo and Houssa from the east-ward, speak a different language from that of Bambarra, or any other kingdom with which they are acquainted. But even these merchants, it would seem, are ignorant of the termination of the river, for such of them as can speak Arabic describe the amazing length of its course in very general terms, saying only that they believe it *runs to the world's end.*

The names of many kingdoms to the eastward of Houssa are familiar to the inhabitants of Bambarra. I was shown quivers and arrows of very curious workmanship, which I was informed came from the kingdom of Kassina.

On the northern bank of the Niger, at a short distance from Silla, is the kingdom of Masina, which is inhabited by Foulahs. They employ themselves there, as in other places, chiefly in pasturage, and pay an annual tribute to the king of Bambarra for the lands which they occupy.

To the north-east of Masina is situated the kingdom of Timbuctoo, the great object of European research—the capital of this kingdom being one of the principal marts for that extensive commerce which the Moors carry on with the Negroes. The hopes of acquiring wealth in this pursuit, and zeal for propagating their religion, have filled this extensive city with Moors and Mahomedan converts; the king himself, and all the chief officers of state are Moors, and they are said to be more severe and intolerant in their principles than any other of the Moorish tribes in this part of Africa. I was informed by a venerable old Negro that when he first visited Timbuctoo, he took up his lodging at a sort of public inn, the landlord of which, when he conducted him into his hut, spread a mat on the floor, and laid a rope upon it, saying, " If you are a Mussulman you are my friend, sit down; but if you are a Kafir, you are my slave, and with this rope I will lead you to market." The present king of Timbuctoo is named *Abu Abrahima;* he is reported to possess immense riches. His wives and concubines are said to be clothed in silk, and the chief officers of state live in considerable splendour. The whole expense of his government is defrayed, as I was told, by a tax upon merchandise, which is collected at the gates of the city.

The city of Houssa (the capital of a large kingdom of the same name, situated to the eastward of Timbuctoo), is another great mart for Moorish commerce. I conversed with many merchants who had visited that city, and they all agreed that it is larger and more populous than Timbuctoo. The trade, police, and government, are nearly the same in both; but in Houssa the Negroes are in greater proportion to the Moors, and have some share in the government.

Concerning the small kingdom of Jinbala, I was not able

to collect much information. The soil is said to be remarkably fertile, and the whole country so full of creeks and swamps, that the Moors have hitherto been baffled in every attempt to subdue it. The inhabitants are Negroes, and some of them are said to live in considerable affluence, particularly those near the capital, which is a resting-place for such merchants as transport goods from Timbuctoo to the western parts of Africa.

To the southward of Jinbala is situated the Negro kingdom of Gotto, which is said to be of great extent. It was formerly divided into a number of petty states, which were governed by their own chiefs; but their private quarrels invited invasion from the neighbouring kingdoms. At length a politic chief, of the name of Moosee, had address enough to make them unite in hostilities against Bambarra, and on this occasion he was unanimously chosen general—the different chiefs consenting for a time to act under his command. Moosee immediately dispatched a fleet of canoes, loaded with provisions, from the banks of the lake Dibbie up the Niger, towards Jenné, and with the whole of his army pushed forwards into Bambarra. He arrived on the banks of the Niger opposite to Jenné before the townspeople had the smallest intimation of his approach, his fleet of canoes joined him the same day, and having landed the provisions, he embarked part of his army, and in the night took Jenné by storm. This event so terrified the king of Bambarra that he sent messengers to sue for peace, and in order to obtain it, consented to deliver to Moosee a certain number of slaves every year, and return everything that had been taken from the inhabitants of Gotto. Moosee, thus triumphant, returned to Gotto, where he was declared king, and the capital of the country is called by his name.

On the west of Gotto is the kingdom of Baedoo, which was conquered by the present king of Bambarra about seven years ago, and has continued tributary to him ever since.

West of Baedoo is Maniana, the inhabitants of which, according to the best information I was able to collect, are cruel and ferocious, carrying their resentment towards their enemies so far as never to give quarter, and even to indulge themselves with unnatural and disgusting banquets of human flesh.

I am well aware that the accounts which the Negroes give of their enemies ought to be received with great caution, but I heard the same account in so many different kingdoms, and from such variety of people, whose veracity I had no occasion to suspect, that I am disposed to allow it some degree of credit. The inhabitants of Bambarra, in the course of a long and bloody war, must have had frequent opportunities of satisfying themselves as to the fact; and if the report had been entirely without foundation, I cannot conceive why the term *Madummulo* (man-eaters) should be applied exclusively to the inhabitants of Maniana.

CHAPTER XVII.

Park Returns Homewards—Arrives at Modiboo, and recovers his Old Horse—Finds great difficulty in travelling, in consequence of the rains, and overflowing of the Niger—Is shunned by the Inhabitants—Avoids Sego, and prosecutes his journey along the banks of the Niger—Incidents on the Road—Cruelties attendant on African wars—Crosses the river Frina, and arrives at Tafiara.

A.D. 1796.

HAVING, for the reasons assigned in the last chapter, determined to proceed no farther eastward than Silla, I acquainted the Dooty with my intention of returning to Sego, proposing to travel along the southern side of the river; but he informed me, that from the number of creeks and swamps on that side, it was impossible to travel by any other route than along the northern bank; and even that route, he said, would soon be impassable on account of the overflowing of the river. However, as he commended my determination to return westward, he agreed to speak to some one of the fishermen to carry me over to Moorzan. I accordingly stepped into a canoe about eight o'clock in the morning of July 30th, and in about an hour was landed at Moorzan. At this place I hired a canoe for sixty cowries, and in the afternoon arrived at Kea, where, for forty cowries more, the Dooty permitted me to sleep in the same hut with one of his slaves. This poor Negro, perceiving that I was sickly, and that my clothes were very ragged, humanely lent me a large cloth to cover me for the night.

The Dooty's brother was now about to proceed to Modiboo, I therefore embraced the opportunity of accompanying him thither, there being no beaten road. He promised to carry my saddle, which I had left at Kea when my horse fell down in the woods, as I now proposed to present it to the king of Bambarra.

About a mile to the westward of Kea, we observed on the bank of the river a great number of earthen jars piled up together. They were very neatly formed, but not glazed; and were evidently of that sort of pottery which is manufactured at Downie (a town to the west of Timbuctoo), and sold to great advantage in different parts of Bambarra. As we approached towards the jars, my companion plucked up a large handful of herbage and threw it upon them; making signs for me to do the same, which I did. He then, with great seriousness, told me that these jars belonged to some supernatural power, that they were found in their present situation about two years ago; and as no person had claimed them, every traveller as he passed them, from respect to the invisible proprietor, threw some grass, or the branch of a tree, upon the heap, to defend the jars from the rain.

Thus conversing, we travelled in the most friendly manner until, unfortunately, we perceived the footsteps of a lion, quite fresh in the mud, near the river side. My companion now proceeded with great circumspection, and at last, coming to some thick underwood, he insisted that I should walk before him. I endeavoured to excuse myself, by alleging that I did not know the road; but he obstinately persisted, and after a few high words and menacing looks threw down the saddle and went away. This very much disconcerted me, but as I had given up all hopes of obtaining a horse, I could not think of encumbering myself with the saddle; and taking off the stirrups and girths, I threw the saddle into the river. The Negro no sooner saw me throw the saddle into the water, than he came running from among the bushes where he had concealed himself, jumped into the river, and by help of his spear, brought out the saddle, and ran away with it. I continued my course along the bank; but as the wood was remarkably thick, and I had reason to believe that a lion was at no great distance, I became much alarmed, and took a long circuit through the bushes to avoid him,

In the afternoon I reached Modiboo, where I found my saddle. The guide, who had got there before me, being afraid that I should inform the king of his conduct, had brought the saddle with him in a canoe.

While I was conversing with the Dooty, and remonstrating against the guide for having left me in such a situation, I heard a horse neigh in one of the huts, and the Dooty inquired with a smile if I knew who was speaking to me. He explained himself by telling me that my horse was still alive, and somewhat recovered from his fatigue; but he insisted that I should take him along with me, adding that he had once kept a Moor's horse for four months, and when the horse had recovered and got into good condition, the Moor returned and claimed it, and refused to give him any reward for his trouble.

I departed from Modiboo, driving my horse before me, and reached Nyamee, where I remained three days; during which time it rained without intermission, and with such violence that no person could venture out of doors.

Proceeding onwards from Nyamee, the country was so deluged that I was frequently in danger of losing the road, and had to wade across the savannas for miles together, knee deep in water. Even the corn ground, which is the driest land in the country, was so completely flooded that my horse twice stuck fast in the mud, and was not got out without the greatest difficulty.

Arrived at Nyara I was well received by the Dooty, and as the weather was rainy I did not depart until the next day, by which time the water had swelled to such a height that in many places the road was scarcely passable ; and though I waded breast deep across the swamps, I could only reach a small village called Nemaboo. Here, for a hundred cowries, I procured from some Foulahs plenty of corn for my horse, and milk for myself.

The difficulties I had now experienced made me anxious to engage a fellow-traveller, particularly, as I was assured that, in the course of a few days, the country would be so completely overflowed as to render the road utterly impassable ; but though I offered two hundred cowries for a guide nobody would accompany me. One morning, however (August 9), a Moor and his wife, riding upon two bullocks, and bound for Sego with salt, passed the village, and agreed to take me along with them ; but I found them of little service, for they were wholly unacquainted with the road, and being accustomed to a sandy soil, were very bad travellers. Instead of wading before the bullocks, to feel if the ground was solid, the woman boldly entered the first swamp, riding upon the top of the load; but when she had proceeded about two hundred yards, the bullock sunk into a hole, and threw both the load and herself among the reeds. The frightened husband stood for some time seemingly petrified with horror, and suffered his wife to be almost drowned before he went to her assistance.

On reaching Sibity, the Dooty received me very coolly ; and when I solicited a guide to Sansanding, he told me his people were otherwise employed. I was shown into a damp old hut, where I passed a very uncomfortable night ; for when the walls of the hut are softened by the rain they frequently become too weak to support the weight of the roof. I heard three huts fall during the night, and was apprehensive that the hut I lodged in would be the fourth. In the morning, as I went to pull some grass for my horse, I counted fourteen huts which had fallen in this manner since the commencement of the rainy season.

On the 11th of August the Dooty compelled me to depart from the town, and I set out for Sansanding, without any great hopes of faring better there than I had done at Sibity ; for I learned from people who came to visit me, that a report prevailed, and was universally believed, that I had come to Bambarra as a spy ; and as Mansong had not admitted me into his presence, the Dooties of the different towns were at liberty to treat me in what manner they pleased. From repeatedly hearing the same story, I had no doubt of the truth of it ; but as there was no alternative, I determined to proceed, and a little before sunset I arrived at Sansanding. My reception was what I expected. Counti Mamadi, who had been so kind to me formerly, scarcely gave me welcome. Every one wished to shun me, and my landlord sent a person to inform me that a very unfavourable report was received from Sego concerning me, and that he wished me to depart early in the morning. About ten o'clock at night Counti Mamadi himself came privately to me, and informed me that Mansong had dispatched a canoe to Janné to bring me back ; and he was afraid I should find great difficulty in going to the west country. He advised me, therefore, to depart from Sansanding before daybreak ; and cautioned me against stopping at Diggani, or any town near Sego.

I therefore departed from Sansanding, and reached Kabba in the afternoon of the 12th of August. As I approached the town, I was surprised to see several people assembled at the gate ; one of whom, as I advanced, came running towards me, and taking my horse by the bridle, led me round the walls of the town ; and then pointing to the west, told me to go along, or it would fare worse with me. It was in vain that I represented the danger of being benighted in the woods, exposed to the inclemency of the weather and to the fury of wild beasts. "Go along," was all the answer ; and a number of people coming up, and urging me in the same manner with great earnestness, I suspected that some of the king's messengers, who were sent in search of me, were in the town ; and that these Negroes, from mere kindness, conducted me past it with a view to facilitate my escape. I accordingly took the road for Sego, with the uncomfortable prospect of passing the night on the branches of a tree. After travelling about three miles I came to a small village near the road. The Dooty was splitting sticks by the gate, but I found I could have no admittance ; and when I attempted to enter, he jumped up, and with the stick he held in his hand threatened to strike me off the horse, if I presumed to advance another step.

At a little distance from this village, and farther from the road, is another small one. I conjectured that being rather out of the common route, the inhabitants might have fewer objections to give me house-room for the night ; and having crossed some corn fields, I sat down under a tree by the well. Two or three women came to draw water, and one of them, perceiving I was a stranger, inquired whether I was going. I told her I was going for Sego, but being benighted on the road I wished to stay at the village until morning, and begged she would acquaint the Dooty with my situation. In a little time the Dooty sent for me, and permitted me to sleep in a large baloon, in one corner of which was constructed a kiln for drying the fruit of the Shea-trees; it contained about half a cart-load of fruit, under which was kept up a clear wood fire. I was informed that in three days the fruit would be ready for pounding and boiling, and that the butter thus manufactured is preferable to that which is prepared from fruit dried in the sun, especially in the rainy season, when the process by isolation is always tedious, and oftentimes ineffectual.

About ten o'clock the following day I reached a small village within half a mile of Sego, where I endeavoured, but in vain, to procure some provisions. Every one seemed anxious to avoid me, and I could plainly perceive, by the looks and behaviour of the inhabitants, that some very unfavourable accounts had been circulated concerning me. I was again informed that Mansong had sent people to apprehend me, and the Dooty's son told me I had no time to lose if I wished to get safe out of Bambarra. I now fully saw the danger of my situation, and determined to avoid Sego altogether. I accordingly mounted my horse, and taking the road for Diggani, travelled as fast as I could, until I was out of sight of the villagers, when I struck to the westward, through high grass and swampy ground. About noon, I stopped under a tree to consider what course to take, for I had now no doubt but that the Moors and Slatees had misinformed the king respecting the object of my mission, and that the people were absolutely in search of me to convey me a prisoner to Sego. Sometimes I had thoughts of swimming my horse across the Niger and going to the southward for Cape Coast; but reflecting that I had ten days to travel before I should reach Kong, and afterwards an extensive country to traverse, inhabited by various nations, with whose language and manners I was totally unacquainted, I relinquished this scheme, and judged that I should better answer the purpose of my mission by proceeding to the westward along the Niger, endeavouring to ascertain how far the river was navigable in that direction. Having resolved upon this course, I proceeded accordingly, and a little before sunset arrived at a Foulah village called Sooboo, where, for two hundred cowries, I procured lodging for the night.

I continued my course along the bank of the river, through a populous and well-cultivated country. I passed a walled town called Kamalia,* without stopping; and at noon rode through a large town called Samee, where there happened to be a market, and a number of people assembled in an open place in the middle of the town selling cattle, cloth, corn, etc. I rode through the midst of them without being much observed; every one taking me for a Moor. I at length arrived at a small village called Binni, where I agreed with the Dooty's son, for one hundred cowries, to allow me to stay for

---

* There is another town of this name hereafter to be mentioned.

the night; but when the Dooty returned, he insisted that I should instantly leave the place; and if his wife and son had not interceded for me, I must have complied.

On the 15th August I passed a large town called Sai, which very much excited my curiosity. It is completely sur-rounded by two very deep trenches at about two hundred yards distant from the walls. On the top of the trenches are a number of square towers, and the whole has the appearance of a regular fortification. Inquiring into the origin of this extraordinary entrenchment, I learned from two of the towns-people the following particulars, which, if true, furnish a mournful picture of the enormities of African wars. About fifteen years ago, when the present king of Bambarra's father desolated Maniana, the Dooty of Sai had two sons slain in battle, fighting in the king's cause. He had a third son living, and when the king demanded a further reinforcement of men, and this youth among the rest, the Dooty refused to send him. This conduct so enraged the king, that when he returned from Maniana, about the beginning of the rainy season, and found the Dooty protected by the inhabitants, he sat down before Sai with his army, and surrounded the town with the trenches I had now seen. After a siege of two months, the towns-people became involved in all the horrors of famine; and whilst the king's army were feasting in their trenches, they saw, with pleasure, the miserable inhabitants of Sai devour the leaves and bark of the Bentang-tree that stood in the middle of the town. Finding, however, that the besieged would sooner perish than surrender, the king had recourse to treachery. He promised, that if they would open the gates, no person should be put to death, nor suffer any injury but the Dooty alone. The poor old man determined to sacrifice himself for the sake of his fellow-citizens, and immediately walked over to the king's army, where he was put to death. His son, in attempting to escape, was caught and massacred in the trenches, and the rest of the townspeople were carried away captives, and sold as slaves to the different Negro traders.

About noon I came to the village of Kaimoo, situated upon the bank of the river; and as the corn I had purchased at Sibili was exhausted, I endeavoured to purchase a fresh supply, but was informed that corn was become very scarce all over the country; and though I offered fifty cowries for a small quantity, no person would sell me any. As I was about to depart, however, one of the villagers (who probably mistook me for a Moorish shereef) brought me some as a present, only desiring me in return to bestow my blessing upon him, which I did in plain English, and he received it with a thousand acknowledgments. Of this present I made my dinner, and it was the third successive day that I had subsisted entirely upon raw corn.

In the evening, I arrived at a small village called Song, the surly inhabitants of which would not receive me, nor so much as permit me to enter the gate: but as lions were very numerous in this neighbourhood, and I had frequently, in the course of the day, seen the impression of their feet on the road, I resolved to stay in the vicinity of the village. Having collected some grass for my horse, I accordingly lay down under a tree by the gate. About ten o'clock I heard the hollow roar of a lion at no great distance, and attempted to open the gate; but the people from within told me that no person must attempt to enter the gate without the Dooty's permission. I begged them to inform the Dooty that a lion was approaching the village, and I hoped he would allow me to come within the gate. I waited for an answer to this message with great anxiety, for the lion kept prowling round the village, and once advanced so very near me that I heard him rustling among the grass, and climbed the tree for safety. About midnight, the Dooty, with some of his people, opened the gate, and desired me to come in. They were convinced, they said, that I was not a Moor, for no Moor ever waited any time at the gate of a village without cursing the inhabitants.

Next day I passed a considerable town with a mosque called Jabbe. Here the country begins to rise into hills, and I could see the summits of high mountains to the westward. I had very disagreeable travelling all this day on account of the swampiness of the roads, for the river was now risen to such a height as to overflow great part of the flat land on both sides, and from the muddiness of the water it was difficult to discern its depth. In crossing one of these swamps a little to the westward of a town called Gangu, my horse being up to the belly in water slipt suddenly into a deep pit, and was almost drowned before he could disengage his feet from the stiff clay at the bottom. Indeed, both the horse and its rider were so completely covered with mud, that in passing the village of Callimana, the people compared us to two dirty elephants. About noon I stopped at a small village near Yamina, where I purchased some corn and dried my papers and clothes.

The town of Yamina, at a distance, has a very fine appearance. It covers nearly the same extent of ground as Sansanding; but having been plundered by Daisy, king of Kaarta, about four years ago, it has not yet resumed its former prosperity—nearly one half of the town being nothing but a heap of ruins : however, it is still a considerable place, and is so much frequented by the Moors that I did not think it safe to lodge in it; but, in order to satisfy myself respecting its population and extent, I resolved to ride through it; in doing which, I observed a great many Moors sitting upon the Bentangs, and other places of public resort. Everybody looked at me with astonishment, but as I rode briskly along they had no time to ask questions.

I arrived in the evening at Farra, a walled village, where, without much difficulty, I procured a lodging for the night.

I pursued my journey early next morning, and at eight o'clock passed a considerable town called Balaba ; after which the road quits the plain, and stretches along the side of the hill. I passed in the course of this day the ruins of three towns, the inhabitants of which were all carried away by Daisy, king of Kaarta, on the same day that he took and plundered Yamina. Near one of these ruins I climbed a tamarind tree, but found the fruit quite green and sour, and the prospect of the country was by no means inviting; for the high grass and bushes seemed completely to obstruct the road, and the low lands were all so flooded by the river that the Niger had the appearance of an extensive lake. In the evening I arrived at Kanika, where the Dooty, who was sitting upon an elephant's hide at the gate, received me kindly, and gave me for supper some milk and meal, which I considered (as to a person in my situation it really was) a very great luxury.

August 18th.—By mistake I took the wrong road, and did

not discover my error until I had travelled near four miles, when coming to an eminence, I observed the Niger considerably to the left. Directing my course towards it, I travelled through long grass and bushes with great difficulty until two o'clock in the afternoon, when I came to a comparatively small but very rapid river, which I took at first for a creek, or one of the streams of the Niger. However, after I had examined it with more attention, I was convinced that it was a distinct river; and as the road evidently crossed it (for I could see the pathway on the opposite side), I sat down upon the bank, in hopes that some traveller might arrive, who would give me the necessary information concerning the fording-place; for the banks were so covered with reeds and bushes, that it would have been almost impossible to land on the other side, except at the pathway, which, on account of the rapidity of the stream, it seemed very difficult to reach. No traveller, however, arriving, and there being a great appearance of rain, I examined the grass and bushes for some way up the bank, and determined upon entering the river considerably above the pathway, in order to reach the other side before the stream had swept me too far down. With this view I fastened my clothes upon the saddle, and was standing up to the neck in water, pulling my horse by the bridle to make him follow me, when a man came accidentally to the place, and seeing me in the water, called to me with great vehemence to come out. The alligators, he said, would devour both me and my horse if we attempted to swim over. When I had got out, the stranger who had never before seen a European, seemed wonderfully surprised. He twice put his hand to his mouth, exclaiming in a low tone of voice, "God

preserve me! who is this?" but when he heard me speak the
Bambarra tongue, and found that I was going the same way
as himself, he promised to assist me in crossing the river, the
name of which he told me was Frina.   He then went a little
way along the bank, and called to some person who answered
from the other side.   In a short time, a canoe with two boys
came paddling from among the reeds; these boys agreed for
fifty cowries to transport me and my horse over the river,
which was effected without much difficulty, and I arrived in
the evening at Taffara, a walled town, and soon discovered that
the language of the natives was improved from the corrupted
dialect of Bambarra, to the pure Mandingo.

CHAPTER XVIII.

Inhospitable Reception at Taffara—Inhuman Negro—Park's Route
  along the Banks of the Niger—Comes to Koolikorro—Supports
  himself by writing Saphies—Reaches Marraboo—Loses the Road,
  and after many difficulties arrives at Bammakoo—Takes the
  Road for Sibidooloo—Meets with great Kindness at a Village
  called Kooma—Is afterwards robbed, stripped, and plundered by
  Banditti—Influence of Religion under distress—Arrives in
  safety at Sibidooloo.

A.D. 1796.

ON my arrival at Taffara I inquired for the Dooty, but
was informed that he had died a few days before my
arrival, and that there was at that moment a meeting of the
chief men for electing another, there being some dispute
about the succession. It was probably owing to the unsettled
state of the town that I experienced such a want of hospitality
in it, for though I informed the inhabitants that I should
only remain with them for one night, and assured them that
Mansong had given me some cowries to pay for my lodging,
yet no person invited me to come in ; and I was forced to sit
alone under the Bentang-tree exposed to the rain and wind of
a tornado, which lasted with great violence until midnight.
At this time the stranger who had assisted me in crossing the
river paid me a visit, and observing that I had not found a
lodging, invited me to take part of his supper which he had

brought to the door of his hut; for being a guest himself he could not, without his landlord's consent, invite me to come in. After this I slept upon some wet grass in the corner of a court. My horse fared still worse than myself, the corn I had purchased being all expended, and I could not procure a supply.

I passed the town of Jaba (August 20th), and stopped a few minutes at a village called Somino, where I begged and obtained some coarse food which the natives prepare from the husks of corn and call *Boo*. About two o'clock I came to the village of Sooha, and endeavoured to purchase some corn from the Dooty, who was sitting by the gate, but without success. I then requested a little food by way of charity, but was told he had none to spare. Whilst I was examining the countenance of this inhospitable old man, and endeavouring to find out the cause of the sullen discontent which was visible in his eye, he called to a slave who was working in the corn-field at a little distance, and ordered him to bring his hoe along with him. The Dooty then told him to dig a hole in the ground, pointing to a spot at no great distance. The slave, with his hoe, began to dig a pit in the earth; and the Dooty, who appeared to be a man of a very fretful disposition, kept muttering and talking to himself until the pit was almost finished, when he repeatedly pronounced the words *dankatoo* (good for nothing), *jankra lemen* (a real plague); which expressions I thought could be applied to nobody but myself, and as the pit had very much the appearance of a grave, I thought it prudent to mount my horse, and was about to decamp, when the slave, who had before gone into the village, to my surprise returned with the corpse of a boy about nine or ten years of age, quite naked.

The Negro carried the body by a leg and an arm, and threw it into the pit with a savage indifference which I had never before seen. As he covered the body with earth the Dooty often expressed himself, *naphula attiniata* (money lost), whence I concluded that the boy had been one of his slaves.

Departing from this shocking scene I travelled by the side of the river until sunset, when I came to Koolikorro, a considerable town and a great market for salt. Here I took up my lodging at the house of a Bambarran, who had formerly been the slave of a Moor, and in that character had travelled to Aoran, Towdinni, and many other places in the Great Desert; but turning Mussulman, and his master dying at Jenné, he obtained his freedom and settled at this place, where he carries on a considerable trade in salt, cotton cloth, etc. His knowledge of the world had not lessened that superstitious confidence in saphies and charms which he had imbibed in his earlier years; for when he heard that I was a Christian, he immediately thought of procuring a saphie, and for this purpose brought out his *walha*, or writing-board, assuring me that he would dress me a supper of rice if I would write him a saphie to protect him from wicked men. The proposal was of too great consequence to me to be refused. I therefore wrote the board full from top to bottom on both sides; and my landlord, to be certain of having the whole force of the charm, washed the writing from the board into a calabash with a little water, and having said a few prayers over it, drank this powerful draught: after which, lest a single word should escape, he licked the board until it was quite dry. A saphie writer was a man of too great consequence to be long concealed; the important information was carried to the Dooty, who sent his son with half a sheet of writing paper, desiring me to write him a *naphula saphie* (a charm to procure wealth). He brought me as a present some meal and milk, and when I had finished the saphie and read it to him with an audible voice, he seemed highly satisfied with his bargain, and promised to bring me in the morning some milk for my breakfast. When I had finished my supper of rice and salt, I laid myself down upon a bullock's hide and slept very quietly until morning, this being the first good meal and refreshing sleep that I had enjoyed for a long time.

At daybreak (August 21st) I departed from Koolikorro, and about noon passed the villages of Kayoo and Toolumbo. In the afternoon I arrived at Marraboo, a large town and, like Koolikorro, famous for its salt. I was conducted to the house of a Kaartan of the tribe of Jower, by whom I was well received. This man had acquired a considerable property in the slave trade, and from his hospitality to strangers was called, by way of pre-eminence, *Jattee* (the landlord), and his house was a sort of public inn for all travellers. Those who had money were well lodged, for they always made him some return for his kindness ; but those who had nothing to give, were content to accept whatever he thought proper ; and as I could not rank myself among the monied men, I was happy to take up my lodging in the same hut with seven poor fellows who had come from Kancaba in a canoe. But our landlord sent us some victuals.

Next day one of the landlord's servants went with me a little way from the town to show me what road to take, but whether from ignorance or design I know not, he directed me wrong ; and I did not discover my mistake until the day was

far advanced ; when, coming to a deep creek, I had some
thoughts of turning back, but as by that means I foresaw that
I could not possibly reach Bammakoo before night, I resolved
to cross it ; and leading my horse close to the brink I went
behind him and pushed him headlong into the water, and
then taking the bridle in my teeth swam over to the other
side. This was the third creek I had crossed in this manner
since I had left Sego, but having secured my notes and
memorandums in the crown of my hat, I received little or no
inconvenience from such adventures. The rain and heavy
dew kept my clothes constantly wet, and the roads being very
deep and full of mud, such a washing was sometimes pleasant
and oftentimes necessary. I continued travelling through
high grass without any beaten road, and about noon came to
the river, the banks of which are here very rocky, and the
force and roar of the water were very great. The king of
Bambarra's canoes, however, frequently pass these rapids, by
keeping close to the bank ; persons being stationed on the
shore with ropes fastened to the canoe, while others push it
forward with long poles. At this time, however, it would, I
think, have been a matter of great difficulty for any European
boat to have crossed the stream. About four o'clock in the
afternoon, having altered my course from the river towards
the mountains, I came to a small pathway which led to a
village called Frookaboo, where I slept.

Early next morning I set out for Bammakoo, at which
place I arrived about five o'clock in the afternoon (August 23d).
I had heard Bammakoo much talked of as a great market for
salt, and I felt rather disappointed to find it only a middling
town, not quite so large as Marraboo ; however, the smallness

of its size is more than compensated by the riches of its inhabitants; for when the Moors bring their salt through Kaarta
or Bambarra they constantly rest a few days at this place, and
the Negro merchants here, who are well acquainted with the
value of salt in different kingdoms, frequently purchase by
wholesale, and retail it to great advantage. Here I lodged at
the house of a Serawooli Negro, and was visited by a number
of Moors. They spoke very good Mandingo, and were more
civil to me than their countrymen had been. One of them
had travelled to Rio Grande, and spoke very highly of the
Christians. He sent me in the evening some boiled rice and
milk. I now endeavoured to procure information concerning
my route to the westward from a slave merchant who had
resided some years on the Gambia. He gave me some imperfect account of the distance, and enumerated the names of
a great many places that lay in the way, but withal told me
that the road was impassable at this season of the year. He
was even afraid, he said, that I should find great difficulty in
proceeding any farther, as the road crossed the Joliba at a
town about half a day's journey to the westward of Bammakoo;
and there being no canoes at that place large enough to receive
my horse, I could not possibly get him over for some months
to come. This was an obstruction of a very serious nature;
but as I had no money to maintain myself even for a few
days, I resolved to push on, and if I could not convey my
horse across the river, to abandon him and swim over myself.
In thoughts of this nature I passed the night, and in the
morning consulted with my landlord how I should surmount
the present difficulty. He informed me that one road still
remained, which was indeed very rocky and scarcely passable

for horses, but that if I had a proper guide over the hills to a town called Sibidooloo, he had no doubt, but with patience and caution, I might travel forwards through Manding. I immediately applied to the Dooty, and was informed that a *Jilli Kea* (singing-man) was about to depart for Sibidooloo, and would show me the road over the hills. With this man, who undertook to be my conductor, I travelled up a rocky glen about two miles, when we came to a small village, and here my musical fellow-traveller found out that he had brought me the wrong road. He told me that the horse-road lay on the other side of the hill, and throwing his drum upon his back, mounted up the rocks, where indeed no horse could follow him, leaving me to admire his agility and trace out a road for myself. As I found it impossible to proceed, I rode back to the level ground, and directing my course to the eastward came about noon to another glen, and discovered a path on which I observed the marks of horses' feet. Following this path I came in a short time to some shepherds' huts, where I was informed that I was in the right road, but that I could not possibly reach Sibidooloo before night. Soon after this I gained the summit of a hill, from whence I had an extensive view of the country. Towards the south-east appeared some very distant mountains, which I had formerly seen from an eminence near Marraboo, where the people informed me that these mountains were situated in a large and powerful kingdom called Kong, the sovereign of which could raise a much greater army than the king of Bambarra. Upon this height the soil is shallow, the rocks are ironstone and schistus, with detached pieces of white quartz.

A little before sunset I descended on the north-west side

of this ridge of hills, and as I was looking about for a convenient tree under which to pass the night (for I had no hopes of reaching any town), I descended into a delightful valley, and soon afterwards arrived at a romantic village called Kooma. This village is surrounded by a high wall, and is the sole property of a Mandingo merchant who fled hither with his family during a former war. The adjacent fields yield him plenty of corn, his cattle roam at large in the valley, and the rocky hills secure him from the depredations of war. In this obscure retreat he is seldom visited by strangers, but whenever this happens he makes the weary traveller welcome. I soon found myself surrounded by a circle of the harmless villagers. They asked me a thousand questions about my country, and, in return for my information, brought corn and milk for myself and grass for my horse, kindled a fire in the hut where I was to sleep, and appeared very anxious to serve me.

I departed from Kooma (August 25th), accompanied by two shepherds who were going towards Sibidooloo. The road was very steep and rocky, and as my horse had hurt his feet much in coming from Bammakoo, he travelled slowly and with great difficulty, for in many places the ascent was so sharp and the declivities so great, that if he had made one false step he must inevitably have been dashed to pieces. The shepherds, being anxious to proceed, gave themselves little trouble about me or my horse, and kept walking on at a considerable distance. It was about eleven o'clock, as I stopped to drink a little water at a rivulet (my companions being nearly a quarter of a mile before me), that I heard some people calling to each other, and presently a loud screaming as from a person in great distress. I immediately conjectured that a lion had taken one of the shepherds, and mounted my horse to have a better view of what had happened. The noise however ceased, and I rode slowly towards the place from whence I thought it had proceeded, calling out but without receiving any answer. In a little time, however, I perceived one of the shepherds lying among the long grass near the road, and though I could see no blood upon him I concluded he was dead. But when I came close to him he whispered me to stop, telling me that a party of armed men had seized upon his companion, and shot two arrows at himself as he was making his escape. I stopped to consider what course to take, and looking round saw at a little distance a man sitting on the stump of a tree. I distinguished also the heads of six or seven more, sitting upon the grass with muskets in their hands. I had now no hopes of escaping, and therefore determined to ride forward towards them. As I approached them I was in hopes they were elephant hunters, and by way of opening the conversation inquired if they had shot anything; but without returning an answer, one of them ordered me to dismount, and then, as if recollecting himself, waved with his hand for me to proceed. I accordingly rode past, and had with some difficulty crossed a deep rivulet, when I heard somebody holloa, and looking behind, saw those I had taken for elephant hunters running after me, and calling out to me to turn back. I stopped until they were all come up, when they informed me that the king of the Foulahs had sent them on purpose to bring me, my horse, and every thing that belonged to me, to Fooladoo, and that therefore I must turn back, and go along with them. Without hesitating a moment,

I turned round and followed them, and we travelled together near a quarter of a mile without exchanging a word; when, coming to a dark place of the wood, one of them said, in the Mandingo language, "This place will do;" and immediately snatched my hat from my head. Though I was by no means free of apprehension, yet I resolved to show as few signs of fear as possible, and therefore told them, that unless my hat was returned to me I should proceed no further. But before I had time to receive an answer, another drew his knife, and seizing upon a metal button which remained upon my waistcoat, cut it off, and put it into his pocket. Their intentions were now obvious, and I thought that the easier they were permitted to rob me of everything the less I had to fear. I therefore allowed them to search my pockets without resistance, and examine every part of my apparel, which they did with the most scrupulous exactness. But observing that I had one waistcoat under another, they insisted that I should cast them both off; and at last, to make sure work, stripped me quite naked. Even my half boots (though the sole of one of them was tied on to my foot with a broken bridle rein) were minutely inspected. Whilst they were examining the plunder, I begged them, with great earnestness, to return my pocket compass; but when I pointed it out to them, as it was lying on the ground, one of the banditti, thinking I was about to take it up, cocked his musket, and swore that he would lay me dead on the spot if I presumed to put my hand upon it. After this, some of them went away with my horse, and the remainder stood considering whether they should leave me quite naked, or allow me something to shelter me from the sun. Humanity at last prevailed ; they returned me the worst of the two shirts, and a pair of trousers; and as they went away, one of them threw back my hat, in the crown of which I kept my memorandums; and this was probably the reason they did not wish to keep it. After they were gone I sat for some time looking around me with amazement and terror. Whichever way I turned, nothing appeared but danger and difficulty. I saw myself in the midst of a vast wilderness, in the depth of the rainy season, naked and alone; surrounded by savage animals, and men still more savage. I was five hundred miles from the nearest European settlement. All these circumstances crowded at once on my recollection, and I confess that my spirits began to fail me. I considered my fate as certain, and that I had no alternative but to lie down and perish. The influence of religion, however, aided and supported me. I reflected that no human prudence or foresight could possibly have averted my present sufferings. I was indeed a stranger in a strange land, yet I was still under the protecting eye of that Providence who has condescended to call himself the stranger's friend. At this moment, painful as my reflections were, the extraordinary beauty of a small moss, in fructification, irresistibly caught my eye. I mention this to show from what trifling circumstances the mind will sometimes derive consolation; for though the whole plant was not larger than the top of one of my fingers, I could not contemplate the delicate conformation of its roots, leaves, and capsula, without admiration. *Can that Being (thought I) who planted, watered, and brought to perfection, in this obscure part of the world, a thing which appears of so small importance, look with unconcern upon the situation and sufferings of creatures formed after his own image?—surely not!* Reflections like these would not allow me to despair. I started up, and disregarding both hunger and fatigue, travelled forwards, assured that relief was at hand; and I was not disappointed. In a short time I came to a small village, at the entrance of which I overtook the two shepherds who had come with me from Kooma. They were much surprised to see me; for they said they never doubted that the Foulahs, when they had robbed, had murdered me. Departing from this village, we travelled over several rocky ridges, and at sunset arrived at Sibidooloo, the frontier town of the kingdom of Manding.

CHAPTER XIX.

*Town of Sibidooloo—Government of Manding—Reception by the Mansa,
or chief man of Sibidooloo, who takes measures for the recovery of
Park's horse and effects—Removes to Wonda—Great Scarcity and
its afflicting Consequences—Recovers his horse and clothes—Presents
his horse to the Mansa; and prosecutes his journey to Kamalia—
Some account of that Town—Kind reception by Karfa Taura, a
Slatee, who proposes to go to the Gambia in the next dry season
with a caravan of Slaves—Park's sickness.*

THE town of Sibidooloo is situated in a fertile valley, surrounded with high rocky hills. It is scarcely accessible
for horses, and during the frequent wars between the Bambarrans, Foulahs, and Mandingoes, has never once been plundered by an enemy. When I entered the town, the people
gathered round me, and followed me into the baloon, where I
was presented to the Dooty or chief man, who is here called
Mansa, which usually signifies king. Nevertheless, it appeared
to me that the government of Manding was a sort of republic,
or rather an oligarchy—every town having a particular Mansa,
and the chief power of the state, in the last resort, being lodged
in the assembly of the whole body. I related to the Mansa
the circumstances of my having been robbed of my horse and
apparel, and my story was confirmed by the two shepherds.
He continued smoking his pipe all the time I was speaking;
but I had no sooner finished than, taking the pipe from his

mouth and tossing up the sleeve of his coat, with an indignant air, "Sit down," said he, "you shall have everything restored to you—I have sworn it;"—and then turning to an attendant, "Give the white man," said he, "a draught of water, and with the first light of the morning go over the hills, and inform the Dooty of Bammakoo that a poor white man, the king of Bambarra's stranger, has been robbed by the king of Fooladoo's people."

I little expected, in my forlorn condition, to meet with a man who could thus feel for my sufferings. I heartily thanked the Mansa for his kindness, and accepted his invitation to remain with him until the return of the messenger. I was conducted into a hut, and had some victuals sent me; but the crowd of people which assembled to see me, all of whom commiserated my misfortunes and vented imprecations against the Foulahs, prevented me from sleeping until past midnight. Two days I remained without hearing any intelligence of my horse or clothes; and as there was at this time a great scarcity of provisions, approaching even to famine, all over this part of the country, I was unwilling to trespass any further on the Mansa's generosity, and begged permission to depart to the next village. Finding me very anxious to proceed, he told me that I might go as far as a town called Wonda, where he hoped I would remain a few days, until I heard some account of my horse.

I departed accordingly on the next morning (the 28th) and stopped at some small villages for refreshment. I was presented at one of them with a dish which I had never before seen. It was composed of the blossoms or *antheræ* of the maize, stewed in milk and water. It is eaten only in time of great scarcity. On the 30th, about noon, I arrived at Wonda, a small town with a mosque, and surrounded by a high wall. The Mansa, who was a Mahomedan, acted in two capacities— as chief magistrate of the town, and schoolmaster to the children. He kept his school in an open shed, where I was desired to take up my lodging until some account should arrive from Sibidooloo concerning my horse and clothes; for though the horse was of little use to me, yet the few clothes were essential. The little raiment upon me could neither protect me from the sun by day nor the dews and mosquitoes by night; indeed, my shirt was not only worn thin like a piece of muslin, but withal was so very dirty that I was happy to embrace an opportunity of washing it; which having done, and spread it upon a bush, I sat down naked, in the shade, until it was dry.

Ever since the commencement of the rainy season my health had been greatly on the decline. I had often been affected with slight paroxysms of fever, and from the time of leaving Bammakoo the symptoms had considerably increased. As I was sitting in the manner described, the fever returned with such violence that it very much alarmed me; the more so, as I had no medicine to stop its progress, nor any hope of obtaining that care and attention which my situation required.

I remained at Wonda nine days, during which time I experienced the regular return of the fever every day. And though I endeavoured as much as possible to conceal my distress from my landlord, and frequently lay down the whole day, out of his sight, in a corn field, conscious how burdensome I was to him and his family in a time of such great scarcity, yet I found that he was apprized of my situation; and one morning, as I feigned to be asleep by the fire, he observed to his wife that they were likely to find me a very troublesome and chargeable guest, for that, in my present sickly state, they should be obliged for the sake of their good name, to maintain me until I recovered or died.

The scarcity of provisions was certainly felt at this time most severely by the poor people, as the following circumstance most painfully convinced me. Every evening during my stay I observed five or six women come to the Mansa's house, and receive each of them a certain quantity of corn. As I knew how valuable this article was at this juncture, I inquired of the Mansa whether he maintained these poor women from pure bounty, or expected a return when the harvest should be gathered in. " Observe that boy," said he (pointing to a fine child of five years of age) ; "his mother has sold him to me for forty days' provision for herself and the rest of her family. I have bought another boy in the same manner." " Good God!" thought I, " what must a mother suffer before she sells her own child!" I could not get this melancholy subject out of my mind, and the next night, when the women returned for their allowance, I desired the boy to point out to me his mother, which he did. She was much emaciated, but had nothing cruel or savage in her countenance ; and when she had received her corn she came and talked to her son with as much cheerfulness as if he had still been under her care.

Two people arrived at length from Sibidooloo, bringing with them my horse and clothes ; but I found that my pocket-compass was broken to pieces. This was a great loss, which I could not repair. Another loss occurred to me at the same time. As my horse was grazing near the brink of a well, the ground gave way and he fell in. The well was about ten feet diameter, and so very deep that, when I saw my horse snorting in the water, I thought it was impossible to save him. The inhabitants of the village, however, immediately assembled, and having tied together a number of withes,* they lowered a man down into the well, who fastened those withes round the body of the horse ; and the people, having first drawn up the man, took hold of the withes, and to my surprise pulled the horse out with the greatest facility. The poor animal was now reduced to a mere skeleton, and the roads were scarcely passable, being either very rocky, or else full of mud and water ; I therefore found it impracticable to travel with him any farther, and was happy to leave him in the hands of one who I thought would take care of him. I accordingly presented him to my landlord, and desired him to send my saddle and bridle as a present to the Mansa of Sibidooloo, being the only return I could make him for having taken so much trouble in procuring my horse and clothes.

I now thought it necessary, sick as I was, to take leave of my hospitable landlord. On the morning of Sept. 8th, when I was about to depart, he presented me with his spear as a token of remembrance, and a leather bag to contain my clothes. Having converted my half-boots into sandals, I travelled with more ease, and slept that night at a village called Ballanti. On the 9th I reached Nemacoo; but the Mansa of the village thought fit to make me sup upon the cameleon's dish. By way of apology, however, he assured me the next morning that the scarcity of corn was such that he could not possibly allow me any. I could not accuse him of unkindness, as all the people actually appeared to be starving.

* From a plant called *kabba*, that climbs like a vine upon the trees.

At this time I was visited by a Negro, named Modi Lemina Taura, a great trader, who, suspecting my distress, brought me some victuals, and promised to conduct me to his house at Kinyeto the day following. I accordingly departed from Nemacoo, and arrived at Kinyeto (Sept. 11th) in the evening; but having hurt my ankle in the way, it swelled and inflamed so much that I could neither walk nor set my foot to the ground the next day without great pain. My landlord observing this, kindly invited me to stop with him a few days; and I accordingly remained at his house until the 14th, by which time I felt much relieved and could walk with the help of a staff. I now set out, thanking my landlord for his great care and attention, and being accompanied by a young man who was travelling the same way, I proceeded for Jerijang, a beautiful and well-cultivated district, the Mansa of which is reckoned the most powerful chief of any in Manding.

On the 15th I reached Dosita, a large town, where I staid one day on account of the rain; but continued very sickly, and was slightly delirious in the night. On the 17th I set out for Mansia, a considerable town, where small quantities of gold are collected. The road led over a high rocky hill, and my strength and spirits were so much exhausted, that before I could reach the top of the hill I was forced to lie down three times, being very faint and sickly. I reached Mansia in the afternoon. The Mansa of this town had the character of being very inhospitable; he, however, sent me a little corn for my supper, but demanded something in return; and when I assured him that I had nothing of value in my possession, he told me (as if in jest) that my white skin should not defend me if I told him lies. He then showed me the hut wherein I was to sleep, but took away my spear, saying that it would be returned to me in the morning. This trifling circumstance, when joined to the character I had heard of the man, made me rather suspicious of him; and I privately desired one of the inhabitants of the place, who had a bow and quiver, to sleep in the same hut with me. About midnight I heard somebody approach the door, and observing the moonlight strike suddenly into the hut I started up, and saw a man stepping cautiously over the threshold. I immediately snatched up the Negro's bow and quiver, the rattling of which made the man withdraw; and my companion looking out, assured me that it was the Mansa himself, and advised me to keep awake until the morning. I closed the door, and placed a large piece of wood behind it, and was wondering at this unexpected visit, when somebody pressed so hard against the door that the Negro could scarcely keep it shut. But when I called to him to open the door, the intruder ran off as before.

As soon as it was light, the Negro, at my request, went to the Mansa's house and brought away my spear. He told me that the Mansa was asleep; and lest this inhospitable chief should devise means to detain me, he advised me to set out before he was awake, which I immediately did; and about two o'clock reached Kamalia, a small town situated at the bottom of some rocky hills, where the inhabitants collect gold in considerable quantities. The Bushreens here live apart from the Kafirs, and have built their huts in a scattered manner at a short distance from the town. They have a place set apart for performing their devotions in, to which they give the name of *missura* or mosque; but it is, in fact, nothing more than a square piece of ground made level, and surrounded with the trunks of trees, having a small projection towards the east, where the Marraboo, or priest, stands, when he calls the people to prayers. Mosques of this description are very common among the converted Negroes; but having neither walls nor roof, they can only be used in fine weather. When it rains, the Bushreens perform their devotions in their huts.

On my arrival at Kamalia I was conducted to the house of a Bushreen named Karfa Taura, the brother of him to whose hospitality I was indebted at Kinyeto. He was collecting a coffle of slaves, with a view to sell them to the Europeans on the Gambia, as soon as the rains should be over. I found him sitting in his baloon, surrounded by several Slatees who proposed to join the coffle. He was reading to them from an Arabic book, and inquired, with a smile, if I understood it. Being answered in the negative, he desired one of the Slatees to fetch the little curious book which had been brought from the west country. On opening this small volume, I was surprised and delighted to find it our *Book of Common Prayer;* and Karfa expressed great joy to hear that I could read it; for some of the Slatees, who had seen the Europeans upon the coast, observing the colour of my skin (which was now become very yellow from sickness), my long beard, ragged clothes, and extreme poverty, were unwilling to admit that I was a white man, and told Karfa that they suspected I was some Arab in disguise. Kara, however, perceiving that I could read this book, had no doubt concerning me, and kindly promised me every assistance in his power. At the same time he informed me that it was impossible to cross the Jallonka wilderness for many months yet to come, as no less than eight rapid rivers, he said, lay in the way. He added, that he intended to set out himself for Gambia as soon as the rivers were fordable and the grass burnt, and advised me to stay and accompany him. He remarked, that when a caravan of the natives could not travel through the country, it was idle for a single white man to attempt it. I readily admitted that such an attempt was an act of rashness; but I assured him that I had now no alternative, for, having no money to support myself, I must either beg my subsistence by travelling from place to place, or perish from want. Karfa now looked at me with great earnestness, and inquired if I could eat the common victuals of the country—assuring me that he had never before seen a white man. He added, that if I would remain with him until the rains were over, he would give me plenty of victuals in the meantime, and a hut to sleep in; and that after he had conducted me in safety to the Gambia, I might then make him what return I thought proper. I asked him if the value of one prime slave would satisfy him. He answered in the affirmative, and immediately ordered one of the huts to be swept for my accommodation. Thus was I delivered by the friendly care of this benevolent Negro from a situation truly deplorable. Distress and famine pressed hard upon me. I had before me the gloomy wilds of Jallonkadoo, where the traveller sees no habitation for five successive days. I had observed at a distance the rapid course of the river Kokoro. I had almost marked out the place where I was doomed, I thought, to perish, when this friendly Negro stretched out his hospitable hand for my relief.

In the hut which was appropriated for me, I was provided

with a mat to sleep on, an earthen jar for holding water, and a small calabash to drink out of; and Karfa sent me from his own dwelling two meals a day, and ordered his slaves to supply me with firewood and water. But I found that neither the kindness of Karfa, nor any sort of accommodation, could put a stop to the fever which weakened me, and which became every day more alarming. I endeavoured as much as possible to conceal my distress; but on the third day after my arrival, as I was going with Karfa to visit some of his friends, I found myself so faint that I could scarcely walk, and before we reached the place I staggered and fell into a pit from which the clay had been taken to build one of the huts. Karfa endeavoured to console me with the hopes of a speedy recovery, assuring me, that if I would not walk out in the wet I should soon be well. I determined to follow his advice, and confine myself to my hut, but was still tormented with the fever, and my health continued to be in a very precarious state for five ensuing weeks. Sometimes I could crawl out of the hut and sit a few hours in the open air, at other times I was unable to rise, and passed the lingering hours in a very gloomy and solitary manner. I was seldom visited by any person except my benevolent landlord, who came daily to inquire after my health. When the rains became less frequent, and the country began to grow dry, the fever left me, but in so debilitated a condition that I could scarcely stand upright, and it was with great difficulty that I could carry my mat to the shade of a tamarind tree at a short distance, to enjoy the refreshing smell of the corn-fields, and delight my eyes with a prospect of the country. I had the pleasure, at length, to find myself in a state of convalescence, towards which the benevolent and simple manners of the Negroes, and the perusal of Karfa's little volume, greatly contributed.

In the meantime, many of the Slatees who resided at Kamalia having spent all their money and become in a great measure dependent upon Karfa's hospitality, beheld me with an eye of envy, and invented many ridiculous and trifling stories to lessen me in Karfa's esteem. A Serawoolli Slatee, too, who had arrived from Sego with five slaves, spread a number of malicious reports concerning me; but Karfa paid no attention to them, and continued to show me the same kindness as formerly. As I was one day conversing with the slaves which this Slatee had brought, one of them begged me to give him some victuals. I told him I was a stranger, and had none to give. He replied, "I gave *you* victuals when you was hungry. Have you forgot the man who brought you milk at Karankalla? But (added he, with a sigh) *the irons were not then upon my legs !*" I immediately recollected him, and begged some ground nuts from Karfa to give him as a return for his former kindness. He told me that he had been taken by the Bambarrans the day after the battle at Joka, and sent to Sego, where he had been purchased by his present master, who was carrying him down to Kajaaga. Three more of these slaves were from Kaarta, and one from Wassela, all of them prisoners of war. They stopped four days at Kamalia, and were then taken to Bala, where they remained until the river Kokoro was fordable and the grass burnt.

In the beginning of December, Karfa proposed to complete his purchase of slaves, and for this purpose collected all the debts which were owing to him in his own country. And on the 19th, being accompanied by three Slatees, he departed for

Kancaba, a large town on the banks of the Niger, and a great slave-market. Most of the slaves who are sold at Kancaba come from Bambarra ; for Mansong, to avoid the expense and danger of keeping all his prisoners at Sego, commonly sends them in small parties to be sold at the different trading towns ; and as Kancaba is much resorted to by merchants, it is always well supplied with slaves, who are sent thither up the Niger in canoes. When Karfa departed from Kamalia, he proposed to return in the course of a month, and during his absence I was left to the care of a good old Bushreen who acted as school-master to the young people of Kamalia.

Being now left alone, and at leisure to indulge my own reflections, it was an opportunity not be neglected of augmenting and extending the observations I had already made on the climate and productions of the country, and of acquiring a more perfect knowledge of the natives, than it was possible for me to obtain in the course of a transient and perilous journey through the country. I endeavoured likewise to collect all the information I could concerning those important branches of African commerce—the trade for gold, ivory, and slaves. Such was my employment during the remainder of my stay at Kamalia ; and I shall now proceed to lay before my readers the result of my researches and inquiries, avoiding as far as I can a repetition of those circumstances and observations which were related, as occasion arose, in the narrative of my journey.

CHAPTER XX.

The Negroes considered in a Moral light—Prominent Features in their Mental Character—Marriages, Religion, etc.

THE whole of my route, both in going and returning, having been confined to a tract of country bounded nearly by the 12th and 15th parallels of latitude, the reader must imagine that I found the climate in most places extremely hot, but nowhere did I feel the heat so intense and oppressive as in the camp at Benowm, of which mention has been made in a former place. In some parts, where the country ascends into hills, the air is at all times comparatively cool; yet none of the districts which I traversed could properly be called mountainous. About the middle of June the hot and sultry atmosphere is agitated by violent gusts of wind (called *tornadoes*), accompanied with thunder and rain. These usher in what is denominated the *rainy season*, which continues until the month of November. During this time the diurnal rains are very heavy, and the prevailing winds are from the south-west. The termination of the rainy season is likewise attended with violent tornadoes, after which the wind shifts to the north-east, and continues to blow from that quarter during the rest of the year.

WINDS.

When the wind sets in from the north-east it produces a

wonderful change in the face of the country ; the grass soon becomes dry and withered ; the rivers subside very rapidly, and many of the trees shed their leaves. About this period is commonly felt the *harmattan*, a dry and parching wind blowing from the north-east, and accompanied by a thick smoky haze, through which the sun appears of a dull red colour. This wind, in passing over the great desert of Sahara, acquires a very strong attraction for humidity, and parches up everything exposed to its current. It is, however, reckoned very salutary, particularly to Europeans, who generally recover their health during its continuance. I experienced immediate relief from sickness, both at Dr. Laidley's and at Kamalia, duri ʳ the *harmattan*. Indeed, the air during the rainy season is so loaded with moisture, that clothes, shoes, trunks, and everything that is not close to the fire, become damp and mouldy, and the inhabitants may be said to live in a sort of vapour bath ; but this dry wind braces up the solids which were before relaxed, gives a cheerful flow of spirits, and is even pleasant to respiration. Its ill effects are, that it produces chaps in the lips, and afflicts many of the natives with sore eyes.

BURNING THE GRASS.

Whenever the grass is sufficiently dry the Negroes set it on fire ; but in Ludamar, and other Moorish countries, this practice is not allowed, for it is upon the withered stubble that the Moors feed their cattle until the return of the rains. The burning the grass in Manding exhibits a scene of terrific grandeur. In the middle of the night I could see the plains and mountains, as far as my eye could reach, variegated with lines of fire, and the light reflected on the sky made the heavens appear in a blaze. In the day time pillars of smoke were seen in every direction, while the birds of prey were observed hovering round the conflagration, and pouncing down upon the snakes, lizards, and other reptiles, which attempted to escape from the flames. This annual burning is soon followed by a fresh and sweet verdure, and the country is thereby rendered more healthful and pleasant.

Of the most remarkable and important of the vegetable productions mention has already been made, and they are nearly the same in all the districts through which I passed. It is observable however that although many species of the edible roots which grow in the West India Islands are found in Africa, yet I never saw in any part of my journey either the sugar-cane, the coffee, or the cocoa-tree ; nor could I learn on inquiry that they were known to the natives. The pine-apple, and the thousand other delicious fruits which the industry of civilised man (improving the bounties of nature) has brought to such great perfection in the tropical climates of America, are here equally unknown. I observed, indeed, a few orange and banana trees near the mouth of the Gambia ; but whether they were indigenous, or were formerly planted there by some of the white traders, I could not positively learn. I suspect that they were originally introduced by the Portuguese.

PROPERTY IN THE SOIL.

Concerning property in the soil, it appeared to me that the lands in native woods were considered as belonging to the king, or (where the government was not monarchical) to the state. When any individual of free condition had the means of cultivating more land than he actually possessed, he applied to the chief man of the district, who allowed him an extension of territory on condition of forfeiture if the lands were not brought into cultivation by a given period. The condition being fulfilled, the soil became vested in the possessor and, for aught that appeared to me, descended to his heirs.

POPULATION.

The population, however, considering the extent and fertility of the soil, and the ease with which lands are obtained, is not very great in the countries which I visited. I found many extensive and beautiful districts entirely destitute of inhabitants, and in general, the borders of the different kingdoms were either very thinly peopled or entirely deserted. Many places are likewise unfavourable to population, from being unhealthful. The swampy banks of the Gambia, the Senegal, and other rivers towards the coast, are of this description. Perhaps it is on this account chiefly that the interior countries abound more with inhabitants than the maritime districts; for all the Negro nations that fell under my observation, though divided into a number of petty independent states, subsist chiefly by the same means, live nearly in the same temperature, and possess a wonderful similarity of disposition.

CHARACTER OF THE MANDINGOES.

The Mandingoes, in particular, are a very gentle race; cheerful in their dispositions, inquisitive, credulous, simple, and fond of flattery. Perhaps the most prominent defect in their character was that insurmountable propensity which the reader must have observed to prevail in all classes of them, to steal from me the few effects I was possessed of. For this part of their conduct no complete justification can be offered, because theft is a crime in their own estimation; and it must be observed that they are not habitually and generally guilty of it towards each other. This, however, is an important circumstance in mitigation; and before we pronounce them a more depraved people than any other, it were well to consider, whether the lower order of people in any part of Europe would have acted under similar circumstances with greater honesty towards a stranger, than the Negroes acted towards me. It must not be forgotten that the laws of the country afforded me no protection, that every one was at liberty to rob me with impunity; and finally, that some part of my effects were of as great value in the estimation of the Negroes as pearls and diamonds would have been in the eyes of a European. Let us suppose a black merchant of Hindostan to have found his way into the centre of England with a box of jewels at his back, and that the laws of the kingdom afforded him no security; in such a case the wonder would be, not that the stranger was robbed of any part of his riches, but that any part was left for a second depredator. Such, on sober reflection, is the judgment I have formed concerning the pilfering disposition of the Mandingo Negroes towards myself. Notwithstanding I was so great a sufferer by it, I do not consider that their natural sense of justice was perverted or extinguished; it was overpowered only for the moment by the strength of a temptation which it required no common virtue to resist.

On the other hand, as some counterbalance to this depravity in their nature—allowing it to be such—it is impossible for me to forget the disinterested charity and tender solicitude with which many of these poor heathens (from the sovereign of Sego to the poor women who received me at different times into their cottages when I was perishing of hunger) sympathised with me in my sufferings, relieved my distresses, and contributed to my safety. This acknowledgment, however, is perhaps more particularly due to the female part of the nation. Among the men, as the reader must have seen, my reception, though generally kind, was sometimes otherwise. It varied according to the various tempers of those to whom I made application. The hardness of avarice in some, and the blindness of bigotry in others, had closed up the avenues to compassion ; but I do not recollect a single instance of hardheartedness towards me in the women.

AMIABLENESS OF THE WOMEN.

It is surely reasonable to suppose that the soft and amiable sympathy of nature, which was thus spontaneously manifested towards me in my distress, is displayed by these poor people, as occasion requires, much more strongly towards persons of their own nation and neighbourhood, and especially when the objects of their compassion are endeared to them by the ties of consanguinity. Accordingly, the maternal affection (neither suppressed by the restraints, nor diverted by the solicitudes of civilised life) is everywhere conspicuous among them, and creates a correspondent return of tenderness in the child. An illustration of this has been given in the case of my attendant when he exclaimed, " Strike me, but do not curse my mother." The same sentiment I found universally to prevail, and observed in all parts of Africa that the greatest affront which could be offered to a Negro was to reflect on her who gave him birth.

MATERNAL AFFECTION.

It is not strange that this sense of filial duty and affection among the Negroes should be less ardent towards the father than the mother. The system of polygamy, while it weakens the father's attachment, by dividing it among the children of different wives, concentrates all the mother's jealous tenderness to one point—the protection of her own offspring. I perceived with great satisfaction, too, that the maternal solicitude extended not only to the growth and security of the person, but also, in a certain degree, to the improvement of the mind of the infant; for one of the first lessons in which the Mandingo women instruct their children is *the practice of truth.* The reader will probably recollect the case of the unhappy mother, whose son was murdered by the Moorish banditti at Funingkedy. Her only consolation in her uttermost distress was the reflection that the poor boy, in the course of his blameless life, *had never told a lie.* Such testimony from a fond mother, on such an occasion, must have operated powerfully on the youthful part of the surrounding spectators. It was at once a tribute of praise to the deceased, and a lesson to the living.

The Negro women suckle their children until they are able to walk of themselves. Three years' nursing is not uncommon; and during this period the husband devotes his whole attention to his other wives. To this practice it is owing, I presume, that the family of each wife is seldom very numerous. Few women have more than five or six children. As soon as an infant is able to walk, it is permitted to run about with great freedom. The mother is not over solicitous to preserve it from slight falls and other trifling accidents. A little practice soon enables the child to take care of itself, and experience acts the part of a nurse. As they advance in life, the girls are taught to spin cotton and to beat corn, and are instructed in other domestic duties ; and the boys are employed in the field.

RITE OF CIRCUMCISION.

Both sexes, whether Bushreens or Kafirs, on attaining the age of puberty, are circumcised.   This painful operation is not considered by the Kafirs so much in the light of a religious ceremony, as a matter of convenience and utility.   They have, indeed, a superstitious notion that it contributes to render the marriage state prolific.   The operation is performed upon several young people at the same time, all of whom are exempted from every sort of labour for two months afterwards. During this period they form a society called *Solimana*. They visit the towns and villages in the neighbourhood, where they dance and sing, and are well treated by the inhabitants. I had frequently, in the course of my journey, observed parties of this description, but they were all males.   I had, however, an opportunity of seeing a female *Solimana* at Kamalia.

MARRIAGE.

In the course of the celebration, it frequently happens that some of the young women get married.   If a man takes a fancy to any one of them, it is not considered as absolutely necessary that he should make an overture to the girl herself. The first object is to agree with the parents concerning the recompense to be given them for the loss of the company and services of their daughter.   The value of two slaves is a common price, unless the girl is thought very handsome, in which case the parents will raise their demand very considerably.   If the lover is rich enough, and willing to give the sum demanded, he then communicates his wishes to the damsel ; but her consent is by no means necessary to the match ; for if the parents agree to it, and eat a few kolla-nuts, which are presented by the suitor as an earnest of the bargain, the young lady must either have the man of their choice or continue unmarried, for she cannot afterwards be given to another. If the parents should attempt it, the lover is then authorised by the laws of the country to seize upon the girl as his slave. When the day for celebrating the nuptials is fixed on, a select number of people are invited to be present at the wedding ; a bullock or goat is killed, and great plenty of victuals dressed for the occasion. As soon as it is dark, the bride is conducted into a hut, where a company of matrons assist in arranging the wedding-dress, which is always white cotton, and is put on in such a manner as to conceal the bride from head to foot. Thus arrayed, she is seated upon a mat in the middle of the floor, and the old women place themselves in a circle round her. They then give her a series of instructions, and point out, with great propriety, what ought to be her future conduct in life. This scene of instruction, however, is frequently interrupted by girls, who amuse the company with songs and dances, which are rather more remarkable for their gaiety than delicacy. While the bride remains within the hut with the women, the bridegroom devotes his attention to the guests of both sexes, who assemble without doors, and by distributing among them small presents of kolla-nuts, and seeing that every one partakes of the good cheer which is provided, he contributes much to the general hilarity of the evening. When supper is ended, the company spend the remainder of the night in singing and dancing, and seldom separate until daybreak. About midnight, the bride is privately conducted by the women into the hut which is to be her future residence ; and the bridegroom, upon a signal given, retires from his company. The new-married couple, however, are always disturbed towards morning by the women, who assemble to inspect the nuptial sheet (according to the manners of the ancient Hebrews, as recorded in Scripture), and dance round it. This ceremony is thought indispensably necessary, nor is the marriage considered as valid without it.

The Negroes, as has been frequently observed, whether Mahomedan or Pagan, allow a plurality of wives. The Maho-medans alone are by their religion confined to four ; and as the husband commonly pays a great price for each, he requires from all of them the utmost deference and submission, and treats them more like hired servants than companions. They have, however, the management of domestic affairs, and each in rotation is mistress of the household, and has the care of dressing the victuals, overlooking the female slaves, etc. But though the African husbands are possessed of great authority over their wives, I did not observe that in general they treat them with cruelty, neither did I perceive that mean jealousy in their dispositions which is so prevalent among the Moors. They permit their wives to partake of all public diversions, and this indulgence is seldom abused ; for though the Negro women are very cheerful and frank in their behaviour, they are by no means given to intrigue. I believe that instances of conjugal infidelity are not common. When the wives quarrel among themselves, a circumstance which, from the nature of their situation, must frequently happen, the husband decides between them, and sometimes finds it necessary to administer a little corporal chastisement before tranquillity can be restored. But if any one of the ladies complains to the chief of the town that her husband has unjustly punished her, and shown an undue partiality to some other of his wives, the affair is brought to a public trial. In these *palavers*, however, which are conducted chiefly by married men, I was informed that the complaint of the wife is not always considered in a very serious light, and the complainant herself is sometimes convicted of strife and contention, and left without remedy. If she murmurs at the decision of the court, the magic rod of *Mumbo Jumbo* soon puts an end to the business. *Humour*

BAPTISM.

The children of the Mandingoes are not always named after their relations, but frequently in consequence of some remarkable occurrence. Thus, my landlord at Kamalia was called *Karfa*, a word signifying *to replace ;* because he was born shortly after the death of one of his brothers. Other names are descriptive of good or bad qualities, as *Modi*, "a good man ;" *Fadibba*, "father of the town," etc. ; indeed, the very names of their towns have something descriptive in them, as *Sibidooloo*, "the town of ciboa-trees ;" *Kenneyeto*, "victuals here ;" *Dosita*, "lift your spoon." Others seem to be given by way of reproach, as *Bammakoo*, "wash a crocodile ;" *Karankalla*, "no cup to drink from," etc. A child is named when it is seven or eight days old. The ceremony commences by shaving the infant's head ; and a dish called *Dega*, made of pounded corn and sour milk, is prepared for the guests. If the parents are rich, a sheep or goat is commonly added. The feast is called *Ding koon lee*, "the child's head-shaving."

During my stay at Kamalia I was present at four different feasts of this kind, and the ceremony was the same in each, whether the child belonged to a Bushreen or a Kafir. The schoolmaster, who officiated as priest on these occasions, and who is necessarily a Bushreen, first said a long prayer over the *dega*, during which every person present took hold of the brim of the calabash with his right hand. After this the schoolmaster took the child in his arms, and said a second prayer, in which he repeatedly solicited the blessing of God upon the child, and upon all the company. When this prayer was ended, he whispered a few sentences in the child's ear, and spat three times in its face, after which he pronounced its name aloud, and returned the infant to the mother. This part of the ceremony being ended, the father of the child divided the *dega* into a number of balls, one of which he distributed to every person present. And inquiry was then made if any person in the town was dangerously sick—it being usual in such cases to send the party a large portion of the *dega*, which is thought to possess great medical virtues.*

Among the Negroes every individual, besides his own proper name, has likewise a *kontong*, or surname, to denote the family or clan to which he belongs. Some of these families are very numerous and powerful. It is impossible to enumerate the various *kontongs* which are found in different parts of the country, though the knowledge of many of them is of great service to the traveller; for as every Negro plumes himself upon the importance or the antiquity of his clan, he is much flattered when he is addressed by his *kontong*.

---

* Soon after baptism, the children are marked in different parts of the skin, in a manner resembling what is called *tattooing* in the South Sea Islands.

SALUTATIONS.

Salutations among the Negroes to each other, when they meet, are always observed ; but those in most general use among the Kafirs are *Abbe paeretto—E ning seni—Anawari*, etc., all of which have nearly the same meaning, and signify, Are you well ? or to that effect.   There are likewise salutations which are used at different times of the day, as *E ning somo*, Good morning, etc.   The general answer to all salutations is to repeat the *kontong* of the person who salutes, or else to repeat the salutation itself, first pronouncing the word *marhaba*, My friend.

METHOD OF DIVIDING TIME.

The Mandingoes, and, I believe, the Negroes in general, have no artificial method of dividing time.   They calculate the years by the number of *rainy seasons*.   They portion the year into *moons*, and reckon the days by so many *suns*.   The day they divide into morning, mid-day, and evening ; and further subdivide it, when necessary, by pointing to the sun's place in the heavens.   I frequently inquired of some of them what became of the sun during the night, and whether we should see the same sun or a different one in the morning ; but I found that they considered the question as very childish. The subject appeared to them as placed beyond the reach of human investigation ; they had never indulged a conjecture, nor formed any hypothesis about the matter.   The moon, by varying her form, has more attracted their attention.   On the first appearance of the new moon, which they look upon to be newly created, the Pagan natives, as well as Mahomedans, say a short prayer ; and this seems to be the only visible adoration which the Kafirs offer to the Supreme Being. This prayer is pronounced in a whisper—the party holding up his hands before his face ; its purport (as I have been assured by many different people) is to return thanks to God for his kindness through the existence of the past moon, and to solicit a continuation of his favour during that of the new one. At the conclusion they spit upon their hands, and rub them over their faces. This seems to be nearly the same ceremony which prevailed among the heathens in the days of Job.[*]

Great attention, however, is paid to the changes of this luminary in its monthly course, and it is thought very unlucky to begin a journey or any other work of consequence in the last quarter. An eclipse, whether of the sun or moon, is supposed to be effected by witchcraft. The stars are very little regarded ; and the whole study of astronomy appears to them as a useless pursuit, and attended to by such persons only as deal in magic.

NOTIONS OF GEOGRAPHY.

Their notions of geography are equally puerile. They imagine that the world is an extended plain, the termination of which no eye has discovered—it being, they say, overhung with clouds and darkness. They describe the sea as a large river of salt water, on the further shore of which is situated a country called *Tobaubo doo*—" the land of the white people." At a distance from Tobaubo doo, they describe another country, which they allege is inhabited by cannibals of gigantic size, called *Koomi*. This country they call *Jong sang doo*—" the land where the slaves are sold." But of all countries in the world their own appears to them as the best, and their own

* Chapter xxxi. verses 26, 27, 28.

people as the happiest ; and they pity the fate of other nations, who have been placed by Providence in less fertile and less fortunate districts.

RELIGION.

Some of the religious opinions of the Negroes, though blended with the weakest credulity and superstition, are not unworthy of attention. I have conversed with all ranks and conditions upon the subject of their faith, and can pronounce, without the smallest shadow of doubt, that the belief of one God, and of a future state of reward and punishment, is entire and universal among them. It is remakable, however, that, except on the appearance of a new moon as before related, the Pagan natives do not think it necessary to offer up prayers and supplications to the Almighty. They represent the Deity, indeed, as the creator and preserver of all things ; but in general they consider him as a being so remote, and of so exalted a nature, that it is idle to imagine the feeble supplications of wretched mortals can reverse the decrees, and change the purposes of unerring Wisdom. If they are asked, for what reason then do they offer up a prayer on the appearance of the new moon, the answer is, that custom has made it necessary ; they do it because their fathers did it before them. Such is the blindness of unassisted nature ! The concerns of this world, they believe, are committed by the Almighty to the superintendence and direction of subordinate spirits, over whom they suppose that certain magical ceremonies have great influence. A white fowl suspended to the branch of a particular tree, a snake's head, or a few handfuls of fruit, are offerings which ignorance and superstition frequently present, to deprecate the wrath or to conciliate the favour of these tutelary agents. But it is not often that the Negroes make their religious opinions the subject of conversation. When interrogated, in particular concerning their ideas of a future state, they express themselves with great reverence, but endeavour to shorten the discussion by observing—*Mo o mo inta alo*, "no man knows anything about it." They are content, they say, to follow the precepts and examples of their forefathers through the various vicissitudes of life, and when this world presents no objects of enjoyment or comfort, they seem to look with anxiety towards another, which they believe will be better suited to their natures, but concerning which they are far from indulging vain and delusive conjectures.

DURATION OF LIFE.

The Mandingoes seldom attain extreme old age. At forty, most of them become grey-haired and covered with wrinkles ; and but few of them survive the age of fifty-five or sixty. They calculate the years of their lives, as I have already observed, by the number of rainy seasons (there being but one such in the year) ; and distinguish each year by a particular name, founded on some remarkable occurrence which happened in that year. Thus they say the year of the *Farbanna war ;* the year of the *Kaarta war ;* the year on which *Gadou was plundered,* etc. etc. ; and I have no doubt that the year 1796 will in many places be distinguished by the name of *Tabaubo tambi sang,* "the year the white man passed ;" as such an occurrence would naturally form an epoch in their traditional history.

HEALTH AND DISEASE.

But notwithstanding that longevity is uncommon among them, it appeared to me that their diseases are but few in number. Their simple diet and active way of life preserve them from many of those disorders which embitter the days of luxury and idleness. Fevers and fluxes are the most common and the most fatal. For these they generally apply saphies to different parts of the body, and perform a great many other superstitious ceremonies ; some of which are, indeed, well calculated to inspire the patient with the hope of recovery, and divert his mind from brooding over his own danger. But I have sometimes observed among them a more systematic mode of treatment. On the first attack of a fever, when the patient complains of cold, he is frequently placed in a sort of vapour ; this is done by spreading branches of the *Nauclea orientalis* upon hot wood embers, and laying the patient upon them, wrapped up in a large cotton cloth. Water is then sprinkled upon the branches, which, descending to the hot embers, soon covers the patient with a cloud of vapour, in which he is allowed to remain until the embers are almost extinguished. This practice commonly produces a profuse perspiration, and wonderfully relieves the sufferer. For the dysentery they use the bark of different trees reduced to powder, and mixed with the patient's food ; but this practice is in general very unsuccessful.

The other diseases which prevail among the Negroes are the *yaws*, the *elephantiasis*, and a *leprosy* of the very worst kind. This last-mentioned complaint appears, at the beginning, in scurfy spots upon different parts of the body, which finally settle upon the hands or feet, where the skin becomes withered, and cracks in many places. At length, the ends of the fingers swell and ulcerate ; the discharge is acrid and fœtid ; the nails drop off, and the bones of the fingers become carious, and separate at the joints. In this manner the disease continues to spread, frequently until the patient loses all his fingers and toes. Even the hands and feet are sometimes destroyed by this inveterate malady, to which the Negroes give the name of *balla jou*, "incurable." The *Guinea-worm* is likewise very common in certain places, especially at the commencement of the rainy season. The Negroes attribute this disease—which has been described by many writers—to bad water, and allege that the people who drink from wells are more subject to it than those who drink from streams. To the same cause they attribute the swelling of the glands of the neck (goitres), which are very common in some parts of Bambarra. I observed also, in the interior countries, a few instances of simple gonorrhœa, but never the confirmed lues." On the whole, it appeared to me that the Negroes are better surgeons than physicians. I found them very successful in their management of fractures and dislocations, and their splints and bandages are simple and easily removed. The patient is laid upon a soft mat, and the fractured limb is frequently bathed with cold water. All abscesses they open with the actual cautery ; and the dressings are composed of either soft leaves, shea butter, or cow's dung, as the case seems, in their judgment, to require. Towards the coast, where a supply of European lancets can be procured, they sometimes perform phlebotomy ; and in cases of local inflammation a curious sort of cupping is practised. This operation is per-

formed by making incisions in the part, and applying to it
a bullock's horn with a small hole in the end. The operator
then takes a piece of bees'-wax in his mouth, and putting his
lips to the hole, extracts the air from the horn; and by a
dexterous use of his tongue stops up the hole with the wax.
This method is found to answer the purpose, and in general
produces a plentiful discharge.

FUNERALS.

When a person of consequence dies, the relations and
neighbours meet together and manifest their sorrow by loud
and dismal howlings. A bullock or goat is killed for such
persons as come to assist at the funeral, which generally takes
place in the evening of the same day on which the party died.
The Negroes have no appropriate burial-places, and frequently
dig the grave in the floor of the deceased's hut, or in the shade
of a favourite tree. The body is dressed in white cotton, and
wrapped up in a mat. It is carried to the grave, in the dusk
of the evening, by the relations. If the grave is without the
walls of the town, a number of prickly bushes are laid upon
it, to prevent the wolves from digging up the body, but I
never observed that any stone was placed over the grave as
a monument or memorial.

CHAPTER XXI.

Domestic life of the Negroes—Music—Diet—Occupations—Leather Iron—Gold—Ivory, etc.

THE principal musical instruments of the Negroes are the *koonting*, a sort of guitar with three strings; the *korro*, a large harp with eighteen strings; the *simbing*, a small harp with seven strings; the *balafou*, an instrument composed of twenty pieces of hard wood of different lengths, with the shells of gourds hung underneath to increase the sound; the *tang-tang*, a drum, open at the lower end; and lastly, the *tabala*, a large drum, commonly used to spread an alarm through the country. Besides these, they make use of small flutes, bow-strings, elephants' teeth, and bells; and at all their dances and concerts *clapping of hands* appears to constitute a neces-sary part of the chorus.

With the love of music is naturally connected a taste for poetry; and, fortunately for the poets of Africa, they are in a great measure exempted from that neglect and indigence which, in more polished countries, commonly attend the votaries of the Muses. They consist of two classes; the most numerous are the *singing-men*, called *Jilli kea*, mentioned in a former part of my narrative. One or more of these may be found in every town. They sing extempore songs in honour of their chief men, or any other persons who are willing to give "*solid pudding for empty praise."* But a nobler part of their office is to recite the historical events of their country ; hence, in war, they accompany the soldiers to the field, in order, by reciting the great actions of their ancestors, to awaken in them a spirit of glorious emulation. The other class are devotees of the Mahomedan faith, who travel about the country singing devout hymns and performing religious ceremonies, to conciliate the favour of the Almighty, either in averting calamity or ensuring success to any enterprise. Both descriptions of these itinerant bards are much employed and respected by the people, and very liberal contributions are made for them.

DIET.

The usual diet of the Negroes is somewhat different in different districts. In general, the people of free condition breakfast about daybreak upon gruel made of meal and water, with a little of the fruit of the tamarind to give it an acid taste. About two o'clock in the afternoon, a sort of hasty pudding, with a little shea butter, is the common meal ; but the supper constitutes the principal repast, and is seldom ready before midnight. This consists almost universally of kouskous, with a small portion of animal food or shea butter, mixed with it. In eating, the Kafirs, as well as Mahomedans, use the right hand only.

The beverages of the Pagan Negroes are beer and mead ; of each of which they frequently drink to excess. The Mahomedan converts drink nothing but water. The natives of all descriptions take snuff, and smoke tobacco. Their pipes are made of wood, with an earthen bowl of curious workmanship. But in the interior countries the greatest of all luxuries is salt. It would appear strange to a European to see a child suck a piece of rock-salt as if it were sugar. This, however, I have frequently seen; although, in the inland parts, the poorer class of inhabitants are so very rarely indulged with this precious article, that to say *a man eats salt with his victuals* is the same as saying *he is a rich man*. I have myself suffered great inconvenience from the scarcity of this article. The long use of vegetable food creates so painful a longing for salt that no words can sufficiently describe it.

OCCUPATIONS.

The Negroes in general, and the Mandingoes in particular, are considered by the whites on the coast as an indolent and inactive people, I think without reason. The nature of the climate is indeed unfavourable to great exertion; but surely a people cannot justly be denominated habitually indolent, whose wants are supplied, not by the spontaneous productions of nature, but by their own exertions. Few people work harder, when occasion requires, than the Mandingoes; but not having many opportunities of turning to advantage the superfluous produce of their labour, they are content with cultivating as much ground only as is necessary for their own support. The labours of the field give them pretty full employment during the rains; and in the dry season, the people who live in the vicinity of large rivers employ themselves chiefly in fishing.

FISHING.

The fish are taken in wicker baskets, or with small cotton nets, and are preserved by being first dried in the sun and afterwards rubbed with shea butter to prevent them from contracting fresh moisture.

HUNTING.

Others of the natives employ themselves in hunting. Their weapons are bows and arrows, but the arrows in common use are not poisoned. Poisoned arrows are used chiefly in war. The poison, which is said to be very deadly, is prepared from a shrub called *koona* (a species of *echites*), which is very common in the woods. The leaves of this shrub, when boiled with a small quantity of water, yield a thick black juice, into which the Negroes dip a cotton thread ; this thread they fasten round the iron of the arrow in such a manner that it is almost impossible to extract the arrow, when it has sunk beyond the barbs, without leaving the iron point and the poisoned thread in the wound.

They are very dexterous marksmen, and will hit a lizard on a tree, or any other small object, at an amazing distance. They likewise kill Guinea-fowls, partridges, and pigeons, but never on the wing.

WOMEN'S WORK.

While the men are occupied in these pursuits, the women are very diligent in manufacturing cotton cloth. They prepare the cotton for spinning by laying it, in small quantities at a time, upon a smooth stone or piece of wood, and rolling the seeds out with a thick iron spindle, and they spin it with the distaff. The thread is not fine, but well twisted, and makes a very durable cloth. A woman with common diligence will spin from six to nine garments of this cloth in one year, which, according to its fineness, will sell for a minkalli (a quantity of gold nearly equal in value to ten shillings sterling) and a half

or two minkallies each. The weaving is performed by the
men. The loom is made exactly upon the same principle as
that of Europe; but so small and narrow that the web is
seldom more than four inches broad. The shuttle is of the
common construction; but as the thread is coarse, the chamber
is somewhat larger than the European. The women dye this
cloth of a rich and lasting blue colour, by the following simple
process :—The leaves of the indigo, when fresh gathered, are
pounded in a wooden mortar, and mixed in a large earthen jar
with a strong lye of wood ashes. Chamber-lye is sometimes
added. The cloth is steeped in this mixture, and allowed to
remain until it has acquired the proper shade. In Kaarta and
Ludamar, where the indigo is not plentiful, they collect the
leaves and dry them in the sun; and when they wish to use
them they reduce a sufficient quantity to powder, and mix it
with the lye, as before mentioned. Either way the colour is
very beautiful, with a fine purple gloss, and equal, in my
opinion, to the best Indian or European blue. This cloth is
cut into various pieces, and sewed into garments with needles
of the natives' own making.

TANNERS.

As the arts of weaving, dyeing, sewing, etc., may easily be
acquired, those who exercise them are not considered in Africa
as following any particular profession, for almost every slave
can weave, and every boy can sew. The only artists distinctly
acknowledged as such by the Negroes, and who value themselves on exercising appropriate and peculiar trades, are the
manufacturers of *leather* and of *iron*. The first of these are called
Karrankea (or, as the word is sometimes pronounced, *Gaungay*)

They are to be found in almost every town, and they frequently travel through the country in the exercise of their calling. They tan and dress leather with very great expedition, by steeping the hide first in a mixture of wood ashes and water, until it parts with the hair, and afterwards by using the pounded leaves of a tree called *goo* as an astringent. They are at great pains to render the hide as soft and pliant as possible, by rubbing it frequently between their hands, and beating it upon a stone. The hides of bullocks are converted chiefly into sandals, and therefore require less care in dressing than the skins of sheep and goats, which are used for covering quivers and saphies, and in making sheaths for swords and knives, belts, pockets, and a variety of ornaments. These skins are commonly dyed of a red or yellow colour; the red by means of millet-stalks reduced to powder, and the yellow by the root of a plant the name of which I have forgotten.

BLACKSMITHS.

The workers in iron are not so numerous as the *Karrankeas;* but they appear to have studied their business with equal diligence. The Negroes on the coast, being cheaply supplied with iron from the European traders, never attempt the manufacturing of this article themselves; but in the inland parts, the natives smelt this useful metal in such quantities, as not only to supply themselves from it with all necessary weapons and instruments, but even to make it an article of commerce with some of the neighbouring states. During my stay at Kamalia, there was a smelting-furnace at a short distance from the hut where I lodged, and the owner and his workmen made no secret about the manner of conduct-

ing the operation, and readily allowed me to examine the
furnace, and assist them in breaking the ironstone.   The
furnace was a circular tower of clay, about ten feet high and
three in diameter, surrounded in two places with withes, to
prevent the clay from cracking and falling to pieces by the
violence of the heat.   Round the lower part, on a level with
the ground (but not so low as the bottom of the furnace,
which was somewhat concave), were made seven openings,
into every one of which were placed three tubes of clay, and
the openings again plastered up in such a manner that no
air could enter the furnace but through the tubes, by the
opening and shutting of which they regulated the fire.   These
tubes were formed by plastering a mixture of clay and grass
round a smooth roller of wood, which, as soon as the clay
began to harden, was withdrawn, and the tube left to dry in
the sun.   The ironstone which I saw was very heavy, and of
a dull red colour, with greyish specks; it was broken into
pieces about the size of a hen's egg.   A bundle of dry wood
was first put into the furnace and covered with a considerable
quantity of charcoal, which was brought ready burnt from
the woods.   Over this was laid a stratum of ironstone, and
then another of charcoal, and so on, until the furnace was
quite full.   The fire was applied through one of the tubes, and
blown for some time with bellows made of goats' skins.   The
operation went on very slowly at first, and it was some hours
before the flame appeared above the furnace; but after this it
burnt with great violence all the first night, and the people
who attended put in at times more charcoal.   On the day
following the fire was not so fierce, and on the second night
some of the tubes were withdrawn, and the air allowed to

have freer access to the furnace; but the heat was still very great, and a bluish flame rose some feet above the top of the furnace. On the third day from the commencement of the operation all the tubes were taken out, the ends of many of them being vitrified with the heat; but the metal was not removed until some days afterwards, when the whole was perfectly cool. Part of the furnace was then taken down, and the iron appeared in the form of a large irregular mass, with pieces of charcoal adhering to it. It was sonorous; and when any portion was broken off, the fracture exhibited a granulated appearance, like broken steel. The owner informed me that many parts of this cake were useless, but still there was good iron enough to repay him for his trouble. This iron, or rather steel, is formed into various instruments, by being repeatedly heated in a forge, the heat of which is urged by a pair of double bellows of a very simple construction, being made of two goats' skins, the tubes from which unite before they enter the forge, and supply a constant and very regular blast. The hammer, forceps, and anvil, are all very simple, and the workmanship (particularly in the formation of knives and spears) is not destitute of merit. The iron, indeed, is hard and brittle, and requires much labour before it can be made to answer the purpose.

Most of the African blacksmiths are acquainted also with the method of smelting gold, in which process they use an alkaline salt obtained from a lye of burnt corn-stalks evaporated to dryness. They likewise draw the gold into wire, and form it into a variety of ornaments, some of which are executed with a great deal of taste and ingenuity.

In his opinion

GOLD.

Those valuable commodities, gold and ivory, have probably been found in Africa from the first ages of the world. They are reckoned among its most important productions in the earliest records of its history.

It has been observed that gold is seldom or never discovered, except in *mountainous* and *barren* countries; nature, it is said, thus making amends in one way for her penuriousness in the other. This, however, is not wholly true. Gold is found in considerable quantities throughout every part of Manding—a country which is indeed hilly, but cannot properly be called *mountainous,* much less *barren.* It is also found in great plenty in Jallonkadoo (particularly about Boori), another hilly, but by no means an infertile country. It is remarkable that in the place last mentioned (Boori), which is situated about four days' journey to the south-west of Kamalia, the salt-market is often supplied, at the same time, with rock-salt from the Great Desert and sea-salt from the Rio Grande; the price of each at this distance from its source being nearly the same; and the dealers in each, whether Moors from the north, or Negroes from the west, are invited thither by the same motives—that of bartering their salt for gold.

The gold of Manding, so far as I could learn, is never found in any matrix or vein, but always in small grains, nearly in a pure state, from the size of a pin's head to that of a pea, scattered through a large body of sand or clay; and in this state it is called by the Mandingoes *sanoo munko,* "gold-powder." It is, however, extremely probable, by what I could learn of the situation of the ground, that most of it has originally been washed down by repeated torrents from the neighbouring hills. The manner in which it is collected is nearly as follows :—

About the beginning of December, when the harvest is over, and the streams and torrents have greatly subsided, the Mansa or chief man of the town appoints a day to begin *sanoo koo*, "gold-washing ;" and the women are sure to have themselves in readiness by the time appointed. A hoe or spade for digging up the sand, two or three calabashes for washing it in, and a few quills for containing the gold dust, are all the implements necessary for the purpose. On the morning of their departure a bullock is killed for the first day's entertainment, and a number of prayers and charms are used to ensure success ; for a failure on that day is thought a bad omen. The Mansa of Kamalia, with fourteen of his people, were, I remember, so much disappointed in their first day's washing, that very few of them had resolution to persevere, and the few that did had but very indifferent success, which indeed is not much to be wondered at, for instead of opening some untried place, they continued to dig and wash in the same spot were they had dug and washed for years, and where, of course, but few large grains could be left.

The washing the sands of the streams is by far the easiest way of obtaining the gold-dust ; but in most places the sands have been so narrowly searched before, that unless the stream takes some new course, the gold is found but in small quantities. While some of the party are busied in washing the sands, others employ themselves farther up the torrent, where the rapidity of the stream has carried away all the clay, sand, etc., and left nothing but small pebbles. The search among these is a very troublesome task. I have seen women who have had the skin worn off the tops of their fingers in this employment. Sometimes, however, they are rewarded by finding pieces of gold, which they call *sanoo birro*, "gold stones," that amply repay them for their trouble. A woman and her daughter, inhabitants of Kamalia, found in one day two pieces of this kind; one of five drachms, and the other of three drachms weight. But the most certain and profitable mode of washing is practised in the height of the dry season by digging a deep pit, like a draw-well, near some hill which has previously been discovered to contain gold. The pit is dug with small spades or corn-hoes, and the earth is drawn up in large calabashes. As the Negroes dig through the different strata of clay or sand, a calabash or two of each is washed, by way of experiment; and in this manner the labourers proceed, until they come to a stratum containing gold, or until they are obstructed by rocks or inundated by water. In general, when they come to a stratum of fine reddish sand, with small black specks therein, they find gold in some proportion or other, and send up large calabashes full of the sand for the women to wash; for though the pit is dug by the men, the gold is always washed by the women, who are accustomed from their infancy to a similar operation, in separating the husks of corn from the meal.

As I never descended into any of these pits, I cannot say in what manner they are worked under ground. Indeed, the situation in which I was placed made it necessary for me to be cautious not to incur the suspicion of the natives, by examining too far into the riches of their country; but the manner of separating the gold from the sand is very simple, and is frequently performed by the women in the middle of the town ; for when the searchers return from the valleys in the evening, they commonly bring with them each a calabash or two of sand, to be washed by such of the females as remain at home. The operation is simply as follows :—

A portion of sand or clay (for gold is sometimes found in a brown-coloured clay) is put into a large calabash, and mixed with a sufficient quantity of water. The woman whose office it is then shakes the calabash in such a manner as to mix the sand and water together, and give the whole a rotatory motion, at first gently, but afterwards more quick, until a small portion of sand and water, at every revolution, flies over the brim of the calabash. The sand thus separated is only the coarsest particles, mixed with a little muddy water. After the operation has been continued for some time, the sand is allowed to subside and the water poured off ; a portion of coarse sand, which is now uppermost in the calabash, is removed by the hand, and fresh water being added, the operation is repeated until the water comes off almost pure. The woman now takes a second calabash, and shakes the sand and water gently from the one to the other, reserving that portion of sand which is next the bottom of the calabash, and which is most likely to contain the gold. This small quantity is mixed with some pure water, and being moved about in the calabash, is carefully examined. If a few particles of gold are picked out, the contents of the other calabash are examined in the same manner ; but, in general, the party is well contented if she can obtain three or four grains from the contents of both calabashes. Some women, however, by long practice, become so well acquainted with the nature of the sand, and the mode of washing it, that they will collect gold where others cannot find a single particle. The gold-dust is kept in quills, stopped up with cotton ; and the washers are fond of displaying a number of these quills in their hair. Generally speaking, if a person uses common diligence in a proper soil, it is supposed that as much gold may be collected by him in the course of the dry season as is equal to the value of two slaves. Thus simple is the process by which the Negroes obtain gold in Manding ; and it is evident from this account, that the country contains a considerable portion of this precious metal, for many of the smaller particles must necessarily escape the observation of the naked eye ; and as the natives generally search the sands of streams at a considerable distance from the hills, and consequently far removed from the mines where the gold was originally produced, the labourers are sometimes but ill paid for their trouble. Minute particles only of this heavy metal can be carried by the current to any considerable distance ; the larger must remain deposited near the original source from whence they came. Were the gold-bearing streams to be traced to their fountains, and the hills from whence they spring properly examined, the sand in which the gold is there deposited would no doubt be found to contain particles of a much larger size, and even the small grains might be collected to considerable advantage by the use of quicksilver, and other improvements, with which the natives are at present unacquainted.

Part of this gold is converted into ornaments for the women ; but, in general, these ornaments are more to be admired for their weight than their workmanship. They are massy and inconvenient, particularly the ear-rings, which are commonly so heavy as to pull down and lacerate the lobe of the ear; to avoid which they are supported by a thong of red leather, which passes over the crown of the head from one ear to the other. The necklace displays greater fancy; and the proper arrangement of the different beads and plates of gold is the great criterion of taste and elegance. When a lady of consequence is in full dress, her gold ornaments may be worth altogether from fifty to eighty pounds sterling.

A small quantity of gold is likewise employed by the Slatees in defraying the expenses of their journeys to and from the coast; but by far the greater proportion is annually carried away by the Moors in exchange for salt and other merchandise. During my stay at Kamalia, the gold collected by the different traders at that place, for salt alone, was nearly equal to one hundred and ninety-eight pounds sterling; and as Kamalia is but a small town, and not much resorted to by the trading Moors, this quantity must have borne a very small proportion to the gold collected at Kancaba, Kancaree, and some other large towns. The value of salt in this part of Africa is very great. One slab, about two feet and a half in length, fourteen inches in breadth, and two inches in thickness, will sometimes sell for about two pounds ten shillings sterling, and from one pound fifteen shillings to two pounds may be considered as the common price. Four of these slabs are considered as a load for an ass, and six for a bullock. The value of European merchandise in Manding varies very much, according to the supply from the coast or the dread of war in the country; but the return for such articles is commonly made in slaves. The price of a prime slave when I was at Kamalia

was from *nine* to *twelve* minkallies, and European commodities
had then nearly the following value :—

18 gun-flints,
48 leaves of tobacco,
20 charges of gunpowder,
A cutlass,
⎫
⎬ one minkalli.
⎭

A musket from three to four minkallies.

The produce of the country, and the different necessaries
of life, when exchanged for gold, sold as follows :—

Common provisions for one day, the weight of one *teelee-
kissi* (a black bean, six of which make the weight of one minkalli ; a chicken, one teelee-kissi ; a sheep, three teelee-kissi ;
a bullock, one minkalli ; a horse, from ten to seventeen minkallies.

The Negroes weigh the gold in small balances, which they
always carry about them. They make no difference in point
of value between gold-dust and wrought gold. In bartering
one article for another, the person who receives the gold always
weighs it with his own teelee-kissi. These beans are sometimes fraudulently soaked in shea butter, to make them heavy ;
and I once saw a pebble ground exactly into the form of one
of them ; but such practices are not very common.

IVORY.

Nothing creates a greater surprise among the Negroes on
the sea-coast than the eagerness displayed by the European
traders to procure elephants' teeth ; it being exceedingly difficult to make them comprehend to what use it is applied.
Although they are shown knives with ivory hafts, combs, and
toys of the same material, and are convinced that the ivory thus

manufactured was originally parts of a tooth, they are not satisfied. They suspect that this commodity is more frequently converted in Europe to purposes of far greater importance, the true nature of which is studiously concealed from them, lest the price of ivory should be enhanced. They cannot, they say, easily persuade themselves, that ships would be built, and voyages undertaken, to procure an article which had no other value than that of furnishing handles to knives, etc., when pieces of wood would answer the purpose equally well.

Elephants are very numerous in the interior of Africa, but they appear to be a distinct species from those found in Asia. It has been said that the African elephant is of a less docile nature than the Asiatic, and incapable of being tamed. The Negroes certainly do not at present tame them; but when we consider that the Carthaginians had always tame elephants in their armies, and actually transported some of them to Italy in the course of the Punic wars, it seems more likely that they should have possessed the art of taming their own elephants, than have submitted to the expense of bringing such vast animals from Asia. Perhaps the barbarous practice of hunting the African elephants for the sake of their teeth has rendered them more untractable and savage than they were found to be in former times.

The greater part of the ivory which is sold on the Gambia and Senegal rivers is brought from the interior country. The lands towards the coast are too swampy, and too much intersected with creeks and rivers, for so bulky an animal as the elephant to travel through without being discovered; and when once the natives discern the marks of his feet in the earth, the whole village is up in arms. The thoughts of feasting on his

flesh, making sandals of his hide, and selling the teeth to the
Europeans, inspire every one with courage, and the animal
seldom escapes from his pursuers; but in the plains of Bambarra and Kaarta, and the extensive wilds of Jallonkadoo, the
elephants are very numerous; and from the great scarcity of
gunpowder in those districts they are less annoyed by the
natives.

Scattered teeth are frequently picked up in the woods, and
travellers are very diligent in looking for them. It is a common practice with the elephant to thrust his teeth under the
roots of such shrubs and bushes as grow in the more dry and
elevated parts of the country where the soil is shallow. These
bushes he easily overturns, and feeds on the roots, which are
in general more tender and juicy than the hard woody branches
or the foliage; but when the teeth are partly decayed by age
and the roots more firmly fixed, the great exertions of the animal in this practice frequently causes them to break short.
At Kamalia I saw two teeth, one a very large one, which were
found in the woods, and which were evidently broken off in this
manner. Indeed, it is difficult otherwise to account for such
a large proportion of broken ivory as is daily offered for sale at
the different factories; for when the elephant is killed in hunting, unless he dashes himself over a precipice, the teeth are
always extracted entire.

ELEPHANT HUNTERS.

There are certain seasons of the year when the elephants
collect into large herds, and traverse the country in quest of
food or water; and as all that part of the country to the north
of the Niger is destitute of rivers, whenever the pools in the

woods are dried up, the elephants approach towards the banks
of that river. Here they continue until the commencement
of the rainy season in the months of June or July; and
during this time they are much hunted by such of the Bambarrans as have gunpowder to spare. The elephant-hunters
seldom go out singly; a party of four or five join together;
and having each furnished himself with powder and ball, and
a quantity of corn-meal in a leather bag, sufficient for five or
six days' provision, they enter the most unfrequented parts of
the wood, and examine with great care everything that can
lead to the discovery of the elephants. In this pursuit,
nothwithstanding the bulk of the animal, very great nicety of
observation is required. The broken branches, the scattered
dung of the animal, and the marks of his feet, are carefully
inspected; and many of the hunters have, by long experience
and attentive observation, become so expert in their search,
that as soon as they observe the footmarks of an elephant, they
will tell almost to a certainty at what time it passed, and at
what distance it will be found.

When they discover a herd of elephants, they follow them at
a distance until they perceive some one stray from the rest and
come into such a situation as to be fired at with advantage.
The hunters then approach with great caution, creeping
amongst the long grass until they have got near enough to be
sure of their aim. They then discharge all their pieces at once,
and throw themselves on their faces among the grass. The
wounded elephant immediately applies his trunk to the
different wounds, but being unable to extract the balls, and
seeing nobody near him, becomes quite furious, and runs
about amongst the bushes, until by fatigue and loss of blood

he has exhausted himself, and affords the hunters an opportunity of firing a second time at him, by which he is generally brought to the ground.

The skin is now taken off and extended on the ground with pegs to dry; and such parts of the flesh as are most esteemed are cut up into thin slices and dried in the sun, to serve for provisions on some future occasion. The teeth are struck out with a light hatchet which the hunters always carry along with them, not only for that purpose, but also to enable them to cut down such trees as contain honey; for though they carry with them only five or six days' provisions, they will remain in the woods for months if they are successful, and support themselves upon the flesh of such elephants as they kill, and wild honey

The ivory thus collected is seldom brought down to the coast by the hunters themselves. They dispose of it to the itinerant merchants, who come annually from the coast with arms and ammunition to purchase this valuable commodity. Some of these merchants will collect ivory in the course of one season sufficient to load four or five asses. A great quantity of ivory is likewise brought from the interior by the slave coffles; there are, however, some Slatees of the Mahomedan persuasion, who, from motives of religion, will not deal in ivory, nor eat of the flesh of the elephant, unless it has been killed with a spear.

The quantity of ivory collected in this part of Africa is not so great, nor are the teeth in general so large as in the countries nearer the line; few of them weigh more than eighty or one hundred pounds; and upon an average, a bar of European merchandise may be reckoned as the price of a pound of ivory.

I have now, I trust, in this and the preceding chapters, explained with sufficient minuteness the nature and extent of the commercial connection which at present prevails, and has long subsisted, between the Negro natives of those parts of Africa which I visited, and the nations of Europe ; and it appears that slaves, gold, and ivory, together with the few articles enumerated in the beginning of my work, viz. bees'-wax and honey, hides, gums, and dye-woods, constitute the whole catalogue of exportable commodities. Other productions, however, have been incidentally noticed as the growth of Africa ; such as grain of different kinds, tobacco, indigo, cotton-wool, and perhaps a few others ; but all of these (which can only be obtained by cultivation and labour) the natives raise sufficient only for their own immediate expenditure ; nor under the present system of their laws, manners, trade, and government, can anything farther be expected from them. It cannot, however, admit of a doubt, that all the rich and valuable productions, both of the East and West Indies, might easily be naturalised and brought to the utmost perfection in the tropical parts of this immense continent. Nothing is wanting to this end but example, to enlighten the minds of the natives ; and instruction, to enable them to direct their industry to proper objects. It was not possible for me to behold the wonderful fertility of the soil, the vast herds of cattle, proper both for labour and food, and a variety of other circumstances favourable to colonisation and agriculture—and reflect, withal, on the means which presented themselves of a vast inland navigation, without lamenting that a country so abundantly gifted and favoured by nature, should remain in its present savage and neglected state. Much more did I lament that a people of manners and disposition so gentle and benevolent, should either be left as they now are, immersed in the gross and uncomfortable blindness of pagan superstition, or permitted to become converts to a system of bigotry and fanaticism which, without enlightening the mind, often debases the heart. On this subject many observations might be made ; but the reader will probably think that I have already digressed too largely.

CHAPTER XXIII.

Slavery in Africa.

COMMUNITY OF LABOUR.

IN all the laborious occupations previously described, the master and his slaves work together, without any distinction of superiority. Hired servants—by which I mean, persons of a free condition, voluntarily working for pay—are unknown in Africa ; and this observation naturally leads me to consider the condition of the slaves, and the various means by which they are reduced to so miserable a state of servitude. This unfortunate class are found, I believe, in all parts of this extensive country, and constitute a considerable branch of commerce with the states on the Mediterranean, as well as with the nations of Europe.

A state of subordination and certain inequalities of rank and condition are inevitable in every stage of civil society ; but when this subordination is carried to so great a length, that the persons and services of one part of the community are entirely at the disposal of another part, it may then be denominated a state of slavery ; and in this condition of life a great body of the Negro inhabitants of Africa have continued from the most early period of their history, with this aggravation, that their children are born to no other inheritance.

The slaves in Africa, I suppose, are nearly in the proportion of three to one to the free men. They claim no reward for their services except food and clothing, and are treated with kindness or severity according to the good or bad disposition of their masters. Custom, however, has established certain rules with regard to the treatment of slaves which it is thought dishonourable to violate. Thus, the domestic slaves, or such as are born in a man's own house, are treated with more lenity than those which are purchased with money. The authority of the master over the domestic slave, as I have else-where observed, extends only to reasonable correction ; for the master cannot sell his domestic without having first brought him to a public trial before the chief men of the place.* But these restrictions on the power of the master extend not to the case of prisoners taken in war, nor to that of slaves purchased with money. All these unfortunate beings are considered as strangers and foreigners, who have no right to the protection of the law, and may be treated with severity, or sold to a stranger, according to the pleasure of their owners. There are, indeed, regular markets where slaves of this description are bought and sold ; and the value of a slave in the eye of an African purchaser increases in proportion to his distance from his native kingdom ; for when slaves are only a few days' journey from the place of their nativity they frequently effect their escape, but when one or more kingdoms intervene, escape being more difficult, they are more readily

---

* In time of famine, the master is permitted to sell one or more of his domestics, to purchase provisions for his family ; and in case of the master's insolvency, the domestic slaves are sometimes seized upon by the creditors, and if the master cannot redeem them, they are liable to be sold for payment of his debts. These are the only cases that I recollect, in which the domestic slaves are liable to be sold, without any misconduct or demerit of their own.

reconciled to their situation. On this account, the unhappy slave is frequently transferred from one dealer to another, until he has lost all hopes of returning to his native kingdom. The slaves which are purchased by the Europeans on the coast are chiefly of this description; a few of them are collected in the petty wars which take place near the coast, but by far the greater number are brought down in large caravans from the inland countries, of which many are unknown even by name to the Europeans. The slaves thus brought from the interior may be divided into two distinct classes; *first*, such as were slaves from their birth, having been born of enslaved mothers; *secondly*, such as were born free, but who afterwards, by whatever means, became slaves. Those of the first description are by far the most numerous; for prisoners taken in war (at least such as are taken in open and declared war, when one kingdom avows hostilities against another) are generally of this description. The comparatively small proportion of free people to the enslaved throughout Africa has already been noticed; and it must be observed that men of free condition have many advantages over the slaves, even in war time. They are in general better armed and well mounted, and can either fight or escape with some hopes of success; but the slaves, who have only their spears and bows, and of whom great numbers are loaded with baggage, become an easy prey. Thus, when Mansong, king of Bambarra, made war upon Kaarta (as I have related in a former chapter), he took in one day nine hundred prisoners, of which number not more than seventy were free men. This account I received from Daman Jumma, who had thirty slaves at Kemmoo, all of whom were made prisoners by

Mansong. Again, when a free man is taken prisoner, his friends will sometimes ransom him by giving two slaves in exchange ; but when a slave is taken, he has no hopes of such redemption. To these disadvantages, it is to be added that the Slatees, who purchase slaves in the interior countries, and carry them down to the coast for sale, constantly prefer such as have been in that condition of life from their infancy, well knowing that these have been accustomed to hunger and fatigue, and are better able to sustain the hardships of a long and painful journey than free men ; and on their reaching the coast, if no opportunity offers of selling them to advantage, they can easily be made to maintain themselves by their labour, neither are they so apt to attempt making their escape as those who have once tasted the blessings of freedom.

CAUSES.

Slaves of the second description generally become such by *Captivity, Famine, Insolvency,* or *Crime.* A free man may, by the established customs of Africa, become a slave by being taken in war. War is, of all others, the most productive source, and was probably the origin of slavery ; for when one nation had taken from another a greater number of captives than could be exchanged on equal terms, it is natural to suppose that the conquerors, finding it inconvenient to maintain their prisoners, would compel them to labour ; at first, perhaps, only for their own support, but afterwards to support their masters. Be this as it may, it is a known fact, that prisoners of war in Africa are the slaves of the conquerors ; and when the weak or unsuccessful warrior begs for mercy beneath the uplifted spear of his opponent, he gives up at the same time his claim to liberty, and purchases his life at the expense of his freedom.

In a country divided into a thousand petty states, mostly independent and jealous of each other, where every free man is accustomed to arms and fond of military achievements, where the youth, who has practised the bow and spear from his infancy, longs for nothing so much as an opportunity to display his valour, it is natural to imagine that wars frequently originate from very frivolous provocation. When one nation is more powerful than another a pretext is seldom wanting for commencing hostilities. Thus the war between Kajaga and Kasson was occasioned by the detention of a fugitive slave; that between Bambarra and Kaarta by the loss of a few cattle. Other cases of the same nature perpetually occur, in which the folly or mad ambition of their princes, and the zeal of their religious enthusiasts, give full employment to the scythe of desolation.

PRISONERS OF DECLARED WAR.

The wars of Africa are of two kinds, which are distinguished by different appellations; that species which bears the greatest resemblance to our European contests is denominated *killi*, a word signifying "to call out," because such wars are openly avowed and previously declared. Wars of this description in Africa commonly terminate, however, in the course of a single campaign. After a battle of this description has been fought, the vanquished seldom think of rallying; the whole inhabitants become panic struck, and the conquerors have only to bind the slaves, and carry off their plunder and their victims. Such of the prisoners as, through age or infirmity, are unable to endure fatigue, or are found unfit for sale, are considered as useless, and I have no doubt are frequently put to death. The same fate commonly awaits a chief, or any other person who has taken a very distinguished part in the war. And here it may be observed that, notwithstanding this exterminating system, it is surprising to behold how soon an African town is rebuilt and repeopled. The circumstance arises probably from this, that their pitched battles are few, the weakest know their own situation, and seek safety in flight.

When their country has been desolated, and their ruined towns and villages deserted by the enemy, such of the inhabitants as have escaped the *sword* and the *chain*, generally return, though with cautious steps, to the place of their nativity ; for it seems to be the universal wish of mankind to spend the evenings of their days where they passed their infancy. The poor Negro feels this desire in its full force. To him no water is sweet but what is drawn from his own well, and no tree has so cool and pleasant a shade as the *tabba* tree * of his native village. When war compels him to abandon the delightful spot in which he first drew his breath, and seek for safety in some other kingdom, his time is spent in talking about the country of his ancestors ; and no sooner is peace restored than he turns his back upon the land of strangers, rebuilds with haste his fallen walls, and exults to see the smoke ascend from his native village.

* This is a large spreading tree (a species of *sterculia*) under which the Bentang is commonly placed.

PRISONERS OF HEREDITARY FEUD.

The other species of African warfare is distinguished by the appellation of *tegria*, " plundering or stealing." It arises from a sort of hereditary feud which the inhabitants of one nation or district bear towards another. No immediate cause of hostility is assigned, or notice of attack given, but the inhabitants of each watch every opportunity to plunder and distress the objects of their animosity by predatory excursions. These are very common, particularly about the beginning of the dry season, when the labour of the harvest is over and provisions are plentiful. Schemes of vengeance are then meditated. The chief man surveys the number and activity of his vassals as they brandish their spears at festivals, and, elated with his own importance, turns his whole thoughts towards revenging some depredation or insult which either he or his ancestors may have received from a neighbouring state. Wars of this description are generally conducted with great secrecy. A few resolute individuals, headed by some person of enterprise and courage, march quietly through the woods, surprise in the night some unprotected village, and carry off the inhabitants and their effects before their neighbours can come to their assistance. One morning, during my stay at Kamalia, we were all much alarmed by a party of this kind. The king of Fooladoo's son, with five hundred horsemen, passed secretly through the woods, a little to the southward of Kamalia, and on the morning following plundered three towns belonging to Madigai, a powerful chief in Jallonkadoo.

The success of this expedition encouraged the governor of Bangassi, a town in Fooladoo, to make a second inroad upon

another part of the same country. Having assembled about
two hundred of his people, he passed the river Kokoro in the
night, and carried off a great number of prisoners. Several
of the inhabitants, who had escaped these attacks, were afterwards seized by the Mandingoes as they wandered about in
the woods, or concealed themselves in the glens and strong
places in the mountains.

These plundering excursions always produce speedy
retaliation; and when large parties cannot be collected for
this purpose, a few friends will combine together, and advance
into the enemy's country, with a view to plunder or carry off
the inhabitants. A single individual has been known to take
his bow and quiver, and proceed in like manner. Such an
attempt is doubtless in him an act of rashness; but when it
is considered that in one of these predatory wars he has probably been deprived of his child or his nearest relation, his
situation will rather call for pity than censure. The poor
sufferer, urged on by the feelings of domestic or paternal
attachment, and the ardour of revenge, conceals himself
among the bushes until some young or unarmed person
passes by. He then, tiger-like, springs upon his prey, drags
his victim into the thicket, and in the night carries him off
as a slave.

When a Negro has, by means like these, once fallen into
the hands of his enemies, he is either retained as the slave of
his conqueror, or bartered into a distant kingdom; for an
African, when he has once subdued his enemy, will seldom
give him an opportunity of lifting up his hand against him
at a future period. A conqueror commonly disposes of his
captives according to the rank which they held in their native

kingdom. Such of the domestic slaves as appear to be of a mild disposition, and particularly the young women, are retained as his own slaves. Others that display marks of discontent are disposed of in a distant country, and such of the free men or slaves as have taken an active part in the war, are either sold to the Slatees, or put to death. War, therefore, is certainly the most general and most productive source of slavery, and the desolations of war often (but not always) produce the second cause of slavery, *famine*, in which case a free man becomes a slave to avoid a greater calamity.

CAUSED BY FAMINE.

Perhaps by a philosophic and reflecting mind, death itself would scarcely be considered as a greater calamity than slavery ; but the poor Negro, when fainting with hunger, thinks like Esau of old ; "*Behold I am at the point to die, and what profit shall this birthright do to me ?*" There are many instances of free men voluntarily surrendering up their liberty to save their lives. During a great scarcity, which lasted for three years, in the countries of the Gambia, great numbers of people became slaves in this manner. Dr. Laidley assured me, that at that time many free men came and begged with great earnestness *to be put upon his slave-chain*, to save them from perishing of hunger. Large families are very often exposed to absolute want ; and as the parents have almost unlimited authority over their children, it frequently happens in all parts of Africa that some of the latter are sold to purchase provisions for the rest of the family. When I was at Jarra, Daman Jumma pointed out to me three young slaves he had purchased in this manner. I have already related another instance which I saw at Wonda, and I was informed that in Fooladoo at that time it was a very common practice.

CAUSED BY INSOLVENCE.

Of all the offences (if insolvency may be so called) to which the laws of Africa have affixed the punishment of slavery, this is the most common. A Negro trader commonly contracts debts on some mercantile speculation, either from his neighbours, to purchase such articles as will sell to advantage in a distant market, or from the European traders on the coast—payment to be made in a given time. In both cases the situation of the adventurer is exactly the same. If he succeeds he may secure an independency. If he is unsuccessful, his person and services are at the disposal of another, for in Africa not only the effects of the insolvent, but even the insolvent himself is sold to satisfy the lawful demands of his creditors.*

CAUSED BY CRIME.

In Africa the only offences on which the laws of the

* When a Negro takes up goods on credit from any of the Europeans on the coast, and does not make payment at the time appointed, the European is authorised, by the laws of the country, to seize upon the debtor himself, if he can find him ; or, if he cannot be found, on any person of his family ; or, in the last resort, on *any native of the same kingdom.* The person thus seized on is detained, while his friends are sent in quest of the debtor. When he is found, a meeting is called of the chief people of the place, and the debtor is compelled to ransom his friend by fulfilling his engagements. If he is unable to do this, his person is immediately secured and sent down to the coast, and the other released. If the debtor cannot be found, the person seized on is obliged to pay double the amount of the debt, or is himself sold into slavery. I was given to understand, however, that t' is part of the law is seldom enforced.

country affix slavery as a punishment, are *murder, adultery,* and *witchcraft;* and I am happy to say that they did not appear to me to be common. In cases of murder, I was informed that the nearest relation of the deceased had it in his power, after conviction, either to kill the offender with his own hand, or sell him into slavery. When adultery occurs it is generally left to the option of the person injured, either to sell the culprit, or accept such a ransom for him as he may think equivalent to the injury he has sustained. By witchcraft is meant pretended magic, by which the lives or healths of persons are affected; in other words, it is the administering of poison. No trial for this offence, however, came under my observation while I was in Africa, and I therefore suppose that the crime and its punishment occur but very seldom.

When a free man has become a slave by any one of these causes he generally continues so for life, and his children (if they are born of an enslaved mother) are brought up in the same state of servitude. There are, however, a few instances of slaves obtaining their freedom, and sometimes even with the consent of their masters—as by performing some singular piece of service, or by going to battle and bringing home two slaves as a ransom; but the common way of regaining freedom is by escape; and when slaves have once set their minds on running away they often succeed. Some of them will wait for years before an opportunity presents itself, and during that period show no signs of discontent. In general, it may be remarked, that slaves who come from a hilly country, and have been much accustomed to hunting and travel, are more apt to attempt their escape than such as are born in a flat country, and have been employed in cultivating the land.

Such are the general outlines of that system of slavery which prevails in Africa, and it is evident from its nature and extent that it is a system of no modern date. It probably had its origin in the remote ages of antiquity, before the Mahomedans explored a path across the desert. How far it is maintained and supported by the slave traffic which for two hundred years the nations of Europe have carried on with the natives of the coast, it is neither within my province nor in my power to explain. If my sentiments should be required concerning the effect which a discontinuance of that commerce would produce on the manners of the natives, I should have no hesitation in observing, that, in the present unenlightened state of their minds, the effect would neither be so extensive or beneficial as many wise and worthy persons fondly expect.

CHAPTER XXIII.

Negro Children's Schools—Return of Karfa—Purchase and Treatment of Slaves—Fast of Rhamadan—Departure of the Caravan—Arrival at Kinytakooro.

THE schoolmaster, to whose care I was entrusted during the absence of Karfa, was a man of a mild disposition and gentle manners ; his name was Fankooma, and although he himself adhered strictly to the religion of Mahomet, he was by no means intolerant in his principles towards others who differed from him. He spent much of his time in reading, and teaching appeared to be his pleasure as well as employment. His school consisted of seventeen boys, most of whom were sons of Kafirs, and two girls, one of whom was Karfa's own daughter. The girls received their instructions in the day-time, but the boys always had their lessons by the light of a large fire before daybreak, and again late in the evening ; for being considered during their scholarship as the domestic slaves of the master, they were employed in planting corn, bringing fire-wood, and in other servile offices through the day.

Exclusive of the Koran, and a book or two of commentaries thereon, the schoolmaster possessed a variety of manuscripts, which had partly been purchased from the trading Moors, and partly borrowed from Bushreens in the neighbourhood, and copied with great care. Other manuscripts had been produced

to me at different places in the course of my journey, and on
recounting those I had before seen, and those which were now
shown to me, and interrogating the schoolmaster on the subject,
I discovered that the Negroes are in possession (among others)
of an Arabic version of the Pentateuch of Moses, which they
call *Taureta la Moosa*. This is so highly esteemed that it is
often sold for the value of one prime slave. They have likewise a version of the Psalms of David (*Zabora Dawidi*). And
lastly, the book of Isaiah, which they call *Lingeeli la Isa*, and
it is in very high esteem. I suspect, indeed, that in all these
copies there are interpolations of some of the peculiar tenets
of Mahomet, for I could distinguish in many passages the name
of the Prophet. It is possible, however, that this circumstance
might otherwise have been accounted for, if my knowledge of
the Arabic had been more extensive. By means of those books
many of the converted Negroes have acquired an acquaintance
with some of the remarkable events recorded in the Old Testa-
ment. The account of our first parents; the death of Abel;
the deluge; the lives of Abraham, Isaac, and Jacob; the story
of Joseph and his brethren; the history of Moses, David, Solo-
mon, etc. All these have been related to me in the Mandingo
language with tolerable exactness, by different people, and my
surprise was not greater on hearing these accounts from the lips
of the Negroes, than theirs on finding that I was already acquainted with them; for, although the Negroes in general have
a very great idea of the wealth and power of the Europeans, I
am afraid that the Mahomedan converts among them think
but very lightly of our superior attainments in religious knowledge. The white traders in the maritime districts take no
pains to counteract this unhappy prejudice; always performing

their own devotions in secret, and seldom condescending to converse with the Negroes in a friendly and instructive manner. To me, therefore, it was not so much the subject of wonder as matter of regret, to observe, that while the superstition of Mahomet has, in this manner, scattered a few faint beams of learning among these poor people, the precious light of Christianity is altogether excluded.   I could not but lament, that although the coast of Africa has now been known and frequented by the Europeans for more than two hundred years, yet the Negroes still remain entire strangers to the doctrines of our holy religion. We are anxious to draw from obscurity the opinions and records of antiquity, the beauties of Arabian and Asiatic literature, etc.; but while our libraries are thus stored with the learning of various countries, we distribute with a parsimonious hand the blessings of religious truth to the benighted nations of the earth. The natives of Asia derive but little advantage in this respect from an intercourse with us; and even the poor Africans, whom we affect to consider as barbarians, look upon us, I fear, as little better than a race of formidable but ignorant heathens.   When I produced Richardson's Arabic Grammar to some Slatees on the Gambia, they were astonished to think that any European should understand and write the sacred language of their religion. At first they suspected that it might have been written by some of the slaves carried from the coast; but on a closer examination they were satisfied that no Bushreen could write such beautiful Arabic; and one of them offered to give me an ass and sixteen bars of goods, if I would part with the book.   Perhaps a short and easy introduction to Christianity, such as is found in some of the catechisms for children, elegantly printed in Arabic, and distributed on different parts of the coast, might have a wonderful effect. The expense would be but trifling; curiosity would induce many to read it; and the evident superiority which it would possess over their present manuscripts, both in point of elegance and cheapness, might at last obtain it a place among the school-books of Africa.

The reflections which I have thus ventured to submit to my readers on this important subject naturally suggested themselves to my mind on perceiving the encouragement which was given to learning (such as it is) in many parts of Africa. I observed, as the pupils at Kamalia were most of them the children of Pagans, their parents, therefore, could have had no predilection for the doctrines of Mahomet. Their aim was their children's improvement; and if a more enlightened system had presented itself, it would probably have been preferred. The children too, did not want a spirit of emulation, which it is the aim of the tutor to encourage. When any one of them has read through the Koran, and performed a certain number of public prayers, a feast is prepared by the schoolmaster, and the scholar undergoes an examination, or (in European terms) *takes out his degree.* I attended at three different inaugurations of this sort, and heard with pleasure the distinct and intelligent answers which the scholars frequently gave to the Bushreens who assembled on those occasions, and acted as examiners. When the Bushreens had satisfied themselves respecting the learning and abilities of the scholar, the last page of the Koran was put into his hand, and he was desired to read it aloud; after the boy had finished this lesson he pressed the paper against his forehead and pronounced the word *Amen;* upon which all the Bushreens rose, and shaking him cordially by the hand bestowed upon him the title of Bushreen.

When a scholar has undergone this examination his parents are informed that he has completed his education, and that it is incumbent on them to redeem their son, by giving to the schoolmaster a slave, or the price of a slave, in exchange ; which is always done, if the parents can afford to do it ; if not, the boy remains the domestic slave of the schoolmaster until he can, by his own industry, collect goods sufficient to ransom himself.

About a week after the departure of Karfa, three Moors arrived at Kamalia with a considerable quantity of salt and other merchandise, which they had obtained on credit from a merchant of Fezzan who had lately arrived at Kancaba. Their engagement was to pay him his price when the goods were sold, which they expected would be in the course of a month. Being rigid Bushreens, they were accommodated with two of Karfa's huts, and sold their goods to very great advantage.

On the 24th of January, Karfa returned to Kamalia with a number of people and thirteen prime slaves which he had purchased. He likewise brought with him a young girl whom he had married at Kancaba as his fourth wife, and had given her parents three prime slaves for her. She was kindly received at the door of the baloon by Karfa's other wives, who conducted their new acquaintance and copartner into one of the best huts, which they had caused to be swept and whitewashed on purpose to receive her.*

My clothes were by this time become so very ragged that I was almost ashamed to appear out of doors ; but Karfa, on the day after his arrival, generously presented me with

* The Negroes whitewash their huts with a mixture of bone ashes and water, to which is commonly added a little gum.

such a garment and trousers as are commonly worn in the country.

The slaves which Karfa had brought with him were all of them prisoners of war ; eleven of them confessed to me that they had been slaves from their infancy ; but the other two refused to give any account of their former condition. They were all very inquisitive ; but they viewed me at first with looks of horror, and repeatedly asked if my countrymen were cannibals. They were very desirous to know what became of the slaves after they had crossed the salt water. I told them that they were employed in cultivating the land, but they would not believe me ; and one of them, putting his hand upon the ground, said, with great simplicity, "Have you really got such ground as this to set your feet upon ?" A deeply-rooted idea that the whites purchase Negroes for the purpose of devouring them, or of selling them to others that they may be devoured hereafter, naturally makes the slaves contemplate a journey towards the coast with great terror, insomuch that the Slatees are forced to keep them constantly in irons, and watch them very closely to prevent their escape. They are commonly secured by putting the right leg of one, and the left of another into the same pair of fetters. By supporting the fetters with a string, they can walk, though very slowly. Every four slaves are likewise fastened together by the necks with a strong rope of twisted thongs ; and in the night an additional pair of fetters is put on their hands, and sometimes a light iron chain passed round their necks.

Such of them as evince marks of discontent are secured in a different manner. A thick billet of wood is cut about three feet long, and a smooth notch being made upon one side of it, the ankle of the slave is bolted to the smooth part by means of a strong iron staple, one prong of which passes on each side of the ankle. All these fetters and bolts are made from native iron ; in the present case they were put on by the blacksmith as soon as the slaves arrived from Kancaba, and were not taken off until the morning on which the coffle departed for Gambia.

In other respects, the treatment of the slaves during their stay at Kamalia was far from being harsh or cruel. They were led out in their fetters every morning to the shade of the tamarind-tree, where they were encouraged to play at games of hazard, and sing diverting songs, to keep up their spirits ; for though some of them sustained the hardships of their situation with amazing fortitude, the greater part were very much dejected, and would sit all day in a sort of sullen melancholy, with their eyes fixed upon the ground. In the evening their irons were examined and their hand-fetters put on, after which they were conducted into two large huts, where they were guarded during the night by Karfa's domestic slaves. But notwithstanding all this, about a week after their arrival, one of the slaves had the address to procure a small knife, with which he opened the rings of his fetters, cut the rope, and made his escape ; more of them would probably have got off had they assisted each other ; but the slave no sooner found himself at liberty than he refused to stop and assist in breaking the chain which was fastened round the necks of his companions.

As all the Slatees and slaves belonging to the coffle were now assembled, either at Kamalia or some of the neighbouring villages, it might have been expected that we sh uld have set

out immediately for Gambia ; but though the day of our
departure was frequently fixed, it was always found expedient
to change it.   Some of the people had not prepared their dry
provisions ; others had gone to visit their relations, or collect
some trifling debts; and last of all, it was necessary to consult
whether the day would be a lucky one.   On account of one of
these, or other such causes, our departure was put off day
after day until the month of February was far advanced,
after which all the Slatees agreed to remain in their present
quarters until the *fast moon was over*.   And here I may remark
that loss of time is an object of no great importance in the
eyes of a Negro.   If he has anything of consequence to perform, it is a matter of indifference to him whether he does it
to-day or to-morrow, or a month or two hence ; so long as he
can spend the present moment with any degree of comfort he
gives himself very little concern about the future.

The fast of Rhamadan was observed with great strictness
by all the Bushreens ; but instead of compelling me to follow
their example, as the Moors did on a similar occasion, Karfa
told me that I was at liberty to pursue my own inclination.
In order, however, to manifest a respect for their religious
opinions, I voluntarily fasted three days, which was thought
sufficient to screen me from the reproachful epithet of Kafir.
During the fast, all the Slatees belonging to the coffle assembled every morning in Karfa's house, where the schoolmaster read to them some religious lesson from a large folio
volume, the author of which was an Arab of the name of
Sheiffa.   In the evening, such of the women as had embraced
Mahomedanism assembled and said their prayers publicly at
the Misura.   They were all dressed in white, and went through

the different prostrations prescribed by their religion with becoming solemnity. Indeed, during the whole fast of Rhamadan the Negroes behaved themselves with the greatest meekness and humility, forming a striking contrast to the savage intolerance and brutal bigotry which at this period characterise the Moors.

When the fast month was almost at an end, the Bushreens assembled at the Misura to watch for the appearance of the new moon; but the evening being rather cloudy they were for sometime disappointed, and a number of them had gone home, with a resolution to fast another day, when on a sudden this delightful object showed her sharp horns from behind a cloud, and was welcomed with the clapping of hands, beating of drums, firing muskets, and other marks of rejoicing. As this moon is reckoned extremely lucky, Karfa gave orders that all the people belonging to the coffle should immediately pack up their dry provisions, and hold themselves in readiness; and on the 16th of April the Slatees held a consultation, and fixed on the 19th of the same month as the day on which the coffle should depart from Kamalia. This resolution freed me from much uneasiness; for our departure had already been so long deferred that I was apprehensive it might still be put off until the commencement of the rainy season; and although Karfa behaved towards me with the greatest kindness, I found my situation very unpleasant. The Slatees were unfriendly to me, and the trading Moors who were at this time at Kamalia continued to plot mischief against me from the first day of their arrival. Under these circumstances, I reflected that my life in a great measure depended on the good opinion of an individual who was daily hearing malicious stories concerning the Europeans; and I could hardly expect that he would always judge with impartiality between me and his country-men. Time had, indeed, reconciled me, in some degree, to their mode of life, and a smoky hut or a scanty supper gave me no great uneasiness; but I became at last wearied out with a constant state of alarm and anxiety, and felt a painful longing for the manifold blessings of civilised society.

On the morning of the 17th, a circumstance occurred which wrought a considerable change in my favour. The three trading Moors who had lodged under Karfa's protection ever since their arrival at Kamalia, and had gained the esteem of all the Bushreens by an appearance of great sanctity, suddenly packed up their effects, and without once thanking Karfa for his kindness towards them, marched over the hills to Bala. Every one was astonished at this unexpected removal; but the affair was cleared up in the evening by the arrival of the Fezzan merchant from whom they had got their goods, who assured Karfa that these Moors had borrowed all their salt and goods from him, and had sent for him to come to Kamalia and receive payment. When he was told that they had fled to the westward, he wiped a tear from each eye with the sleeve of his cloak and exclaimed, "These *shirrukas* (robbers) are Mahomedans, but they are not men; they have robbed me of two hundred minkallies."

The long-wished-for day of our departure (April 19th) was at length arrived, and the Slatees, having taken the irons from their slaves, assembled with them at the door of Karfa's house, where the bundles were all tied up, and every one had his load assigned him. The coffle consisted of twenty-seven slaves for sale, the property of Karfa and four other Slatees; but we were afterwards joined by five at Marraboo, and three at Bala, making in all thirty-five slaves. The free men were fourteen in number, but most of them had one or two wives and some domestic slaves, and the schoolmaster, who was now upon his return for Woradoo, the place of his nativity, took with him eight of his scholars, so that the number of free people and domestic slaves amounted to thirty-eight, and the whole amount of the coffle was seventy-three. Among the free men were six Jillikeas (singing-men), whose musical talents were frequently exerted either to divert our fatigue, or obtain us a welcome from strangers. When we departed from Kamalia we were followed for about half-a-mile by most of the inhabitants of the town, some of them crying, and others shaking hands with their relations who were now about to leave them; and when we had gained a piece of rising ground, from which we had a view of Kamalia, all the people belonging to the coffle were ordered to sit down in one place with their faces toward the west, and the townspeople were desired to sit down in another place with their faces towards Kamalia. In this situation the schoolmaster, with two of the principal Slatees, having taken their places between the two parties, pronounced a long and solemn prayer; after which they walked three times round the coffle, making an impression on the ground with the ends of their spears, and muttering something by way of charm. When this ceremony was ended, all the people belonging to the coffle sprang up, and without taking a formal farewell of their friends, set forwards. As many of the slaves had remained for years in irons, the sudden exertion of walking quick with heavy loads upon their heads, occasioned spasmodic contractions of their legs, and we had not proceeded

above a mile before it was found necessary to take two of
them from the rope, and allow them to walk more slowly
until we reached Marraboo, a walled village, where some
people were waiting to join the coffle. Here we stopped
about two hours, to allow the strangers time to pack up their
provisions, and then continued our route to Bala, which town
we reached about four in the afternoon. The inhabitants of
Bala, at this season of the year, subsist chiefly on fish, which
they take in great plenty from the streams in the neighbourhood. We proceeded by Worumbang, the frontier village of
Manding, towards Jallonkadoo. As we proposed shortly to
enter the Jallonka wilderness, the people of this village furnished us with great plenty of provisions. On the morning
of the 21st we entered the woods to the westward of Worumbang, and after having travelled some little way, a consultation
was held whether we should continue our route through the
wilderness, or save one day's provisions by going to Kinytakooro, a town in Jallonkadoo. After debating the matter
for some time, it was agreed that we should take the road for
Kinytakooro ; but as that town was a long day's journey
distant, it was necessary to take some refreshment. Accordingly, every person opened his provision-bag, and brought a
handful or two of meal to the place where Karfa and the
Slatees were sitting. When every one had brought his quota,
and the whole was properly arranged in small gourd shells,
the schoolmaster offered up a short prayer, the substance of
which was, that God and the holy Prophet might preserve us
from robbers and all bad people, that our provisions might
never fail us, nor our limbs become fatigued. This ceremony
being ended, every one partook of the meal, and drank a little

water; after which we set forward (rather running than walking) until we came to the river Kokoro, a branch of the Senegal, where we halted about ten minutes. The banks of this river are very high; and from the grass and brushwood which had been left by the stream, it was evident that at this place the water had risen more than twenty feet perpendicular during the rainy season. At this time it was only a small stream, such as would turn a mill, swarming with fish; and on account of the number of crocodiles and the danger of being carried past the ford by the force of the stream in the rainy season, it is called *Kokoro* (dangerous). From this place we continued to travel with the greatest expedition, and in the afternoon crossed two small branches of the river. About sunset we came in sight of Kinytakooro, a considerable town, nearly square, situated in the middle of a large and well-cultivated plain. Before we entered the town we halted until the people who had fallen behind came up.

During this day's travel, two slaves, a woman and a girl belonging to a Slatee of Bala, were so much fatigued that they could not keep up with the coffle; they were severely whipped, and dragged along until about three o'clock in the afternoon, when they were both affected with vomiting, by which it was discovered that they had *eaten clay*. This practice is by no means uncommon amongst the Negroes; but whether it arises from a vitiated appetite, or from a settled intention to destroy themselves, I cannot affirm. They were permitted to lie down in the woods, and three people remained with them until they had rested themselves; but they did not arrive at the town until past midnight, and were then so much exhausted that the Slatee gave up all thoughts of taking them across the

woods in their present condition, and determined to return
with them to Bala, and wait for another opportunity.

As this was the first town beyond the limits of Manding,
greater etiquette than usual was observed.   Every person was
ordered to keep in his proper station, and we marched towards
the town in a sort of procession, nearly as follows :—In front
five or six singing-men, all of them belonging to the coffle ;
these were followed by the other free people ; then came the
slaves, fastened in the usual way by a rope round their necks,
four of them to a rope, and a man with a spear between each
four ; after them came the domestic slaves, and in the rear
the women of free condition, wives of the Slatees, etc.   In
this manner we proceeded until we came within a hundred
yards of the gate, when the singing-men began a loud song,
well calculated to flatter the vanity of the inhabitants, by extolling their known hospitality to strangers, and their particular friendship for the Mandingoes.   When we entered the
town we proceeded to the Bentang, where the people gathered
round us to hear our *dentegi* (history); this was related
publicly by two of the singing-men ; they enumerated every
little circumstance which had happened to the coffle, beginning
with the events of the present day, and relating everything in
a backward series until they reached Kamalia.   When this
history was ended, the master of the town gave them a small
present, and all the people of the coffle, both free and enslaved,
were invited by some person or other, and accommodated with
lodging and provisions for the night.

CHAPTER XXIV.

The Coffle crosses the Jallonka Wilderness—Miserable Fate of one of the Female Slaves—Arrival at Sooseta—Journey to Manna—Some account of the Jallonkas—Crossing the main Stream of the Senegal—Bridge of a singular Construction—Arrival at Mala-cotta—Remarkable conduct of the King of the Jaloffs.

A.D. 1796.

WE continued at Kinytakooro until noon of the 22d of April, when we removed to a village about seven miles to the westward, the inhabitants of which, being apprehensive of hostilities from the Foulahs of Fooladoo, were at this time employed in constructing small temporary huts among the rocks, on the side of a high hill close to the village. The situation was almost impregnable, being everywhere surrounded with high precipices, except on the eastern side, where the natives had left a pathway sufficient to allow one person at a time to ascend. Upon the brow of the hill, immediately over this path, I observed several heaps of large loose stones which the people told me were intended to be thrown down upon the Foulahs if they should attempt the hill.

At daybreak next day we departed from this village and entered the Jallonka wilderness. We passed in the course of the morning the ruins of two small towns which had lately been burned by the Foulahs. The fire must have been very intense, for I observed that the walls of many of the huts were slightly vitrified, and appeared at a distance as if covered with a red varnish. About ten o'clock we came to the river Wonda, which is somewhat larger than the river Kokoro, but the stream was at this time rather muddy, which Karfa assured me was occasioned by amazing shoals of fish. They were indeed seen in all directions, and in such abundance that I fancied the water itself tasted and smelt fishy. As soon as we had crossed the river, Karfa gave orders that all the people of the coffle should in future keep close together and travel in their proper station; the guides and young men were accordingly placed in the van, the women and slaves in the centre, and the free men in the rear. In this order we travelled with uncommon expedition through a woody but beautiful country, interspersed with a pleasing variety of hill and dale, and abounding with partridges, guinea-fowl, and deer. At sunset we arrived at a most romantic stream called Co-meissang. My arms and neck having been exposed to the sun during the whole day, and irritated by the rubbing of my dress in walking, were now very much inflamed and covered with blisters, and I was happy to embrace the opportunity, while the coffle rested on the bank of this river, to bathe myself in the stream. This practice, together with the cool of the evening, much diminished the inflammation. About three miles to the westward of the Co-meissang we halted in a thick wood, and kindled our fires for the night. We were all by this time very much fatigued, having, as I judged, travelled thirty miles in one day; but no person was heard to complain. Whilst supper was preparing Karfa made one of the slaves break some branches from the trees for my bed. When we had finished our supper of kouskous, moistened with some boiling water, and put the slaves in irons, we all lay down to sleep; but we were frequently disturbed in the night by the howling of wild beasts, and we found the small brown ants very troublesome.

Before daybreak the Bushreens said their morning prayers, and most of the free people drank a little *moening* (a sort of gruel), part of which was likewise given to such of the slaves as appeared least able to sustain the fatigues of the day. One of Karfa's female slaves was very sulky, and when some gruel was offered to her she refused to drink it. As soon as day dawned we set out, and travelled the whole morning over a wild and rocky country, by which my feet were very much bruised, and I was sadly apprehensive that I should not be able to keep up with the coffle during the day, but I was in a great measure relieved from this anxiety when I observed that others were more exhausted than myself. In particular, the woman slave who had refused victuals in the morning began now to lag behind, and complained dreadfully of pains in her legs. Her load was taken from her and given to another slave, and she was ordered to keep in the front of the coffle. About eleven o'clock, as we were resting by a small rivulet, some of the people discovered a hive of bees in a hollow tree, and they were proceeding to obtain the honey, when the largest swarm I ever beheld flew out, and attacking the people of the coffle made us fly in all directions. I took the alarm first, and I believe was the only person who escaped with impunity. When our enemies thought fit to desist from pursuing us, and every person was employed in picking out the stings he had received, it was discovered that the poor woman above mentioned, whose name was Nealee, was not come up ; and as many of the slaves in their retreat had left their bundles behind them, it became necessary for some persons to return and bring them. In order to do this with safety, fire was set to the grass, a considerable way to the eastward of the hive, and the wind driving the fire furiously along, the party pushed through the smoke and recovered the bundles. They likewise brought with them poor Nealee, whom they found lying by the rivulet. She was very much exhausted, and had crept to the stream in hopes to defend herself from the bees by throwing water over her body, but this proved ineffectual, for she was stung in the most dreadful manner.

When the Slatees had picked out the stings as far as they could, she was washed with water, and then rubbed with bruised leaves ; but the wretched woman obstinately refused to proceed any farther, declaring that she would rather die than walk another step. As entreaties and threats were used in vain, the whip was at length applied ; and after bearing patiently a few strokes, she started up and walked with tolerable expedition for four or five hours longer, when she made an attempt to run away from the coffle, but was so very weak that she fell down in the grass. Though she was unable to rise, the whip was a second time applied, but without effect ; upon which Karfa desired two of the Slatees to place her upon the ass which carried our dry provisions ; but she could not sit erect, and the ass being very refractory it was found impossible to carry her forward in that manner. The Slatees, however, were unwilling to abandon her, the day's journey being nearly ended ; they therefore made a sort of litter of bamboo

ROGERS SC

The general cry was "Cut her throat!" an operation which I did not wish to see performed, and therefore marched onwards with the foremost.—Page 309.

canes, upon which she was placed, and tied on it with slips of bark. This litter was carried upon the heads of two slaves, one walking before the other, and they were followed by two others, who relieved them occasionally. In this manner the woman was carried forward until it was dark, when we reached a stream of water at the foot of a high hill called Gankaran-Kooro, and here we stopped for the night and set about preparing our supper. As we had eaten only one handful of meal since the preceding night, and travelled all day in a hot sun, many of the slaves, who had loads upon their heads, were very much fatigued, and some of them *snapt their fingers*, which among the Negroes is a sure sign of desperation. The Slatees immediately put them all in irons ; and such of them as had evinced signs of great despondency were kept apart from the rest and had their hands tied. In the morning they were found greatly recovered.

At daybreak (April 25th) poor Nealee was awakened, but her limbs were now become so stiff and painful that she could neither walk nor stand; she was therefore lifted like a corpse upon the back of the ass, and the Slatees endeavoured to secure her in that situation by fastening her hands together under the ass's neck, and her feet under the belly, with long slips of bark ; but the ass was so very unruly that no sort of treatment could induce him to proceed with his load, and as Nealee made no exertion to prevent herself from falling, she was quickly thrown off, and had one of her legs much bruised. Every attempt to carry her forward being thus found ineffectual, the general cry of the coffle was, *Kang-tegi, kang-tegi*, "Cut her throat, cut her throat," an operation I did not wish to see performed, and therefore marched onwards with the foremost of the coffle. I had not walked above a mile when one of Karfa's domestic slaves came up to me with poor Nealee's garment upon the end of his bow, and exclaimed *Nealee affeeleeta* (Nealee is lost). I asked him whether the Slatees had given him the garment as a reward for cutting her throat? He replied, that Karfa and the schoolmaster would not consent to that measure, but had left her on the road, where undoubtedly she soon perished, and was probably devoured by wild beasts.

The sad fate of this wretched woman, notwithstanding the outcry before mentioned, made a strong impression on the minds of the whole coffle, and the schoolmaster fasted the whole of the ensuing day in consequence of it. We proceeded in deep silence, and soon afterwards crossed the river Furkoomah, which was about as large as the river Wonda. We now travelled with great expedition, every one being apprehensive he might otherwise meet with the fate of poor Nealee. It was, however, with great difficulty that I could keep up, although I threw away my spear and everything that could in the least obstruct me. About noon we saw a large herd of elephants, but they suffered us to pass unmolested, and in the evening we halted near a thicket of bamboo but found no water, so that we were forced to proceed four miles farther to a small stream, where we stopt for the night. We had marched this day, as I judged, about twenty-six miles.

This morning (April 26th) two of the schoolmaster's pupils complained much of pains in their legs, and one of the slaves walked lame, the soles of his feet being very much blistered and inflamed. We proceeded, notwithstanding, and about eleven o'clock began to ascend a rocky hill called Boki-Kooro, and it was past two in the afternoon before we reached the level ground on the other side. This was the most rocky road we had yet encountered, and it hurt our feet much. In a short time we arrived at a pretty large river called Boki, which we forded; it ran smooth and clear over a bed of whinstone. About a mile to the westward of the river we came to a road which leads to the north-east towards Gadou, and seeing the marks of many horses' feet upon the soft sand the Slatees conjectured that a party of plunderers had lately rode that way, to fall upon some town of Gadou; and lest they should discover upon their return that we had passed, and attempt to pursue us by the marks of our feet, the coffle was ordered to disperse, and travel in a loose manner through the high grass and bushes. A little before it was dark, having crossed the ridge of hills to the westward of the river Boki, we came to a well called *cullong qui* (white sand well), and here we rested for the night.

We departed from the well early in the morning, and walked on with the greatest alacrity, in hopes of reaching a town before night. The road during the forenoon led through extensive thickets of dry bamboos. About two o'clock we came to a stream called Nunkolo, where we were each of us regaled with a handful of meal, which, according to a superstitious custom, was not to be eaten until it was first moistened with water from this stream. About four o'clock we reached Sooseeta, a small Jallonka village situated in the district of Kullo, which comprehends all that tract of country lying along the banks of the Black River, or main branch of the Senegal. These were the first human habitations we had seen since we left the village to the westward of Kinytakooro, having travelled in the course of the last five days upwards of one hundred miles. Here, after a great deal of entreaty, we were provided with huts to sleep in, but the master of the village plainly told us that he could not give us any provisions, as there had lately been a great scarcity in this part of the country. He assured us that before they had gathered in their present crops the whole inhabitants of Kullo had been for twenty-nine days without tasting corn, during which time they supported themselves entirely upon the yellow powder which is found in the pods of the *nitta*, so called by the natives—a species of mimosa—and upon the seeds of the bamboo-cane, which, when properly pounded and dressed, taste very much like rice. As our dry provisions were not yet exhausted, a considerable quantity of kouskous was dressed for supper, and many of the villagers were invited to take part of the repast; but they made a very bad return for this kindness, for in the night they seized upon one of the schoolmaster's boys, who had fallen asleep under the Bentang-tree, and carried him away. The boy fortunately awoke before he was far from the village, and setting up a loud scream, the man who carried him put his hands upon his mouth and ran with him into the woods; but afterwards, understanding that he belonged to the schoolmaster, whose place of residence is only three days' journey distant, he thought, I suppose, that he could not retain him as a slave without the schoolmaster's knowledge, and therefore stripped off the boy's clothes and permitted him to return.

Early in the morning (April 28th), we departed from Sooseeta, and about ten o'clock came to an unwalled town called **Manna**, the inhabitants of which were employed in collecting the fruit of the nitta trees, which are very numerous in this neighbourhood. The pods are long and narrow, and contain a few black seeds enveloped in the fine mealy powder beforementioned ; the meal itself is of a bright yellow colour, resembling the flour of sulphur, and has a sweet mucilaginous taste ; when eaten by itself it is clammy, but when mixed with milk or water it constitutes a very pleasant and nourishing article of diet.

The language of the people of Manna is the same that is spoken all over that extensive and hilly country called Jallonkadoo. Some of the words have a great affinity to the Mandingo, but the natives themselves consider it as a distinct language. Their numerals are these : One, *kidding;* two, *fidding;* three, *sarra;* four, *nani;* five, *soolo;* six, *seni;* seven, *soolo ma fidding;* eight, *soolo ma sarra;* nine, *soolo ma nani;* ten, *nuff.*

The Jallonkas, like the Mandingoes, are governed by a number of petty chiefs, who are, in a great measure, independent of each other. They have no common sovereign ; and the chiefs are seldom upon such terms of friendship as to assist each other even in war time. The chief of Manna, with a number of his people, accompanied us to the banks of the Bafing, or Black river (a principal branch of the Senegal), which we crossed upon a bridge of bamboos of a very singular construction. The river at this place is smooth and deep, and has very little current. Two tall trees, when tied together by the tops, are sufficiently long to reach from one side to the other ; the roots resting upon the rocks, and the tops floating in the water. When a few trees have been placed in this direction, they are covered with dry bamboos, so as to form a floating bridge, with a sloping gangway at each end, where the trees rest upon the rocks. This bridge is carried away every year by the swelling of the river in the rainy season, and is constantly rebuilt by the inhabitants of Manna, who on that account expect a small tribute from every passenger.

In the afternoon we passed several villages, at none of which could we procure a lodging; and in the twilight we received information that two hundred Jallonkas had assembled near a town called Melo, with a view to plunder the coffle. This induced us to alter our course, and we travelled with great secrecy until midnight, when we approached a town called Koba. Before we entered the town, the names of all the people belonging to the coffle were called over, and a free man and three slaves were found to be missing. Every person immediately concluded that the slaves had murdered the free man, and made their escape. It was therefore agreed that six people should go back as far as the last village, and endeavour to find his body or collect some information concerning the slaves. In the meantime the coffle was ordered to lie concealed in a cotton-field near a large nitta tree, and nobody to speak except in a whisper. It was towards morning before the six men returned, having heard nothing of the man or the slaves. As none of us had tasted victuals for the last twenty-four hours, it was agreed that we should go into Koba, and endeavour to procure some provisions. We accordingly entered the town before it was quite day, and Karfa purchased from the chief man, for three strings of beads, a considerable quantity of ground-nuts, which we roasted and ate for breakfast; we were afterwards provided with huts, and rested here for the day.

About eleven o'clock, to our great joy and surprise, the free man and slaves who had parted from the coffle the preceding night entered the town. One of the slaves, it seems, had hurt his foot, and the night being very dark, they soon lost sight of the coffle. The free man, as soon as he found himself alone with the slaves, was aware of his own danger, and insisted on putting them in irons. The slaves were at first rather unwilling to submit; but when he threatened to stab them one by one with his spear they made no further resistance, and he remained with them among the bushes until morning, when he let them out of irons, and came to the town in hopes of hearing which route the coffle had taken. The information that we received concerning the Jallonkas who intended to rob the coffle was this day confirmed, and we were forced to remain here until the afternoon of the 30th, when Karfa hired a number of people to protect us, and we proceeded to a village called Tinkingtang. Departing from this village on the day following, we crossed a high ridge of mountains to the west of the Black River, and travelled over a rough stony country until sunset, when we arrived at Lingicotta, a small village in the district of Woradoo. Here we shook out the last handful of meal from our dry provision bags; this being the second day (since we crossed the Black River) that we had travelled from morning until night without tasting one morsel of food.

We departed from Lingicotta (May 2d), but the slaves being very much fatigued, we halted for the night at a village about nine miles to the westward, and procured some provisions through the interest of the schoolmaster, who now sent forward a messenger to Malacotta, his native town, to inform his friends of his arrival in the country, and to desire them to provide the necessary quantity of victuals to entertain the coffle for two or three days.

About noon next day we arrived at a village near a considerable stream of water which flows to the westward. Here we determined to stop for the return of the messenger who had been sent to Malacotta the day before ; and as the natives assured me there were no crocodiles in this stream I went and bathed myself. Very few people here can swim ; for they came in numbers to dissuade me from venturing into a pool where they said the water would come over my head. About two o'clock the messenger returned from Malacotta, and the schoolmaster's elder brother being impatient to see him, came along with the messenger to meet him at this village. The interview between the two brothers, who had not seen each other for nine years, was very natural and affecting. They fell upon each other's neck, and it was sometime before either of them could speak. At length, when the schoolmaster had a little recovered himself, he took his brother by the hand, and turning round—"This is the man," said he, pointing to Karfa, "who has been my father in Manding ; I would have pointed him out sooner to you, but my heart was too full."

We reached Malacotta in the evening, where we were well received. This is an unwalled town ; the huts for the most part are made of split cane twisted into a sort of wicker-work, and plastered over with mud. Here we remained three days, and were each day presented with a bullock from the schoolmaster ; we were likewise well entertained by the townspeople, who appear to be very active and industrious. They make very good soap by boiling ground-nuts in water, and then adding a lye of wood ashes. They likewise manufacture excellent iron, which they carry to Bondou to barter for salt. A party of the townspeople had lately returned from a trading expedition of this kind, and brought information concerning a war between Almami Abdulkader, king of Foota Torra, and Damel, king of the Jaloffs. The events of this war soon became a favourite subject with the singing-men, and the common topic of conversation in all the kingdoms bordering upon the Senegal and Gambia; and as the account is somewhat singular, I shall here abridge it for the readers' information. The king of Foota Torra, inflamed with a zeal for propagating his religion, had sent an embassy to Damel, similar to that which he had sent to Kasson, as previously related. The ambassador, on the present occasion, was accompanied by two of the principal Bushreens, who carried each a large knife fixed on the top of a long pole. As soon as he had procured admission into the presence of Damel, and announced the pleasure of his sovereign, he ordered the Bushreens to present the emblems of his mission. The two knives were accordingly laid before Damel, and the ambassador explained himself as follows :—" With this knife," said he, "Abdulkader will condescend to shave the head of Damel, if Damel will embrace the Mohammedan faith; and with this other knife, Abdulkader will cut the throat of Damel, if Damel refuses to embrace it; take your choice." Damel coolly told the ambassador that he had no choice to make; he neither chose to have his head shaved nor his throat cut; and with this answer the ambassador was civilly dismissed. Abdulkader took his measures accordingly, and with a powerful army invaded Damel's country. The inhabitants of the towns and

villages filled up their wells, destroyed their provisions, carried
off their effects, and abandoned their dwellings as he approached.
By this means he was led on from place to place, until he had
advanced three days' journey into the country of the Jaloffs.
He had, indeed, met with no opposition ; but his army had
suffered so much from the scarcity of water that several of his
men had died by the way.   This induced him to direct his
march towards a watering-place in the woods, where his men,
having quenched their thirst and being overcome with fatigue,
lay down carelessly to sleep among the bushes.   In this situation they were attacked by Damel before daybreak and completely routed.   Many of them were trampled to death, as
they lay asleep, by the Jaloff horses ; others were killed in
attempting to make their escape ; and a still greater number
were taken prisoners.   Among the latter was Abdulkader
himself.   This ambitious or rather frantic prince, who but a
month before had sent the threatening message to Damel, was
now himself led into his presence a miserable captive.   The
behaviour of Damel on this occasion is never mentioned by
the singing-men but in terms of the highest approbation ; and
it was indeed so extraordinary in an African prince that the
reader may find it difficult to give credit to the recital.   When
his royal prisoner was brought before him in irons, and thrown
upon the ground, the magnanimous Damel, instead of setting
his foot upon his neck, and stabbing him with his spear, according to custom in such cases, addressed him as follows :—
"Abdulkader, answer me this question :—If the chance of war
had placed me in your situation, and you in mine, how would
you have treated me ?"   "I would have thrust my spear into
your heart," returned Abdulkader with great firmness ; "and

I know that a similar fate awaits me." "Not so," said Damel; "my spear is indeed red with the blood of your subjects killed in battle, and I could now give it a deeper stain by dipping it in your own; but this would not build up my towns, nor bring to life the thousands who fell in the woods. I will not, therefore, kill you in cold blood, but I will retain you as my slave, until I perceive that your presence in your own kingdom will be no longer dangerous to your neighbours, and then I will consider of the proper way of disposing of you." Abdulkader was accordingly retained, and worked as a slave for three months; at the end of which period, Damel listened to the solicitations of the inhabitants of Foota Torra, and restored to them their king. Strange as this story may appear, I have no doubt of the truth of it; it was told me at Malacotta by the Negroes; it was afterwards related to me by the Europeans on the Gambia; by some of the French at Goree; and confirmed by nine slaves, who were taken prisoners along with Abdulkader, by the watering-place in the woods, and carried in the same ship with me to the West Indies.

CHAPTER XXV.

The Caravan proceeds to Konkadoo, and crosses the Falemé River—
—Its arrival at Baniserile, Kirwani, and Tambacunda—Inci-
dents on the Road—A Matrimonial Case—The Caravan proceed.
through many Towns and Villages, and arrives at length on the
Banks of the Gambia—Passes through Medina, the Capital of
Woolli, and finally stops at Jindey—Park, accompanied by
Karfa, proceeds to Pisania—Various Occurrences previous to
his departure from Africa—Takes his Passage in an American
Ship—Short Account of his Voyage to Great Britain by Way of
the West Indies.

A D. 1796.

ON the 7th of May we departed from Malacotta, and having
crossed the *Ba lee,* "Honey River," a branch of the
Senegal, we arrived in the evening at a walled town called
Bintingala, where we rested two days. From thence, in one
day more, we proceeded to Dindikoo, a small town situated at
the bottom of a high ridge of hills, from which this district is
named *Konkadoo,* "the country of mountains." These hills
are very productive of gold. I was shown a small quantity
of this metal which had been lately collected ; the grains were
about the usual size, but much flatter than those of Manding,
and were found in white quartz, which had been broken to
pieces by hammers. At this town I met with a Negro whose
hair and skin were of a dull white colour. He was of that

sort which are called in the Spanish West Indies *Albinos*, or white Negroes. The skin is cadaverous and unsightly, and the natives considered this complexion (I believe truly) as the effect of disease.

After a toilsome day's travel from Dindikoo we arrived at Satadoo, the capital of a district of the same name. This town was formerly of considerable extent, but many families had left it in consequence of the predatory incursions of the Foulahs of Foota Jalla, who made it a practice to come secretly through the woods and carry off people from the corn-fields, and even from the wells near the town. We then crossed the Falemé River, the same which I had formerly crossed at Bondou in my journey eastward. This river, at this season of the year, is easily forded at this place, the stream being only about two feet deep. The water is very pure, and flows rapidly over a bed of sand and gravel. We lodged for a night at a small village called Medina, the sole property of a Mandingo merchant, who, by a long intercourse with Europeans, has been induced to adopt some of their customs. His victuals were served up in pewter dishes, and even his houses were built after the fashion of the English houses on the Gambia.

As we were preparing to depart, a coffle of slaves belonging to some Serawooli traders crossed the river, and agreed to proceed with us to Baniserile, the capital of Dentila, a very long day's journey from this place. We accordingly set out together (May 13), and travelled with great expedition through the woods until noon, when one of the Serawooli slaves dropt the load from his head, for which he was smartly whipped. The load was replaced, but he had not proceeded above a mile before he let it fall a second time, for which he received the same punishment. After this he travelled in great pain until about two o'clock, when we stopt to breathe a little by a pool of water, the day being remarkably hot. The poor slave was now so completely exhausted that his master was obliged to release him from the rope, for he lay motionless on the ground. A Serawooli, therefore, undertook to remain with him, and endeavour to bring him to the town during the cool of the night. In the meanwhile we continued our route, and after a very hard day's travel arrived at Baniserile late in the evening.

One of our Slatees was a native of this place, from which he had been absent three years. This man invited me to go with him to his house, at the gate of which his friends met him with many expressions of joy—shaking hands with him, embracing him, and singing and dancing before him. As soon as he had seated himself upon a mat by the threshold of his door, a young woman (his intended bride) brought a little water in a calabash, and kneeling down before him desired him to wash his hands : when he had done this, the girl, with a tear of joy sparkling in her eyes, drank the water—this being considered the greatest proof she could give him of her fidelity and attachment. About eight o'clock the same evening, the Serawooli who had been left in the woods to take care of the fatigued slave returned and told us that he was dead : the general opinion, however, was that he himself had killed him or left him to perish on the road, for the Serawoolies are said to be infinitely more cruel in their treatment of slaves than the Mandingoes. We remained at Baniserile two days, in order to purchase native iron, shea-butter, and some other articles for sale on the Gambia; and here the Slatee who had invited me to his house, and who possessed three slaves, part of the coffle, having obtained information that the price on the coast was very low, determined to separate from us, and remain with his slaves where he was, until an opportunity should offer of disposing of them to advantage, giving us to understand that he should complete his nuptials with the young woman before mentioned in the meantime.

We departed from Baniserile (May 16th), and travelled through thick woods until noon, when we saw at a distance the town of Julifunda, but did not approach it, as we proposed to rest for the night at a large town called Kirwani, which we reached about four o'clock in the afternoon. This town stands in a valley, and the country for more than a mile round it is cleared of wood, and well cultivated. The inhabitants appear to be very active and industrious, and seemed to have carried the system of agriculture to some degree of perfection, for they collect the dung of their cattle into large heaps during the dry season, for the purpose of manuring their land with it at the proper time. I saw nothing like this in any other part of Africa. Near the town are several smelting furnaces, from which the natives obtain very good iron. They afterwards hammer the metal into small bars, about a foot in length and two inches in breadth, one of which bars is sufficient to make two Mandingo corn hoes. On the morning after our arrival we were visited by a Slatee of this place, who informed Karfa that among some slaves he had lately purchased was a native of Foota Jalla, and as that country was at no great distance, he could not safely employ him in the labours of the field lest he should effect his escape. The Slatee was therefore desirous of exchanging this slave for one of Karfa's, and offered some cloth and shea-butter to induce Karfa to comply with the proposal, which was accepted. The Slatee thereupon sent a boy to order the slave in question to bring him a few ground-nuts. The poor creature soon afterwards entered the court in which we were sitting, having no suspicion of what was negotiating, until the master caused the gate to be shut, and told him to sit down. The slave now saw his danger, and perceiving the gate to be shut upon him, threw down the nuts and jumped over the fence. He was immediately pursued and overtaken by the Slatee, who brought him back and secured him in irons, after which one of Karfa's slaves was released and delivered in exchange. The unfortunate captive was at first very much dejected, but in the course of a few days his melancholy gradually subsided, and he became at length as cheerful as any of his companions.

Departing from Kirwani on the morning of the 20th, we entered the Tenda wilderness of two days' journey. The woods were very thick, and the country shelved towards the south-west. About ten o'clock we met a coffle of twenty-six people and seven loaded asses returning from the Gambia Most of the men were armed with muskets, and had broad belts of scarlet cloth over their shoulders and European hats upon their heads. They informed us that there was very little demand for slaves on the coast, as no vessel had arrived for some months past. On hearing this, the Serawoolies, who had travelled with us from the Falemé river, separated themselves and their slaves from the coffle. They had not, they said, the means of maintaining their slaves in Gambia until a vessel should arrive, and were unwilling to sell them to disadvantage ; they therefore departed to the northward for Kajaaga. We continued our route through the wilderness, and travelled all day through a rugged country covered with extensive thickets of bamboo. At sunset, to our great joy, we arrived at a pool of water near a large tabba tree, whence the place is called Tabbagee, and here we rested a few hours. The water at this season of the year is by no means plentiful in these woods, and as the days were insufferably hot Karfa proposed to travel in the night. Accordingly, about eleven o'clock the slaves were taken out of their irons, and the people of the coffle received orders to keep close together, as well to prevent the slaves from attempting to escape, as on account of the wild beasts. We travelled with great alacrity until daybreak, when it was discovered that a free woman had parted from the coffle in the night ; her name was called until the woods resounded, but no answer being given, we conjectured that she had either mistaken the road, or that a lion had seized her unperceived. At length it was agreed that four people should go back a few miles to a small rivulet, where some of the coffle had stopped to drink as we passed it in the night, and that the coffle should wait for their return. The sun was about an hour high before the people came back with the woman, whom they found lying fast asleep by the stream. We now resumed our journey, and about eleven o'clock reached a walled town called Tambacunda, where we were well received. Here we remained four days, on account of a *palaver* which was held on the following occasion :—Modi Lemina, one of the Slatees belonging to the coffle, had formerly married a woman of this town, who had borne him two children ; he afterwards went to

Manding, and remained there eight years without sending any account of himself during all that time to his deserted wife, who, seeing no prospect of his return, at the end of three years had married another man, to whom she had likewise borne two children. Lemina now claimed his wife, but the second husband refused to deliver her up, insisting that by the laws of Africa, when a man has been three years absent from his wife, without giving her notice of his being alive, the woman is at liberty to marry again. After all the circumstances had been fully investigated in an assembly of the chief men, it was determined that the wife should make her choice, and be at liberty either to return to the first husband, or continue with the second, as she alone should think proper. Favourable as this determination was to the lady, she found it a difficult matter to make up her mind, and requested time for consideration, but I think I could perceive that *first love* would carry the day. Lemina was indeed somewhat older than his rival, but he was also much richer. What weight this circumstance had in the scale of his wife's affections I pretend not to say.

On the morning of the 26th, as we departed from Tambacunda, Karfa observed to me that there were no shea-trees farther to the westward than this town. I had collected and brought with me from Manding the leaves and flowers of this tree, but they were so greatly bruised on the road that I thought it best to gather another specimen at this place. The appearance of the fruit evidently places the shea-tree in the natural order of *Sapotœ*, and it has some resemblance to the *mudhuca* tree described by Lieutenant Charles Hamilton in the Asiatic Researches. About one o'clock we reached Sibikillin, a walled village; but the inhabitants having the character of inhospitality towards strangers, and of being much addicted to theft, we did not think proper to enter the gate. We rested a short time under a tree, and then continued our route until it was dark, when we halted for the night by a small stream running towards the Gambia. Next day the road led over a wild and rocky country, everywhere rising into hills, and abounding with monkeys and wild beasts. In the rivulets among the hills we found plenty of fish. This was a very hard day's journey, and it was not until sunset that we reached the village of Koomboo, near to which are the ruins of a large town formerly destroyed by war. The inhabitants of Koomboo, like those of Sibikillin, have so bad a reputation that strangers seldom lodge in the village; we accordingly rested for the night in the fields, where we erected temporary huts for our protection, there being great appearance of rain.

We departed from Koomboo (May 28th), and slept at a Foulah town about seven miles to the westward; from which, on the day following, having crossed a considerable branch of the Gambia, called Neola Koba, we reached a well-inhabited part of the country. Here are several towns within sight of each other, collectively called Tenda, but each is distinguished also by its particular name. We lodged at one of them, called Koba Tenda, where we remained the day following, in order to procure provisions for our support in crossing the Simbani woods. On the 30th we reached Jalacotta, a considerable town, but much infested by Foulah banditti, who come through the woods from Bondou and steal everything they can lay their hands on. A few days before our arrival they had stolen twenty head of cattle, and on the day following made a second attempt, but were beaten off, and one of them taken prisoner.

Here one of the slaves belonging to the coffle, who had travelled with great difficulty for the last three days, was found unable to proceed any farther; his master (a singing-man) proposed therefore to exchange him for a young girl belonging to one of the townspeople. The poor girl was ignorant of her fate until the bundles were all tied up in the morning and the coffle ready to depart; when, coming with some other young women to see the coffle set out, her master took her by the hand and delivered her to the singing-man. Never was a face of serenity more suddenly changed into one of the deepest distress; the terror she manifested on having the load put upon her head and the rope fastened round her neck, and the sorrow with which she bade adieu to her companions, were truly affecting. Our route lay across a large plain covered with *ciboa* trees (a species of palm), when we came to the river Nerico, a branch of the Gambia, small at this time, but in the rainy season often dangerous to travellers. As soon as we had crossed this river the singing-men began to vociferate a particular song, expressive of their joy at having got safe into the west country, or, as they expressed it, *the land of the setting sun.* The country was found to be very level, and the soil a mixture of clay and sand. In the afternoon it rained hard, and we had recourse to the common Negro umbrella, a large ciboa leaf, which, being placed upon the head, completely defends the whole body from the rain. We lodged for the night under the shade of a large tabba tree, near the ruins of a village. On the morning following we crossed a stream called Noulico, and about two o'clock, to my infinite joy, I saw myself once more on the banks of the Gambia, which at this place, being deep and smooth, is navigable; but

the people told me that a little lower down the stream is so
shallow that the coffles frequently cross it on foot. On the
south side of the river, opposite to this place, is a large plain
of clayey ground, called Toombi Toorila. It is a sort of morass,
in which people are frequently lost, it being more than a day's
journey across it. In the afternoon we met a man and two
women with bundles of cotton cloth upon their heads. They
were going, they said, for Dentila, to purchase iron, there
being a great scarcity of that article on the Gambia. A little
before it was dark, we arrived at a village in the kingdom of
Woolli, called Seesukunda. Near this village there are great
plenty of nitta trees, and the slaves in passing along had
collected large bunches of the fruit ; but such was the
superstition of the inhabitants that they would not permit
any of the fruit to be brought into the village. They had been
told, they said, that some catastrophe would happen to the
place when people lived upon nittas, and neglected to cultivate
corn.

We departed from Seesukunda (June 2d), and passed a
number of villages, at none of which was the coffle permitted
to stop, although we were all very much fatigued ; it was four
o'clock in the afternoon before we reached Baraconda, where
we rested one day. Departing from Baraconda on the morning of the 4th, we reached in a few hours Medina, the capital
of the king of Woolli's dominions, from whom the reader may
recollect I received a hospitable reception in the beginning of
December 1795 in my journey eastward. I immediately inquired concerning the health of my good old benefactor, and
learned with great concern that he was dangerously ill. As
Karfa would not allow the coffle to stop, I could not present

my respects to the king in person ; but I sent him word by the officer to whom we paid customs, that his prayers for my safety had not been unavailing. We continued our route until sunset, when we lodged at a small village a little to the westward of Kootakunda, and on the day following arrived at Jindey, where, eighteen months before, I had parted from my friend Dr. Laidley, an interval during which I had not beheld the face of a Christian, nor once heard the delightful sound of my native language.

Being now arrived within a short distance of Pisania, from whence my journey originally commenced, and learning that my friend Karfa was not likely to meet with an immediate opportunity of selling his slaves on the Gambia, it occurred to me to suggest to him that he would find it for his interest to leave them at Jindey until a market should offer. Karfa agreed with me in this opinion, and hired, from the chief man of the town, huts for their accommodation, and a piece of land on which to employ them in raising corn and other provisions for their maintenance. With regard to himself, he declared that he would not quit me until my departure from Africa. We set out accordingly, Karfa, myself, and one of the Foulahs belonging to the coffle, early on the morning of the 9th June ; but although I was now approaching the end of my tedious and toilsome journey, and expected in another day to meet with countrymen and friends, I could not part, for the last time, with my unfortunate fellow-travellers, doomed, as I knew most of them to be, to a life of captivity and slavery in a foreign land, without great emotion. During a wearisome peregrination of more than five hundred British miles, exposed to the burning rays of a tropical sun, these poor slaves, amidst

their own infinitely greater sufferings, would commiserate
mine; and frequently, of their own accord, bring water to
quench my thirst, and at night collect branches and leaves to
prepare me a bed in the wilderness. We parted with reci-
procal expressions of regret and benediction. My good
wishes and prayers were all I could bestow upon them, and it
afforded me some consolation to be told, that they were sensible I had no more to give.

My anxiety to get forward admitting of no delay on the
road, we reached Tendacunda in the evening, and were hospitably received at the house of an aged black female called
Seniora Camilla, a person who had resided many years at the
English factory, and spoke our language. I was known to her
before I had left the Gambia at the outset of my journey; but
my dress and figure were now so different from the usual
appearance of a European, that she was very excusable in mis-
taking me for a Moor. When I told her my name and country,
she surveyed me with great astonishment, and seemed unwilling to give credit to the testimony of her senses. She
assured me that none of the traders on the Gambia ever
expected to see me again; having been informed long ago
that the Moors of Ludamar had murdered me, as they had
murdered Major Houghton. I inquired for my two attendants,
Johnson and Demba, and learned with great sorrow that neither
of them was returned. Karfa, who had never before heard
people converse in English, listened to us with great attention.
Everything he saw seemed wonderful. The furniture of the
house, the chairs, etc., and particularly beds with curtains,
were objects of his great admiration; and he asked me a
thousand questions concerning the utility and necessity of

different articles, to some of which I found it difficult to give satisfactory answers.

On the morning of the 10th June, Mr. Robert Ainsley, having learnt that I was at Tendacunda, came to meet me, and politely offered me the use of his horse. He informed me that Dr. Laidley had removed all his property to a place called Kaye, a little farther down the river, and that he was then gone to Doomasansa with his vessel to purchase rice, but would return in a day or two. He therefore invited me to stay with him at Pisania until the Doctor's return. I accepted the invitation, and, accompanied by my friend Karfa, reached Pisania about ten o'clock. Mr. Ainsley's schooner was lying at anchor before the place. This was the most surprising object which Karfa had yet seen. He could not easily comprehend the use of the masts, sails, and rigging, nor did he conceive that it was possible, by any sort of contrivance, to make so large a body move forwards by the common force of the wind. The manner of fastening together the different planks which composed the vessel, and filling up the seams so as to exclude the water, was perfectly new to him; and I found that the schooner, with her cable and anchor, kept Karfa in deep meditation the greater part of the day.

About noon, on the 12th June, Dr. Laidley returned from Doomasansa, and received me with great joy and satisfaction, as one risen from the dead. Finding that the wearing apparel which I had left under his care was not sold nor sent to England, I lost no time in resuming the English dress, and disrobing my chin of its venerable incumbrance. Karfa surveyed me in my British apparel with great delight, but regretted exceedingly that I had taken off my beard, the loss of which, he said, had converted me from a man into a boy. Dr. Laidley readily undertook to discharge all the pecuniary engagements I had entered into since my departure from the Gambia, and took my draft upon the Association for the amount. My agreement with Karfa (as I have already related) was to pay him the value of one prime slave, for which I had given him my bill upon Dr. Laidley before we departed from Kamalia; for, in case of my death on the road, I was unwilling that my benefactor should be a loser. But this good creature had continued to manifest towards me so much kindness, that I thought I made him but an inadequate recompense, when I told him that he was now to receive double the sum I had originally promised, and Dr. Laidley assured him that he was ready to deliver the goods to that amount whenever he thought proper to send for them. Karfa was overpowered by this unexpected token of my gratitude, and still more so when he heard that I intended to send a handsome present to the good old schoolmaster Fankooma, at Malacotta. He promised to carry up the goods along with his own, and Dr. Laidlaw assured him that he would exert himself in assisting him to dispose of his slaves to the best advantage, the moment a slave vessel should arrive. These and other instances of attention and kindness shown him by Dr. Laidley, were not lost upon Karfa. He would often say to me, "My journey has indeed been prosperous!" But observing the improved state of our manufactures, and our manifest superiority in the arts of civilised life, he would sometimes appear pensive, and exclaim with an involuntary sigh, *Fato fing inta feng*, "Black men are nothing." At other times he would ask me, with great seriousness, what could possibly have induced me, who was no trader, to think of exploring so miserable a country as Africa? He meant by this, to signify that, after what I must have witnessed in my own country, nothing in Africa could, in his opinion, deserve a moment's attention. I have preserved these little traits of character in this worthy Negro, not only from regard to the man, but also because they appear to me to demonstrate that he possessed a mind *above his condition;* and to such of my readers as love to contemplate human nature in all its varieties, and to trace its progress from rudeness to refinement, I hope the account I have given of this poor African will not be unacceptable.

No European vessel had arrived at Gambia for many months previous to my return from the interior; and as the rainy season was now setting in, I persuaded Karfa to return to his people at Jindey. He parted from me with great tenderness; but as I had little hopes of being able to quit Africa for the remainder of the year, I told him (as the fact was) that I expected to see him again before my departure. In this however I was luckily disappointed, and my narrative now hastens to its conclusion, for on the 15th June, the ship Charlestown, an American vessel commanded by Mr. Charles Harris, entered the river. She came for slaves, intending to touch at Goree to fill up, and to proceed from thence to South Carolina. As the European merchants on the Gambia had at this time a great many slaves on hand, they agreed with the captain to purchase the whole of his cargo, consisting chiefly of rum and tobacco, and deliver him slaves to the amount, in the course of two days. This afforded me such an opportunity of returning (though by a circuitous route) to my native country, as I thought was not to be neglected. I therefore immediately engaged my passage in this vessel for America ; and having taken leave of Dr. Laidley, to whose kindness I was so largely indebted, and my other friends on the river, I embarked at Kaye on the 17th day of June.

Our passage down the river was tedious and fatiguing, and the weather was so hot, moist, and unhealthy, that before our arrival at Goree, four of the seamen, the surgeon, and three of the slaves had died of fevers. At Goree we were detained for want of provisions until the beginning of October.

The number of slaves received on board this vessel, both on the Gambia and at Goree, was one hundred and thirty, of whom about twenty-five had been, I suppose, of free condition in Africa, as most of them, being Bushreens, could write a little Arabic. Nine of them had become captives in the religious war between Abdulkader and Damel, mentioned in the latter part of the preceding chapter ; two of the others had seen me as I passed through Bondou, and many of them had heard of me in the interior countries. My conversation with them in their native language gave them great comfort ; and as the surgeon was dead, I consented to act in a medical capacity in his room for the remainder of the voyage. They had, in truth, need of every consolation in my power to bestow, not that I observed any wanton acts of cruelty practised either by the master or the seamen towards them, but the mode of confining and securing Negroes in the American slave-ships (owing chiefly to the weakness of their crews) being abundantly more rigid and severe than in British vessels employed in the same ·traffic, made these poor creatures to suffer greatly, and a general sickness prevailed amongst them. Besides the three who died on the Gambia and six or eight while we remained at Goree, eleven perished at sea, and many of the survivors were reduced to a very weak and emaciated condition.

In the midst of these distresses, the vessel, after having been three weeks at sea, became so extremely leaky as to require constant exertion at the pumps. It was found necessary, therefore, to take some of the ablest of the Negro men out of irons and employ them in this labour, in which they were often worked beyond their strength. This produced a complication of miseries not easily to be described. We were, however, relieved much sooner than I expected, for the leak continuing to gain upon us, notwithstanding our utmost exertions to clear the vessel, the seamen insisted on bearing away for the West Indies, as affording the only chance of saving our lives. Accordingly, after some objections on the part of the master, we directed our course for Antigua, and fortunately made that island in about thirty-five days after our departure from Goree. Yet even at this juncture we narrowly escaped destruction, for on approaching the north-west side of the island we struck on the Diamond Rock, and got into St. John's harbour with great difficulty. The vessel was afterwards condemned as unfit for sea, and the slaves, as I have heard, were ordered to be sold for the benefit of the owners.

At this island I remained ten days, when I took my passage in the Chesterfield Packet, homeward bound from the Leeward Islands, touching at St. John's for the Antigua mail. We sailed on the 24th of November, and after a short but tempestuous voyage arrived at Falmouth on the 22d of December (1797), from whence I immediately set out for London, having been absent from England two years and seven months.

CHAPTER XXVI.

Park at home—Fowlshiels—Preparation of his Journal—Marriage —Life as a country Doctor—Love of Retirement—Second Ex· pedition to Africa—Intercourse with Sir Walter Scott—Departure from Fowlshiels.

1798—1804.

After his return from Africa, Park remained for a considerable time stationary in London, and was diligently employed in arranging the materials for the publication of his travels.

It was nearly about this time (the spring of the year 1798) that Government, having in contemplation a complete survey of New Holland, made some application to Park, with the view of enlisting his services ; but the proposal was declined.

In June 1798 he visited his mother, who resided at Fowlshiels,* and his other relations in Scotland, and remained with them the whole of the summer and autumn. During all this time he was assiduously employed in compiling and arranging the account of his travels. His materials for this work are stated to have consisted of short notes or memoranda, written on separate pieces of paper, forming an imperfect

---

* Fowlshiels is beautifully situated on the banks of the Yarrow, in the immediate vicinity of Bowhill, a summer residence of the Duke of Buccleuch, and Ashestiel, then the residence of Sir Walter Scott, and at no great distance from the ruins of Newark Castle, and other scenes celebrated in the *Lay of the Last Minstrel.*

journal of his proceedings. Where these were wanting, he supplied the deficiency from his memory.

His family represent him during this period as leading the life of a severe student, employed on his papers during the whole of the mornings, and allowing himself little or no recreation, except a solitary evening walk on the banks of the Yarrow. Occasionally, however, he would indulge himself in longer excursions among the wild and romantic scenery of that neighbourhood, to which he was fondly and almost enthusiastically attached.

He quitted Fowlshiels with great regret towards the latter end of 1798, when it was necessary for him to return to London to prepare his intended publication. He carried back with him a great mass of papers, the produce of his summer's labour, and after his return to London bestowed considerable pains in the correction and retrenchment of his manuscript before it was sent to the press. It was finally published in the spring of the year 1799.

After the publication of his travels, Park began to think of settling himself in life. During the summer and autumn of 1798, he had formed a matrimonial engagement with the eldest daughter of Mr. Anderson of Selkirk, with whom he had served his apprenticeship. He returned, therefore, to Scotland in the summer of 1799, and was married on the 2d of August in that year. This union, which connected him still more closely with a family with which he had long lived in friendship, contributed in a high degree to his future comfort and happiness.

For more than two years after his marriage he resided with his mother and one of his brothers, who lived together and carried on the farm at Fowlshiels. He remained for a long time altogether doubtful and unsettled as to his future plan of life.

An opportunity for medical practice, which was thought sufficiently promising, at length offered itself at Peebles. Thither he went to reside in the month of October 1801, and betook himself in good earnest to the exercise of his profession. His former habits of life had, however, in a great measure disqualified him for his present humble occupation. The situation of a country doctor in Scotland, attended with no distinction or much personal advantage, was little calculated to gratify a man whose mind was full of ambitious views, and of adventurous and romantic undertakings. His visits to distant patients —his long and solitary rides over "cold and lonely heaths" and "gloomy hills, assailed by the wintry tempest," seem to have produced in him feelings of disgust and impatience, which he had perhaps rarely experienced in the deserts of Africa. He frequently expressed his strong sense of the irksomeness of this manner of life, and on one particular occasion, when, previous to undertaking his second African mission, one of his nearest relations expostulated with him on the imprudence of again exposing himself to dangers which he had so very narrowly escaped, and perhaps encountering new and still greater ones, he calmly replied, that a few inglorious winters of country practice at Peebles was a risk as great, and would tend as effectually to shorten life, as the journey which he was about to undertake.

It might have been expected that Park, who had been accustomed to literary and scientific society, and been lately in some degree admitted into the fashionable circles of the metropolis, in which he had become an object of much interest and attention, would have felt great repugnance to the solitude and obscurity of a small market-town. But this does not appear to have been the case. General society, for which indeed he was not particularly suited, was not much to his taste ; and during every period of his life he always looked forward to a state of complete retirement and seclusion in the country as the object and end of all his labours. He had great enjoyment, however, in his own domestic circle, and in the society of select friends ; and his residence at Peebles was, in this respect, highly fortunate for him, since it was the occasion of his becoming acquainted with two distinguished residents in that neighbourhood, Colonel John Murray of Cringletie, a distinguished old officer, then retired from the service, and Dr. Adam Fergusson, with both of whom he became intimate, and passed much of his time.

In the midst of all his occupations, however, Park's thoughts were still turned upon Africa. Soon after the signature of the Preliminary Articles of Peace with France, in October 1801, he received a letter from Sir Joseph Banks, acquainting him "that, in consequence of the peace, the Association would certainly revive their project of sending a mission to Africa, in order to penetrate to and navigate the Niger ;" and he added, " that in case Government should enter into the plan, he would certainly be recommended as the person proper to be employed for carrying it into execution." But the business remained for a considerable time in suspense, nor did any specific proposal follow this communication till the autumn of the year 1803, when he received a letter addressed to him from the office of the Colonial Secretary of

State, desiring his attendance without delay. On his arrival in London he had an interview with the Earl of Buckingham, then Lord Hobart, and Secretary of State for the Colonial Department, who acquainted him with the nature of an expedition to Africa, which was about to take place, and in which it was proposed that he should bear a principal part.

Park's imagination had been indulging itself for some years past upon the visions of discoveries which he was destined to make in the interior of Africa; and the object of his ambition being now within grasp, he hastily announced to Lord Hobart his acceptance of the proposal.

At this time he quitted his house at Peebles, and took his family to the farm at Fowlshiels, where he quietly waited the expected summons of the Secretary of State, employing himself with great diligence in perfecting himself in the use of astronomical instruments, and in the study of the Arabic language, in which he became a tolerable proficient.

Sir Walter Scott was at this time (1804) residing at Ashestiel, in the neighbourhood of Fowlshiels, and naturally sought an acquaintance with Park, which was speedily matured into a sincere and cordial friendship. As might be expected, their conversation often turned upon Africa, and upon one or two occasions Park communicated to his friend several remarkable and very interesting adventures which had happened to him during his journey, but which were not in his printed travels. On being asked the reason of this omission, which appeared to his friend somewhat unaccountable, his reply was striking and characteristic. He said, "That in all cases where he had information to communicate, which he thought of importance to the public, he had stated the facts boldly, leaving it to his readers to give such credit to his statements as they might appear justly to deserve ; but that he would not shock their credulity, or render his travels more marvellous, by introducing circumstances which, however true, were of little or no moment, as they related solely to his own personal adventures and escapes."

Calling one day at Fowlshiels and not finding Park at home, Scott walked in search of him along the banks of the Yarrow, which is here a romantic stream, running among rocks, and forming deep pools and eddies.   In a short time he came upon the traveller, whom he found employed in plunging large stones into the river, and watching with anxious attention the bubbles as they rose to the surface.   On being asked by his friend the reason why he persevered so long in this singular amusement?   "This was the manner," answered Park," in which I used to ascertain the depth of a river in Africa before I ventured to cross it, and of judging whether the attempt would be safe, by the time which the bubbles of air took to ascend."   It was not then known that Park had any thoughts of undertaking a second mission ; but this circumstance left no doubt in Scott's mind that he had formed such an intention.

Notwithstanding his determination again to visit Africa, he acknowledged that the horrors of his captivity in the Moorish camp of Benowm had never ceased to impress his imagination. When he was troubled with indigestion—·a complaint to which, after his return from Africa, he was a good deal subject, and by which his rest was much affected—he used often to start from his sleep in great horror, supposing himself still a prisoner in the tent of Ali.

Scott describes, in strong and feeling terms, the manner of

his last parting with his friend. About the time of his quitting Fowlshiels for the last time, Park paid Scott a farewell visit, and slept at Ashestiel. The next morning Scott accompanied him part of the way on his return to Fowlshiels ; and they rode together over the wild chain of pastoral hills which divide the Tweed from the Yarrow. Park talked much of his new African expedition, and mentioned his determination of going straight from Edinburgh, without returning to take leave of his family. They were then on the top of William-hope ridge, a lofty hill which overlooks the course of the Yarrow ; and the autumnal mist which floated heavily and slowly down the valley beneath them, presented to Scott's imagination a striking emblem of the troubled and uncertain prospect which Park's undertaking afforded. Scott pressed upon his friend the danger likely to result from his being accompanied with a military force, which he *then* thought the most unsafe mode of travelling in Africa ; the number of troops proposed to be employed appearing to be inadequate for conquest, or even for serious defence, yet large enough to excite suspicion. Park answered these objections by describing the manner in which Africa was subdivided among petty sovereigns, who were not likely to form any regular combination for cutting him off, and whose boundaries were soon traversed. He spoke also of the long journeys common in those countries, and of the habit of seeing coffles or caravans of all nations pass through their territories on paying a small duty ; from which he inferred that the march of a small party, such as that which was to be placed under his command, would excite no serious apprehension. This interesting conversation occupied the two friends till they had passed the hills, and come to a road where it had been agreed they should separate. A small ditch divided the moor from the road, and in going over it, Park's horse stumbled and nearly fell. "I am afraid, Mungo," said Mr. Scott, "that is a bad omen;" to which he answered smiling, "*Freits* (*i. e.* omens) follow those who look to them." With this familiar proverb, and afraid of a formal adieu, he rode away and was speedily out of sight.

On leaving Fowlshiels the last time, he was extremely affected, and would not venture to trust his own feelings, or those of his family, with a formal parting. He left them, as if with the intention of returning, alleging that he had particular business at Edinburgh from whence he sent them his final farewell.

CHAPTER XXVII.

Park's Second Journey to Africa.

A.D. 1805.

Starts from Kayee—Extreme Difficulties in Travelling, and Death of several of his Attendants—Threatened by Lions—Death of Mr. Scott and his brother-in law Mr. Anderson—Feels himself for a second time Lonely and Friendless in the Wilds of Africa—Last letter to Mrs. Park—His Death, as related in Amadi Fatoumi's Journal.

THE preparations for the expedition being completed, Park, accompanied by Mr. Anderson and Mr. Scott, proceeded to Portsmouth, where they were joined by four or five artificers from the dockyards, appointed for the service. After waiting some time for a wind, they set sail in the 'Crescent' transport, on the 30th January 1805, and arrived at Port Praya Bay, in the Cape Verd Islands, about the 8th of March. What happened between the time of his embarkation in England to his departure from Kayee on the Gambia for the interior of Africa (a period of about seven weeks) is described in the following letters :—

To Edward Cooke, Esq., Under-Secretary of State for the Colonial Department.

"Jillifree, River Gambia, April 9, 1805.

"We had a very tedious passage to the Cape Verd Islands,

being detained by storms and contrary winds in the Bay of Biscay, so that we did not reach St. Jago till the 8th of March. I immediately set about purchasing the asses, corn, hay, etc., and succeeded so well that on the 18th I had embarked forty-four asses, with plenty of corn and hay. The master of the transport declared that he could not receive any more consistently with the safety of the vessel. We sailed for Goree on the 21st. While we were getting under way, six English ships of the line, one of them a three-decker, came into the bay. They did not hail us ; one of them had an Admiral's blue flag at the mizen.

"We made the coast of Africa on the 25th, and anchored in Goree roads on the morning of 28th. I immediately went on shore, and having delivered the despatches to Major Lloyd, consulted with him respecting the proper encouragement to be offered to the troops. We agreed that nothing would be so great an inducement as double pay during the journey, and a discharge on their return. A garrison order to this effect was accordingly made out, and in the course of a few days almost every soldier in the garrison had volunteered his services. Lieutenant Martyn, of the Royal Artillery Corps, having likewise volunteered, I thought it would be of consequence to have an officer who was acquainted with the men, and who could assist me in choosing such as were best able to stand fatigue. I therefore accepted his services on the conditions mentioned in Lord Camden's letter. Captain Shortland, of the 'Squirrel' frigate, has allowed two of his best seamen to go with me as volunteers, in order to assist in rigging and navigating our *Nigritian men of war.* I have given them the same encouragement as the soldiers, and have had the four carpenters whom I brought from England attested, in order to put the whole under the same discipline and regulations.

"On the morning of the 6th of April we embarked the soldiers, in number thirty-five men. They jumped into the boats in the highest spirits, and bade adieu to Goree with repeated huzzas. I believe that every man in the garrison would have embarked with great cheerfulness ; but no inducement could prevail on a single Negro to accompany me. I must therefore trust to the Gambia for interpreters, and I expect to be able to hire or purchase three or four in going up the river. I will send a particular account of all money matters by the return of the transport.   MUNGO PARK."

To Mrs. Park.

"Kayee, River Gambia, April 26, 1805.

" I have been busy these three days in making preparations for our journey, and I feel rather uneasy when I think that I can receive no letters from you till I return to England ; but you may depend on this that I will avail myself of every opportunity of writing to you, though, from the very nature of the undertaking, these opportunities will be but few. We set off for the interior to-morrow morning, and I assure you, that whatever the issue of the present journey may be, every thing looks favourable. We have been successful thus far, beyond my highest expectations.

"The natives, instead of being frightened at us, look on us as their best friends, and the kings have not only granted us protection, but sent people to go before us. The soldiers are in the highest spirits ; and as many of them (like me) have left a wife and family in England, they are happy to embrace

this opportunity of returning. They never think about difficulties; and I am confident, if there was occasion for it, that
they would defeat any number of Negroes that might come
against us; but of this we have not the most distant expectation. The king of Kataba (the most powerful king in Gambia)
visited us on board the 'Crescent' on the 20th and 21st; he has
furnished us with a messenger to conduct us safely to the
king of Woolli.

"I expect to have an opportunity of writing to you from
Konkodoo or Bamakoo by some of the slave-traders; but as
they travel very slowly, I may probably have returned to the
coast before any of my letters have reached Goree; at any
rate, you need not be surprised if you should not hear from
me for some months; nay, so uncertain is the communication
between Africa and England, that perhaps the next news you
may hear may be my arrival in the latter, which I still think
will be in the month of December. If we have to go round
by the West Indies, it will take us two months more; but as
Government has given me an unlimited credit, if a vessel is
coming direct, I shall of course take a passage in her. I have
enjoyed excellent health, and have great hopes to bring
this expedition to a happy conclusion. In five weeks from
the date of this letter the worst part of the journey will be
over. Kiss all my dear children for me, and let them know
that their father loves them."

In a letter to Mr. Dickson, dated Kayee, April 26th, 1805,
the day before his embarkation, Park writes as follows:—
"Every thing at present looks as favourable as I could wish,
and if all things go well, this day six weeks I expect to drink

all your healths in the water of the Niger. The soldiers are in good health and spirits. They are the most *dashing* men I ever saw; and if they preserve their health, we may keep ourselves perfectly secure from any hostile attempt on the part of the natives. I have little doubt but that I shall be able, with presents and fair words, to pass through the country to the Niger; and if once we are fairly afloat, *the day is won.* Give my kind regards to Sir Joseph and Mr. Greville; and if they should think that I have paid too little attention to natural objects, you may mention that I had forty men and forty-two asses to look after, besides the constant trouble of packing and weighing bundles, palavering with the Negroes, and laying plans for our future success. I never was so busy in my life."

On reading this correspondence it is impossible not to be struck with the satisfaction expressed by Park, and the confidence with which he appears to have looked forward to a favourable termination of his journey. Yet in reality nothing could be much less promising than his actual situation and prospects at the time of writing these letters.

Besides the indifferent quality of the troops, there was another and more serious ground of alarm, from the unfavourable period at which, owing to a series of unforeseen delays, Park found himself obliged to enter on this expedition. This he was about to do, not actually during the rainy season, but with a great probability of being overtaken by it in the course of his journey; and with a positive certainty of encountering, in the meantime, not only the great tropical heats, but also the *tornadoes,* or hurricanes, which always precede and follow the rainy season.   These hurricanes, of which no idea can be formed from the experience of our temperate climates, occur more frequently, and with greater violence, as the rainy period approaches, and are attended with considerable inconvenience, and occasionally with danger, to caravans travelling at that season.

His situation was critical, and he had only a choice of difficulties.   He might either attempt to reach the Niger before the rainy season should be completely set in, or he might postpone his journey till the return of the proper season for travelling, which would be in November or December following. The event has shown that he would have acted more wisely in deferring the expedition.   But in this difficult situation he adopted that alternative which was most congenial to his character and feelings ; and having once formed this resolution he adhered to it with tranquillity and firmness ; dismissing from his own mind all doubts and apprehensions, or at least effectually concealing them from the companions of his journey, and from his friends and correspondents in England.

The persons composing the expedition being assembled at Kayee, a small town on the Gambia, a little below Pisania, Park engaged a Mandingo priest named Isaaco, who was also a travelling merchant, and much accustomed to long inland journeys, to serve as the guide to his caravan.   On the 27th of April 1805 he took his departure from Kayee, and arrived in two days at Pisania, from whence he had set out for the interior of Africa nearly ten years before.   Some of the practical difficulties of the march were apparent during this short journey, and he found it necessary to stop at Pisania six days (a delay which must have been highly inconvenient), to purchase additional beasts of burden, and make other arrangements for the expedition.

He quitted Kayee on the 4th of May, and arrived on the 11th at Madina, the capital of the kingdom of Woolli. The effects of the season had already become apparent, two of the soldiers having fallen ill of dysentery on the 8th. On the 15th he arrived on the banks of the Gambia, and about this time lost one of his soldiers by an epilepsy.

On the 26th the caravan experienced a singular accident (almost unintelligible to a European) from the attack of a large swarm of bees, in consequence of which, besides that many of the people were most severely stung, seven of their beasts of burden perished or were lost; and owing to an accidental fire which was kindled in the confusion, the whole baggage was near being burnt. For half an hour it seemed as if the bees had put an end to the expedition.

On the 28th of May, Park arrived at Badoo, where he mentions having had an opportunity of sending two letters to England by way of the Gambia. These letters were addressed to Sir Joseph Banks and Mrs. Park; the latter is as follows:—

To Mrs. Park.

"Badoo, 29th May 1805.

"I am happy to inform you that we are half through our journey without the smallest accident or unpleasant circumstance. We all of us keep our health, and are on the most friendly terms with the natives. I have seen many of my old acquaintances, and am everywhere well received. By the 27th of June we expect to have finished all our travels by land, and when we have once got afloat on the river, we shall conclude that we are embarking for England. I have **never** had the smallest sickness, and Alexander is quite free from all his stomach complaints.

"The bearer of this to the Gambia is waiting with his asses for a few minutes only. You will therefore inform all friends that we are well, and going on prosperously. I see no reason to think that our stay in the interior will be longer than I first mentioned.

"We carry our own victuals with us, and live very well ; in fact we have only had a pleasant journey, and yet this is what we thought would be the worst part of it.

"I will indulge the hope that my wife, children, and all friends are well. I am in great hopes of finishing this journey with credit in a few months, and then with what joy shall I turn my face towards home! The Slatee is impatient for the letter, and I have only time to subscribe myself," etc.

Notwithstanding this letter, Park's situation was now very critical. The tornadoes had begun to be frequent ; and a few days afterwards it became quite apparent that the rainy season was seriously setting in, before the journey to the Niger was more than half completed. The effect produced on the health of the soldiers by a violent rain on the 10th of June was almost instantaneous ; twelve of them at once were dangerously ill, and from this time the great mortality commenced which was ultimately fatal to the expedition.

At Shrondo, in the kingdom of Dentila, where the caravan shortly afterwards arrived, there are considerable gold mines ; and the journal contains a minute and interesting description both of the manner of collecting the metal, and of the country in which it is found.

After quitting Shrondo, Park mentions that in consequence of a very sudden tornado they were forced to carry their bundles into the huts of the natives, being the first time that the caravan had entered a town since leaving the Gambia. Considering the climate and season, this slight circumstance is alone a sufficient proof of the hardships which must have been sustained by Europeans in such a journey.

At Dindikoo, beyond Shrondo, Park was much struck with the beauty and magnificence of that mountainous tract of country, as well as with the extent to which it was cultivated, and the comparatively happy condition of the inhabitants. Proceeding a little further, he quitted the track he had hitherto followed, by which he had formerly returned from Kamalia to the Gambia, and directed his course towards the north-east, with a view probably of avoiding the Jallonka wilderness. But the difficulties of travelling were now become extreme, partly from the nature of the country, but principally from the increasing prevalence of the disease produced by the continued rains.

On the 4th of July he was nearly losing Isaaco, his guide ; who, in crossing a river, was twice attacked by a crocodile, and saved himself by extraordinary presence of mind, though not without some very severe wounds. This accident detained the caravan several days, and added to the numerous delays which had so unfortunately impeded the expedition.

Several of the soldiers had died during the course of the journey ; and on the 6th of July the whole number of persons composing the caravan (except one) were either actually sick, or in a state of great debility. Yet he still had great difficulties to encounter, in traversing a country where he was obliged to be constantly on the watch against the depredations of the inhabitants, and occasionally the attacks of wild beasts. Under such circumstances it is not wonderful that the few soldiers not disabled by sickness fell back, and it was with great difficulty that any of them could be prevailed on to continue their march. The dangers and sufferings he had now to encounter were such as have been experienced by few travellers, and their narration forms the most interesting part of his second journal, as follows :—

Aug. 6th, 1805.—Having hired two more ass-drivers, at one bar and their victuals per day, we left Koolihori early in the morning, and travelled with considerable despatch till three o'clock, at which time we reached Ganifarra, a small beggarly village. In the course of this march, L. Cahill and J. Bird, two of the soldiers, and William Cox, one of the seamen, fell behind, and lay down. As soon as the front of the coffle had reached Ganifarra it came on a very heavy rain. Being in the rear, I was completely drenched ; and two of the asses, carrying four trunks, in which were the gun-stocks, pistols, looking-glasses, etc., fell down in a stream of water near the town, and all the contents were completely wet. I could purchase nothing here, not so much as a fowl. Served out a short allowance of rice, being very short of that article.

Aug. 7th.—During the night some person had stolen one of our best asses ; and as the load must be left if we could not recover it, Isaaco's people, having traced the footmarks to a considerable distance, agreed to go in search of it. Isaaco gave them the strictest orders, if they came up to the thief in the woods, to shoot him ; and if not, to follow him to a town and demand the ass from the Dooty ; if he refused to give it up, to return as soon as possible.

Spent the day in drying such things as were wet; cleaned and greased with shea-butter all the ornamented pistols, *ten pairs*. Dried the looking-glasses, which were quite spoiled. In the afternoon sent two of the natives away with goods to a neighbouring town to purchase rice and corn. At sun-set Bird came up, but had seen nothing of Cox nor Cahill.

Aug. 8th.—People not yet returned. Opened the trunk which contained the double-barrelled gun stocks; cleaned and greased them. About noon people returned with the rice and corn, but not quite sufficient for one day. Nearly at the same time Isaaco's people came up with the ass; they had traced his footmarks past Koolihori, and found him at Balandoo. Did not see the thief, but learned his name, which Isaaco promised to communicate to his friend Serinummo at Bangassi. In the afternoon agreed with the Dooty for thirty-five bars to carry everything over. Rained heavily all the evening.

Aug. 9th.—Michael May, a soldier, having died during the night, buried him at daybreak. Had all the loads taken to the crossing place by eight o'clock. The Ba Woolli is nearly of the same size as the one we formerly crossed of that name. It appeared to be exceedingly deep, and flowed at the rate of four or five miles per hour. There is a very good canoe here, which can carry over four ass-loads at once. As it threatened rain, sent over three men with one of the tents, and pitched it on the east side, about half a mile from the river, the ground near the bank being marshy. Hired people to carry down the bundles and put them into the canoe, and others to receive them on the other side and carry them up the bank; so that the soldiers had nothing to move, being all weak and sickly.

By one o'clock all the baggage was over; but we found some difficulty in transporting the asses; the rapidity of the stream swept the canoe and the first six past the landing-place; and they went so far down the river that I really thought the asses must be drowned, which would have been an irreparable loss in our situation. However, by the exertions of the Negroes, who swam in with ropes to the canoe, the asses were landed on the other side, where they stood by the water's edge until the Negroes, with their corn-hoes, made a path for them up the steep bank. To prevent such an accident, we took the ropes from several of our loads, and fastened them together so as to reach across the river; with this we hauled over the loaded canoe, and the Negroes paddled it back when empty. In this manner all the asses and horses were swam over without any loss.

When the bundles were all carried up to the tent, we found that we had not more rice than was barely sufficient for the present day; and as no more could be purchased, we had no alternative but to march early in the morning for Bambarra; the distance by all accounts would not exceed fourteen or fifteen miles.

Aug. 10th.—William Ashton declared that he was unable to travel; but as there was no place to leave him at, I advised him to make an exertion and come on, though slowly, till he should reach a place where he could have food. At eight o'clock set forwards, and travelled very expeditiously without halting till four in the afternoon, at which time the front of the coffle reached Dabadoo, a village of Bambarra. Being in the rear, I found many of the men very much fatigued with the length of the journey and the heat of the day. At half-

Here I found many of the soldiers sitting, and Mr. Anderson apparently dying. —Page 357

past four I arrived with the ass I drove at a stream flowing to the westwards.

Here I found many of the soldiers sitting, and Mr. Anderson lying under a bush, apparently dying. Took him on my back and carried him across the stream, which came up to my middle. Carried over the load of the ass which I drove, got over the ass, Mr. Anderson's horse, etc. Found myself much fatigued, having crossed the stream sixteen times. Left here four soldiers with their asses, being unable to carry over their loads. Having loaded my ass and put Mr. Anderson on his horse, we went on to the village; but was sorry to find that no rice could be had, and I was only able to buy one solitary fowl.

Aug. 11th.—Bought a small bullock of the Moorish breed for one barraloolo; and having purchased some corn, had it cleaned and dressed for the people instead of rice. This morning hired Isaaco's people to go back and bring up the loads of the soldiers who had halted by the side of the stream. In the course of the day all the loads arrived; but was sorry to find that in the course of the last two marches we had lost four men, viz., Cox, Cahill, Bird, and Ashton. Mr. Anderson still in a very dangerous way, being unable to walk or sit upright. Mr. Scott much recovered. I found that I must here leave one load, one of the horses being quite finished. Left the seine-nets in charge of the Dooty till I should send for them.

Aug. 12th.—Rained all the morning. About eleven o'clock, the sky being clear, loaded the asses. None of the Europeans being able to lift a load, Isaaco made the Negroes load the whole. Saddled Mr. Anderson's horse, and having put a sick soldier on mine, took Mr. Anderson's horse by the bridle, that

he might have no trouble but sitting upright on the saddle.
We had not gone far before I found one of the asses with a
load of gunpowder, the driver (Dickinson) being unable to
proceed (I never heard of him afterwards); and shortly after
the sick man dismounted from my horse, and lay down by a
small pool of water, refusing to rise. Drove the ass and horse
on before me. Passed a number of sick. At half past twelve
o'clock Mr. Anderson declared he could ride no farther. Took
him down and laid him in the shade of a bush, and sat down
beside him. At half-past two o'clock he made another attempt
to proceed; but had not rode above a hundred yards before I
had to take him down from the saddle, and lay him again in the
shade. I now gave up all thoughts of being able to carry him
forwards till the cool of the evening; and having turned the
horses and ass to feed, I sat down to watch the pulsations of
my dying friend. At four o'clock four of the sick came up;
three of them agreed to take charge of the ass with the
gunpowder; and I put the fourth, who had a sore leg, on
my horse, telling him if he saw Mr. Scott on the road to give
him the horse.

At half-past five o'clock, there being a fine breeze from the
south-west, Mr. Anderson agreed to make another attempt;
and having again placed him on the saddle, I led the horse on
pretty smartly in hopes of reaching Koomikoomi before dark.
We had not proceeded above a mile before we heard on our
left a noise very much like the barking of a large mastiff, but
ending in a hiss like the *fuf* of a cat. I thought it must be
some large monkey; and was observing to Mr. Anderson,
"What a bouncing fellow that must be," when we heard
another bark nearer to us, and presently a third still nearer,

accompanied with a growl. I now suspected that some wild animal meant to attack us, but could not conjecture of what species it was likely to be. We had not proceeded a hundred yards further when, coming to an opening in the bushes, I was not a little surprised to see three lions coming towards us. They were not so red as the lion I formerly saw in Bambarra, but of a dusky colour, like the colour of an ass. They were very large, and came bounding over the long grass, not one after another, but all abreast of each other. I was afraid, if I allowed them to come too near us and my piece should miss fire, that we should be all devoured by them ; I therefore let go the bridle, and walked forwards to meet them. As soon as they were within a long shot of me I fired at the centre one. I do not think I hit him ; but they all stopt, looked at each other, and then bounded away a few paces, when one of them stopt and looked back at me. I was too busy in loading my piece to observe their motions as they went away, and was very happy to see the last of them march slowly off amongst the bushes. We had not proceeded above half a mile farther, when we heard another bark and growl close to us amongst the bushes. This was doubtless one of the lions before seen, and I was afraid they would follow us till dark, when they would have too many opportunities of springing on us unawares. I therefore got Mr. Anderson's call, and made as loud a whistling and noise as possible. We heard no more of them.

Just at dark we descended into a valley where was a small stream of water ; but the ascent on the opposite side was through a species of broken ground, which I have never seen anywhere but in Africa. It is of the following nature : A stratum of stiff yellow clay fourteen or twenty feet thick (which, unless when it rains, is as hard as rock) is washed by the annual rains into fissures of a depth equal to the thickness of the stratum. There is no vegetation on these places, except on the summit or original level. Amongst these horrid gulleys I unfortunately lost sight of the footmarks of the asses which had gone before; and finding no way to get out, led the horse up a very steep place in order to gain the original level, hoping there to find the footpath. But unluckily the ground was all broken as far as I could see; and after travelling some little way, we came to a gully which we could not cross; and finding no possibility of moving without the danger of being killed by falling into some of these ravines, or over some precipice, I thought it advisable to halt till the morning. On this rugged summit we fell in with Jonas Watkins, one of the sick, and with his assistance I lighted a fire. Wrapped Mr. Anderson in his cloak, and laid him down beside it. Watched all night to keep the fire burning, and prevent our being surprised by the lions, which we knew were at no great distance. About two o'clock in the morning two more of the sick joined us. Mr. Anderson slept well during the night, and as soon as day dawned—

Aug. 13th.—Having found the footmarks of the asses, and having with difficulty, even in daylight, traced our way through this labyrinth, we found Mr. Scott and three more of the sick. They too had lost their way, and had slept about half a mile to the east of us. We reached Koomikoomi at ten o'clock. This is an unwalled village, but surrounded with extensive corn-fields.

Aug. 14th.—Jonas Watkins died this morning; buried him. Halted here to-day to see which way Mr. Anderson's fever was likely to terminate ; and in the meantime sent two loaded asses forward to Doombila, the asses to return in the evening and carry loads to-morrow morning. It is a common observation of the Negroes that when the Indian corn is in blossom the rain stops for eleven days. The stopping of the rain evidently depends on the sun approaching the zenith of the place, the sun by this day's observation being only seventy-one miles north of us ; and it is a wonderful institution of Providence, that at this time the maize here is all in full blossom, and on passing through the fields one is like to be blinded with the pollen of the male flowers.

Aug. 15th.—Having slung a cloak like a hammock under a straight stick, had Mr. Anderson put into it, and carried on two men's heads, two more following to relieve them. Mr. Scott complained this morning of sickness and headache. Made one of the soldiers saddle Mr. Anderson's horse for him ; and having seen him mount and given him his canteen with water, I rode forwards to look after four negroes whom I had hired to carry loads on their heads ; but being strangers, I was apprehensive they might run away with them. Found everything going on well ; and we travelled with such expedition that we reached Doombila in four hours and a half, though the distance cannot be less than sixteen or eighteen miles, nearly south. It rained hard all the afternoon, and it was not till dark that all the sick soldiers came up. Only three of the soldiers were able to drive their asses to-day.

When I entered the town I was happy to meet *Karfa Taura*, the worthy Negro mentioned in my former travels. He heard a report at *Boori* (where he now resides) that a coffle of white people were passing through Fooladoo for

Bambarra, and that they were conducted by a person of the name of Park, who spoke Mandingo. He heard this report in the evening ; and in the morning he left his house, determined if possible to meet me at Bambakoo, a distance of six days' travel. He came to Bambakoo with three of his slaves to assist me in going forward to Sego ; but when he found I had not come up, he came forwards to meet me. He instantly recognised me, and you may judge of the pleasure I felt on seeing my old benefactor.

About four o'clock, as Mr. Scott had not come up, and the people in the rear had not seen him lately, I sent one of Isaaco's people back on my horse as far as the next village, suspecting that he might have halted there when the rain came on. The man returned after dark, having been nearly at Koomikoomi without seeing or hearing anything of Mr. Scott. We all concluded that he had returned to Koomikoomi.

Aug. 17th.—Halted at Doombila in order to dry the baggage, and in hopes of Mr. Scott coming up. Told the four Negroes who carried Mr. Anderson, and who returned to Koomikoomi this morning, to make every possible inquiry concerning Mr. Scott ; and if he was able to ride, I would pay them handsomely for coming with him. If he had returned to Koomikoomi, I desired them to assure the Dooty that I would pay for every expense he might incur, and pay for a guide to conduct him to Marraboo. Received from the Dooty of Doombila a small bullock and a sheep. Paid him a barraloolo, five bars of amber, and fifty gun-flints.

Aug. 18th.—Hearing no account of Mr. Scott, concluded he was still at Koomikoomi, but unable to travel. At seven o'clock left Doombila ; and as the asses were now very weak, it was not long before I had to dismount and put a load on my horse. Only one of the soldiers able to drive an ass. Road very bad ; did not reach Toniba till sunset, being a distance of eighteen or twenty miles S.E. by S. Mr. Anderson's bearers halted with him at a village on the road, where there was some good beer. As soon as we had pitched the tent it began to rain, and rained all night ; the soldiers all ran into the village. I passed a very disagreeable night, having to keep our asses from eating the people's corn, which caused me to keep walking about almost the whole night.

In case it should escape my memory, I take this opportunity of observing that the standard law of Africa runs thus : If an ass should break a single stem of corn, the proprietor of the corn has a right to seize the ass ; and if the owner of the ass will not satisfy him for the damage he thinks he has sustained, he can *retain* the ass. He cannot *sell* or *work* him, but he can *kill* him ; and as the Bambarrans esteem ass-flesh as a great luxury, this part of the law is often put in force.

Aug. 19th.—Mr. Anderson's bearers having brought him forward early in the morning, we immediately loaded the asses and departed from Toniba (Serjeant M'Keal appears to be slightly delirious). We kept ascending the mountains to the south of Toniba till three o'clock, at which time, having gained the summit of the ridge which separates the Niger from the remote branches of the Senegal, I went on a little before ; and coming to the brow of the hill, I *once more saw the Niger* rolling its immense stream along the plain !

After the fatiguing march which we had experienced, the sight of this river was no doubt pleasant, as it promised an end to, or to be at least an alleviation of, our toils. But when I

three-fourths of the soldiers had died on their
at in addition to our weakly state we had no car-
rs to build the boats in which we proposed to prosecute
r discoveries, the prospect appeared somewhat gloomy. It
however afforded me peculiar pleasure, when I reflected that
in conducting a party of *Europeans*, with immense baggage,
through an extent of more than five hundred miles, I had
always been able to preserve the most friendly terms with the
natives. In fact, this journey plainly demonstrates,—1st. That
with common prudence any quantity of merchandise may be
transported from the Gambia to the Niger without danger of
being robbed by the natives; 2d. That if this journey be performed in the dry season, one may calculate on losing not
more than three, or at most four, men out of fifty.

But to return to the Niger. The river was much swelled
by the rains, but did not appear to overflow its banks. It certainly is larger even here than either the Senegal or the Gambia.
We descended with difficulty down the steep side of the hill
towards Bambakoo, which place we reached at half-past six
o'clock, and pitched our tents under a tree near the town. Of
thirty-four soldiers and four carpenters who left the Gambia,
only six soldiers and one carpenter reached the Niger. During
the night the wolves carried away two large cloth bundles
from the tent-door to a considerable distance, where they
ate off the skins with which they were covered, and left
them.

Aug. 20th.—Received a bullock from the Dooty as a present.
It was in the afternoon, and we fastened it to the tree close to
the tent, where all the asses were tied. As soon as it was dark
the wolves tore its bowels out, though within ten yards of the

tent-door where we were all sitting. The wolves here are the largest and most ferocious we have yet seen.

Aug. 21st.—Dried a bundle of beads, the strings of which were all rotten with the rain. Opened a leather bag which contained about thirty pounds of gunpowder for present use. Found it all wet and damaged. Spread it out in the sun, resolved to make something of it. Spoke for a canoe to carry down the baggage to Marraboo, the river being navigable over the rapids at this season. In the course of our march from Toniba to Bambakoo, we lost Serjeant M'Keal, Purvey, and Samuel Hill.

Aug. 22d.—Early in the morning had all the bundles put on the asses and carried to the place of embarkation, which is a village called Bossradoo, about a mile and a half east of Bammakoo. It rained hard all the forenoon. The canoes could not carry any of the soldiers, or any person, except two to look after the goods. I resolved to go down with Mr. Anderson, leaving Mr. Martyn to come down with the men by land. They rode on the asses.

We embarked at ten minutes past three o'clock. The current, which is nearly five knots per hour, set us along without the trouble of rowing any more than was necessary to keep the canoe in the proper course. The river is full an English mile over, and at the rapids it is spread out to nearly twice that breadth. The rapids seem to be formed by the river passing through a ridge of hills in a south-easterly direction; they are very numerous, and correspond with the jetting angles of the hills. There are *three* principal ones, where the water breaks with considerable noise in the middle of the river; but the canoe-men easily avoid them by paddling down one of the branches near the shore. Even in this manner the velocity was such as to make me sigh.

We passed two of the principal rapids, and three smaller ones, in the course of the afternoon. We saw on one of the islands in the middle of the river a large elephant; it was of a red clay colour, with black legs. I was very unwell of dysentery, otherwise I would have had a shot at him, for he was quite near us. We saw three hippopotami close to another of these islands. The canoe-men were afraid they might follow us and overset the canoes. The report of a musket will in all cases frighten them away. They blow up the water exactly like a whale. As we were gliding along shore one of the canoe-men speared a fine turtle, of the same species as the one I formerly saw and made a drawing of in Gambia. At sunset we rowed to the shore, landed on some flat rocks, and set about cooking the turtle and rice for our supper; but before this aldermanic repast was half dressed the rain came on us, and continued with great violence all night.

Aug. 23d.—At daybreak embarked again, very wet and sleepy. Passed the third rapid, and arrived at Marraboo at nine o'clock. Our guide soon found a large passage hut in which to deposit our baggage, for one stone of small amber per load. We carried the whole of it up in a few minutes. In the evening Mr. Martyn arrived and all the people, except two, who came up next day.

Aug. 24th.—Received from the Dooty a small black bullock in a present, which our guide would not allow us to kill, it being of a jet-black colour. The Dooty's name is Sokee; and so superstitious was he, that all the time we remained at Marraboo he kept himself in his hut, conceiving that if he saw a white man he would never prosper after.

Aug. 25th.—Paid Isaaco goods to the full value of two prime slaves, according to agreement. I likewise gave him several articles, and told him that when the palaver was adjusted at Sego, he should then have all the asses and horses for his trouble.

Aug. 26.—Took out such things as I meant to give to Mansong—viz. A handsome silver-plated tureen; *two double-barrelled guns, silver-mounted; two pairs of pistols mounted in the same manner; a sabre with morocco scabbard; thirty-two yards scarlet broad cloth; twelve ditto blue; twelve ditto yellow; twelve ditto light green; *half-a-load of gunpowder, or two kegs and a half.

To Mansong's eldest son *Da :*—*A double-barrelled gun, silver-mounted; a pair of pistols, ditto; a sabre, ditto.

I wished to put a stop to the malicious reports of the Moors and Mahomedans at Sego as soon as possible. I therefore resolved to send Isaaco forward to Sego with all the articles before mentioned, except those marked thus, * which I desired him to say to Modibinne would be given as soon as I heard accounts that Mansong would befriend us. This Modibinne is Mansong's prime minister. He is a Mahomedan, but not intolerant in his principles. Isaaco accordingly departed on the 28th with his wife and all his goods. Ever since my arrival at Marraboo I had been subject to attacks of dysentery; and as I found that my strength was failing very fast, I resolved to charge myself with mercury. I accordingly took calomel till it affected my mouth to such a degree that I could not speak or sleep for six days. The salivation put an immediate stop to the dysentery, which had proved fatal to so many of the soldiers. As soon as I recovered, I set about exchanging some amber and coral for cowries, which are the current money of Bambarra.

				Cowries.
Coral No. 4, each stone	.	.	.	60
Amber No. 5	.		.	· 60
Blue agates, per string	.	·.	.	100

With these three articles I bought about twenty thousand cowries. It is curious that in counting the cowries they call eighty a hundred; whilst in all other things they calculate by the common hundred. Sixty is called a Manding hundred.

On the 6th Thomas Dyer (a private) died of fever. I had to pay one thousand shells to Dooty Sokee before he would allow me to bury him; alleging that if the ground was not bought where he was buried it would never grow good corn after.

There is no wood proper for boat-building in this neighbourhood; the best wood is near Kankaree, on a large navigable branch of the Niger, and almost all the Bambarra canoes come from thence; many of them are mahogany.

The travellers from Sego brought us every day some unfavourable news or other. At one time it was reported, and believed all over Marraboo, that Mansong had killed Isaaco with his own hand, and would do the same with all the whites who should come into Bambarra. Our fears were at length dispelled by the arrival of Bookari, Mansong's singing-man, on the 8th, with six canoes. He told us he came by Mansong's orders to convey us and our baggage to Sego; that Mansong thought highly of the presents which Isaaco had brought, and wished us to be brought to Sego before he received them from Isaaco. We accordingly put our baggage in order;

but it was not till the 12th that the singing-man and his
Somonies (canoe people) could be prevailed on to leave Dooty
Sokee's good beef and beer.   We embarked, and left Marraboo
at ten minutes past three o'clock.

Sept. 13th.—Bookari sent four of the Somonies over to a
town on the opposite side of the river, to put in requisition a
canoe for carrying part of our baggage.   The people refused
to give the canoe, and sent the Somonies back without it.
Bookari immediately went with all the Somonies (thirty-eight),
and having cut the owner of the canoe across the forehead
with his sword, and broke his brother's head with a canoe-
paddle, he seized one of his sons, and brought him away as a
slave, along with the canoe.   He, however, set the boy at
liberty, his father paying two thousand shells for his release.

We left Koolikorro at thirty-five minutes past eleven, and
travelled very pleasantly all day.   In fact, nothing can be
more beautiful than the views of this immense river ; sometimes as smooth as a mirror, at other times ruffled with a gentle
breeze, but at all times sweeping us along at the rate of six or
seven miles per hour.   We halted for the night at Deena, a
Somoni village on the south side.   Had a tornado in the night,
which wetted our baggage much.   Most of us slept in the
canoes to prevent theft.

Sept. 14th.—Departed from Deena early in the morning,
and arrived at Yamina at forty-five minutes past four o'clock.
Halted here the 15th, in order to purchase cowries.

On the 16th left Yamina, and in the evening reached
Samee, where we landed our baggage ; and Bookari went
forward to Sego to inform Mansong of our arrival.

Sept. 18th.—No accounts from Sego.

Sept. 19th.—About two o'clock in the morning Isaaco
arrived in a canoe from Sego, with all the articles I had sent
to Mansong. Mansong had never yet seen any of them; and
when he heard that I was arrived at Samee, he desired
Modibinne to inform Isaaco that he had best take the articles
up to Samee; and he would send a person to receive them
from my own hand. Isaaco informed me that Mansong, at
all the interviews he had with him, uniformly declared that
he would allow us to pass; but whenever Isaaco mentioned
us particularly, or related any incident that had happened on
the journey, Mansong immediately began to make squares
and triangles in the sand before him with his finger, and
continued to do so so long as Isaaco spoke about us. Isaaco
said that he thought Mansong was rather afraid of us;
particularly as he never once expressed a wish to see us, but
rather the contrary.

Sept. 22d.—In the evening Modibinne and four more of
Mansong's friends arrived in a canoe. They sent for me, and
Modibinne told me that they were come by Mansong's orders
to hear, from my own mouth, what had brought me into
Bambarra. He said I might think on it during the night, and
they would visit me in the morning; he said Mansong had
sent me a bullock, which he showed me; it was very fat, and
milk-white.

Sept. 23d.—As soon as we had breakfasted, Modibinne and
the four grandees came to visit us. When they had seated
themselves, and the usual compliments passed, Modibinne desired me to acquaint them with the motives which had induced
me to come into their country. I spoke to them in the Bambarra language as follows :—" I am the white man who nine

years ago came into Bambarra. I then came to Sego, and requested Mansong's permission to pass to the eastwards ; he not only permitted me to pass, but presented me with five thousand cowries to purchase provisions on the road ; for you all know that the Moors had robbed me of my goods. This generous conduct of Mansong towards me has made his name much respected in the land of the white people. The king of that country has sent me again into Bambarra, and if Mansong is inclined to protect me, and you, who are sitting, wish to befriend me, I will inform you of the real object of my coming into your country.

(Here Modibinne desired me to speak on, as they were all my friends.) "You all know that the white people are a trading people ; and that all the articles of value which the Moors and the people of Jinnie bring to Sego, are made by us. If you speak of a good gun, who made it?—the *white people*. If you speak of a good pistol or sword, or piece of scarlet or baft, or beads, or gunpowder, who made them?—the *white people*. We sell them to the Moors ; the Moors bring them to Timbuctoo, where they sell them at a *higher rate*. The people of Timbuctoo sell them to the people of Jinnie at a still higher price ; and the people of Jinnie sell them to you. Now, the king of the white people wishes to find out a way by which we may bring our own merchandise to you, and sell everything at a much cheaper rate than you now have them. For this purpose, if Mansong will permit me to pass, I propose sailing down the Joliba to the place where it mixes with the salt water ; and if I find no rocks or danger in the way, the white men's small vessels will come up and trade at Sego, if Mansong wishes it. What I have now spoken I hope and trust you will not men-

tion to any person except Mansong and his son; for if the
Moors should hear of it, I shall certainly be murdered before
I reach the salt water."

Modibinne answered: "We have heard what you have
spoken. Your journey is a good one, and may God prosper
you in it; Mansong will protect you. We will carry your
words to Mansong this afternoon; and to-morrow we will bring
you his answer." I made Isaaco show them the different things
which I allotted for Mansong and his son. They were delighted
with the tureen, the double-barrelled guns, and in fact everything was far superior to anything of the kind they had ever
before seen.

When I had laid out everything for Mansong and his son,
I then made each of the grandees, and Modibinne, a present of
scarlet cloth. Modibinne now said that they had seen what I
laid out for Mansong and his son, and that the present was
great and worthy of Mansong; but, added he, Mansong has
heard so many reports concerning your baggage, that he wishes
us to examine it. "Such of the bundles as are covered with
skin, we will not open: you will tell us what is in them, and
that will be sufficient." I told them that I had nothing but
what was necessary for purchasing provisions; and that it
would please me much if they could dispense with opening the
bundles. They, however, persisted; and I ordered the bundles
to be brought out, taking care, with the assistance of the
soldiers, to secrete all the good amber and coral.

When all the loads were inspected, I asked Modibinne what
he thought of my baggage? If he had seen any more silver
tureens, or double-barrelled guns? He said he had seen nothing
that was *bad*, and nothing but what was necessary for

purchasing provisions; that he would report the same to Mansong. They accordingly went away to Sego; but without taking Mansong's present, till they had heard his answer.

Sept. 24th.—Seed and Barber (soldiers) died during the night; one of fever, the other of dysentery. Paid the Somonies twenty stones of amber for burying them. —) still re cip routy le !

Sept. 25th.—Modibinne and the same people returned with Mansong's answer, a literal translation of which I give as follows :—" Mansong says he will protect you; that a road is open for you everywhere, so far as his hand (power) extends. If you wish to go to the east, no man shall harm you from Sego till you pass Timbuctoo; if you wish to go to the west, you may travel through Fooladoo and Manding, through Kasson and Bondou; the name of Mansong's stranger will be a sufficient protection for you. If you wish to build your boats at Samee or Sego, at Sansanding or Jinnie, name the town, and Mansong will convey you thither." He concluded by observing, that Mansong wished me to sell him four of the blunderbusses, three swords, a fiddle (violin) which belonged to Mr. Scott, and some Birmingham bead necklaces, which pleased above everything; that he had sent us a bullock, and his son another, with a fine sheep. I told Modibinne that Mansong's friendship was of more value to me than the articles he had mentioned, and that I would be happy if Mansong would accept them from me as a further proof of my esteem. I made choice of Sansanding for fitting out our canoe, because Mansong had never said he wished to see me, and because I could live quieter and freer from begging than at Sego. I therefore sent down the bullocks by land to Sansanding.

Sept. 26th.—We departed from Samee. The canoes were

not covered with mats; and there being no wind, the sun became insufferably hot. I felt myself affected with a violent headache, which increased to such a degree as to make me almost delirious. I never felt so hot a day; there was *sensible heat* sufficient to have roasted a *sirloin;* but the thermometer was in a bundle in the other canoe, so that I could not ascertain the *actual* heat. We passed down a small stream to the north of Sego Korro, and halted opposite to Segosee Korro, near the sand-hills, where I formerly waited for a passage. We waited here about an hour for Isaaco, who had gone to Segosee Korro to inform Mansong of our passing. When Isaaco returned, he made a sort of shade over our canoe with four sticks and a couple of cloaks; and in the evening I found myself more collected and less feverish. At sunset we rowed towards the north bank, where there are some flat rocks on which passengers by water often sleep. We found the place occupied by a number of people. I counted between thirty and forty fires; we therefore passed on a little to the eastwards, and slept on a sand-bank covered with verdure.

Sept. 27th.—At daybreak we again proceeded, and in stretching over to gain the middle of the river, we passed a Somoni fishing-village on an island; the huts occupied the whole of the dry ground, and it appeared, even when close to it, like a floating village. We reached Sansanding at ten o'clock. Such crowds of people came to the shore to see us that we could not land our baggage till the people were beaten away with sticks, by Koontie Mamadie's orders, on whose premises we were accommodated with a large hut for sitting in, having another hut opening into it, in which we deposited our baggage.

Oct. 2d.—Marshall and W. Garland (privates) died; one of fever, the other of dysentery. During the night the wolves carried away Garland, the door of the hut where he died being left open. Buried Marshall on the morning following, in a corn-field near the church.

Oct. 4th.—Mansong sent down two broken gun-locks, and a large pewter plate with a hole in the bottom of it, for me to repair; and it was with much difficulty that I could persuade the messenger that none of us knew anything about such occupations.

Oct. 6th.—*Da*, Mansong's eldest son, sent one canoe as a present, and requested me to sell him a blunderbuss and three swords, with some blue and yellow broadcloth. Sent him three swords, and ten spans of yellow cloth; received in return six thousand cowries.

Sansanding contains, according to Koontie Mamadie's account, eleven thousand inhabitants. It has no public buildings except the mosques, two of which, though built of mud, are by no means inelegant. The market-place is a large square, and the different articles of merchandise are exposed for sale on stalls covered with mats, to shade them from the sun. The market is crowded with people from morning to night; some of the stalls contain nothing but beads; others, indigo in balls; others, wood-ashes in balls; others, Houssa and Jinnie cloth. I observed one stall with nothing but antimony in small bits, another with sulphur, and a third with copper and silver rings and bracelets. In the houses fronting the square are sold scarlet, amber, silks from Morocco, and tobacco, which looks like Levant tobacco, and comes by way of Timbuctoo. Adjoining this is the salt-market, part of which occupies one corner of the square. A slab of salt is sold commonly for eight thousand cowries ; a large butcher's stall, or shade, is in the centre of the square, and as good and fat meat sold every day as any in England. The beer-market is at a little distance, under two large trees ; and there are often exposed for sale from eighty to one hundred calabashes of beer, each containing about two gallons. Near the beer-market is the place where red and yellow leather is sold.

Besides these market-places, there is a very large space which is appropriated for the great market every Tuesday. On this day astonishing crowds of people come from the country to purchase articles in wholesale, and retail them in the different villages, etc. There are commonly from sixteen to twenty large fat Moorish bullocks killed on the market morning.

Oct. 8th—As Mansong had delayed much longer in sending the canoes he promised than I expected, I thought it best to be provided with a sufficient quantity of shells to purchase two, particularly when I reflected that the river would subside in the course of a few days, having sunk this morning about four inches by the shore. I therefore opened shop in great style, and exhibited a choice assortment of European articles to be sold in wholesale or retail. I had of course a *great run,* which I suppose drew on me the envy of my brother merchants, for the Jinnie people, the Moors, and the merchants here joined with those of the same description at Sego, and (in presence of Modibinne, from whose mouth I had it) offered to give Mansong a quantity of merchandise of greater value than all the presents I had made him, if he would seize our baggage, and either kill us, or send us back again out of Bambarra.

They alleged that my object was to kill Mansong and his sons by means of charms, that the white people might come and seize on the country. Mansong, much to his honour, rejected the proposal, though it was seconded by two-thirds of the people of Sego, and almost all Sansanding.

From the 8th to the 16th nothing of consequence occurred. I found my shop every day more and more crowded with customers; and such was my run of business that I was sometimes forced to employ *three tellers at once* to count my cash. I turned one market-day twenty-five thousand seven hundred and fifty-six pieces of money (cowries).

The second day after my arrival at Marraboo, as no accounts whatever had arrived concerning Mr. Scott, I sent a messenger to Koomikoomi, desiring him to bring Mr. Scott or some account of him. He returned in four days, and told us that *Mr. Scott was dead,* and that the natives had stolen the pistols out of the holsters; but he had brought the horse to Bambakoo.

When Modibinne inquired of Isaaco what sort of a *return of presents* would be most agreeable to me, Isaaco (being instructed before) said he believed two large canoes; and Modibinne assured me that the canoes would be sent down to Sansanding immediately on our arrival there.

Oct. 16th.—Modibinne and Jower arrived, and told me that they had brought a canoe from Mansong. I went to see it, and objected to one-half of it, which was quite rotten. They sent up to Sego for another half, but when it arrived it would not fit the one already sent. I was therefore forced to send Isaaco again to Sego; and as Mansong had requested me by Modibinne to sell him any spare arms I might have, I sent two blunderbusses, two fowling-pieces, two pairs of pistols, and five unserviceable muskets, requesting in return that Mansong would either send a proper canoe, or permit me to purchase one, that I might proceed on my journey. Isaaco returned on the 20th with a large canoe; but half of it was very much decayed and patched. I therefore set about joining the best half to the half formerly sent, and, with the assistance of Abraham Bolton (private), took out all the rotten pieces, and repaired all the holes and sewed places; and, with eighteen days' hard labour, changed the Bambarra canoe into *His Majesty's schooner Jolibu;* the length forty feet, breadth six feet; being flat-bottomed, draws only one foot water when loaded.

Oct. 28th.—At a quarter past five o'clock in the morning my dear friend, Mr. Alexander Anderson, died, after a sickness of four months. I feel much inclined to speak of his merits; but as his worth was known only to a few friends, I will rather cherish his memory in silence, and imitate his cool and steady conduct, than weary my friends with a panegyric in which they cannot be supposed to join. I shall only observe that no event which took place during the journey ever threw the smallest gloom over my mind till I laid Mr. Anderson in the grave. I then felt myself as if left a second time, lonely and friendless, amidst the wilds of Africa.

Nov. 14th.—The schooner is now nearly ready for our departure. I only wait for Isaaco's return from Sego that I may give him this paper in charge.

Nov. 15th.—Isaaco returned, and told us that Mansong was anxious that I should depart as soon as possible, before the Moors to the east had intimation of my coming. Bought

bullock-hides to form an awning to secure us from the spears
and arrows of the Surka or Soorka and Mahinga, who inhabit
the north bank of the river betwixt Jinnie and Timbuctoo.

Nov. 16th.—All ready, and we sail to-morrow morning or
evening. I will therefore conclude this long epistle with
some miscellaneous information.

Ba Nimma rises in the Kong mountains south of Marraboo; it passes one day's journey south of Sego, and having
received a branch from Miniana, empties itself into the lake
Dibbie. It is not quite half so large as the Niger. I have
not the least doubt of the truth of this, having heard it from
so many people. We shall not see Jinnie in going to Timbuctoo.

Route from Sego to Miniana.

From Sego in one day, Deena, cross the Ba Nimma in
canoes, and halt on the south side; thence in one day,
Dahmaroo, Sijirri, Neaguana, Mullo Soo, Billi Soo; in all
seven days.

The inhabitants of Miniana eat their enemies, and
strangers, if they die in the country. They eat the flesh of
horses, but such is their veneration for the cow that she is
never killed; when she dies they eat the flesh. Miniana is
hilly. All the grains are cultivated the same as in Bambarra.

Route from Sego to Bœdoo.

From Sego in one day. Koogoo, N. goi,* Jeena, Doo-
Wassoo, Choyna, Guandoo on the banks of the Badingfing, a
small river from Miniana. Cheraboo, Baboo, Blendoo, Koolo-
koo, Kay-a, Wangeera, Jibbi, Nemansana, Kooli, Chemosoo,

---

* Thus written in Park's MS.

N. Jeera, Chekora, Koonteela, Doomba, Choongi, Teng: gera, a great Juli town; a Juli is called in Bædoo, Kirko Bimba; Teeleemagee, Soomasoo, Koorinsoo, Jondoo; Juli town, Sala, N. Kannoo, Juli town.

The whole of the foregoing places are in Bambarra.

Totti, a town in Bædoo. Bædoo the capital.

The Julis are people who understand the language of Bædoo and Miniana, and are employed as interpreters and brokers by the salt-merchants. One month's travel south of Bædoo through the kingdom of Gotto will bring the traveller to the country of the Christians, who have their houses on the banks of the *Ba Sea feena.* This water they represent as being incomparably larger than the lake Dibbie, and that the water sometimes flows one way, sometimes another. There are no shea-trees in Kong or Gotto, and very few in Bædoo.

On the 16th of November, the schooner being completed and every preparation made for the voyage, Park put the finishing hand to his journal; and in the course of the succeeding days previous to the embarkation, which appears to have taken place on the 19th, wrote letters to his father-in-law Mr. Anderson, Sir Joseph Banks, Lord Camden, and Mrs. Park. That addressed to the latter, being the most interesting, is here inserted at length, and cannot be read without emotion.

Park's Last Letter to his Wife.

To Mrs. Park.

"Sansanding, 19th November 1805.

" It grieves me to the heart to write anything that may give you uneasiness; but such is the will of Him who *doeth all things well !*   Your brother Alexander, my dear friend, is no more !   He died of fever at Sansanding on the morning of the 28th of October ; for particulars I must refer you to your father.

" I am afraid that, impressed with a woman's fears and the anxieties of a wife, you may be led to consider my situation as a great deal worse than it really is.   It is true, my dear friends Mr. Anderson and George Scott have both bid adieu to the things of this world, and the greater part of the soldiers have died on the march during the rainy season ; but you may believe me, I am in good health.   The rains are completely over, and the healthy season has commenced, so that there is no danger of sickness, and I have still a sufficient force to protect me from any insult in sailing down the river to the sea.

" We have already embarked all our things, and shall sail the moment I have finished this letter.   I do not intend to stop nor land anywhere till we reach the coast, which I suppose will be some time in the end of January.   We shall then embark in the first vessel for England.   If we have to go round by the West Indies the voyage will occupy three months longer, so that we expect to be in England on the 1st of May.   The reason of our delay since we left the coast was the rainy season, which came on us during the journey ; and almost all the soldiers became affected with the fever.

" I think it not unlikely but I shall be in England before you receive this.   You may be sure that I feel happy at turning my face towards home.   We, this morning, have done with all intercourse with the natives ; and the sails are now hoisting for our departure for the coast."

*   *   *   *   *

Here all authentic information concerning Park unfortunately terminates. His letters and journal were brought by Isaaco to the Gambia, and transmitted from thence to England. For some time nothing further was heard of the expedition ; but in the course of the year 1806 unfavourable accounts were brought by the native traders from the interior of Africa to the British settlements on the coast ; and it was currently reported, but upon no distinct authority, that Park and his companions were killed. These rumours increasing, and no intelligence of Park being received, Lieutenant-Colonel Maxwell, then Governor of Senegal, obtained permission from Government to send a proper person to ascertain the truth of the reports, and he was fortunate enough to engage Isaaco, Park's guide, to go upon this mission.

Isaaco left Senegal in January 1810, and was absent about twenty months. He returned on the 1st of September 1811, with a full confirmation of the reports concerning Park's death. As the result of his inquiries into this subject, he delivered to the governor a journal of his whole proceedings, kept by himself in the Arabic language, including another journal which he had received from Amadi Fatoumi, the guide who had accompanied Park from Sansanding down the Niger. The following translation of the principal portion of this singular document of Amadi Fatoumi's was made at Senegal by the directions of Colonel Maxwell, and transmitted by him to the Secretary of State for the Colonial department.

CHAPTER XXVIII.

Amadi Fatoumi's Journal—Continuing Park's Journey to its close.

November 1805.

WE departed from Sansanding in a canoe the 27th day of the moon, and went in two days to Silla, where Mr. Park ended his first voyage.   Mr. Park bought a slave to help him in the navigation of the canoe.   There were Mr. Park, Martyn, three other white men, three slaves, and myself as guide and interpreter, nine in number, to navigate the canoe. Without landing we bought the slave.   We went in two days to Ginne.   We gave the chief one piece of baft and went on. In passing Dibbie three canoes came after us, armed with pikes, lances, bows and arrows, etc., but no firearms.   Being sure of their hostile intentions, we ordered them to go back, but to no effect, and were obliged to repulse them by force.   Passed on. We passed Kabra ; three came up to stop our passage, which we repelled by force.   On passing Timbuctoo we were again attacked by three canoes, which we beat off, always killing many of the natives.   On passing Gouroumo seven canoes came after us, which we likewise beat off.   We lost one white man by sickness.   We were reduced to eight hands, having each of us fifteen muskets, always in order and ready for action.   Passed by a village (of which I have forgotten the name), the residence of King Gotoijege ; after passing which we counted sixty canoes coming after us, which we repulsed, and killed a great number of men. Seeing so many men killed, and our superiority over them, I took hold of Martyn's hand, saying, "Martyn, let us cease firing, for we have killed too many already;" on which Martyn wanted to kill me, had not Mr. Park interfered. After passing Gotoijege a long way, we met a very strong army on one side of the river, composed of the Poul nation; they had no beasts of any kind. We passed on the other side, and went on without hostilities.

On going along we struck on the rocks. A hippopotamus rose near us, and had nearly overset the canoe; we fired on the animal and drove it away. After a great deal of trouble we got off the canoe without any material danger. We came to an anchor before Kaffo, and passed the day there. We had in the canoe, before we departed from Sansanding, a very large stock of provisions, salted and fresh, of all kinds, which enabled us to go along without stopping at any place for fear of accident. The canoe was large enough to contain with ease one hundred and twenty people. In the evening we started and came to before an island. We saw on shore a great quantity of hippopotami; on our approach they went into the water in such confusion that they almost upset our canoe. We passed the island and sailed. In the morning three canoes from Kaffo came after us, which we beat off. We came to near a small island, and saw some of the natives. I was sent on shore to buy some milk. When I got among them I saw two canoes go on board to sell fresh provisions, such as fowls, rice, etc. One of the natives wanted to kill me; at last he took hold of me and said I was his prisoner. Mr. Park, seeing what was passing on shore, suspected the truth. He stopped the two canoes and people, telling the people belonging to them, that if they should kill me, or keep me prisoner on shore, he would kill them all, and carry their canoes away with him. Those on shore suspecting Mr. Park's intentions sent me off in another canoe on board. They were then released ; after which we bought some provisions from them, and made them some presents.

A short time after our departure twenty canoes came after us from the same place. On coming near, they hailed and said, " Amadi Fatoumi, how can you pass through our country without giving us anything?" I mentioned what they had said to Mr. Park, and he gave them a few grains of amber and some trinkets, and they went back peaceably. On coming to a shallow part of the river, we saw on the shore a great many men sitting down. Coming nearer to them they stood up ; we presented our muskets to them, which made them run off to the interior. A little further on we came to a very difficult passage. The rocks had barred the river ; but three passages were still open between them. On coming near one of them, we discovered the same people again standing on the top of a large rock, which caused great uneasiness to us, especially to me, and I seriously promised never to pass there again without making considerable charitable donations to the poor. We returned, and went to a pass of less danger, where we passed unmolested.

We came to before Carmasse, and gave the chief one piece of baft. We went on and anchored before Gourmon. Mr. Park sent me on shore with forty thousand cowries to buy provisions. I went and bought rice, onions, fowls, milk, etc., and departed late in the evening The chief of the village sent a canoe after us, to let us know of a large army encamped on the top of a very high mountain, waiting for us; and that we had better return, or be on our guard. We immediately came to an anchor, and spent there the rest of the day, and all the night. We started in the morning. On passing the above-mentioned mountain, we saw the army, composed of Moors, with horses and camels, but without any firearms. As they said nothing to us, we passed on quietly, and entered the country of Haoussa, and came to an anchor. Mr. Park said to me, "Now Amadi, you are at the end of your journey; I engaged you to conduct me here; you are going to leave me, but before you go, you must give me the names of the necessaries of life, etc., in the language of the countries through which I am going to pass;" to which I agreed, and we spent two days together about it, without landing. During our voyage I was the only one who had landed. We departed and arrived at Yaour.

I was sent on shore the next morning with a musket and sabre, to carry to the chief of the village, also with three pieces of white baft for distribution. I went and gave the chief his present; I also gave one piece to Alhagi, one to Alhagi-biron, and the other to a person whose name I forget, all Marabous. The chief gave us a bullock, a sheep, three jars of honey, and four men's loads of rice. Mr. Park gave me seven thousand cowries, and ordered me to buy provisions, which I did; he told me to go to the chief and give him five silver rings, some powder and flints, and tell him that these presents were given for the king* by the white men, who were taking leave of him before they went away. After the chief had received these things, he inquired if the white men

---

* The king stayed a few hundred yards from the river.

intended to come back. Mr. Park being informed of this inquiry, replied " *that he could not return any more.*"* Mr. Park had paid me for my voyage before we left Sansanding. I said to him, "I agreed to carry you into the kingdom of Haoussa ; we are now in Haoussa. I have fulfilled my engagements with you ; I am therefore going to leave you here and return."

Next day (Saturday) Mr. Park departed, and I slept in the village (Yaour). Next morning I went to the king to pay my respects to him ; on entering the house I found two men who came on horseback ; they were sent by the chief of Yaour. They said to the king " We are sent by the chief of Yaour to let you know that the white men went away, without giving you or him (the chief) anything ; they have a great many things with them, and we have received nothing from them ; and this Amadi Fatoumi, now before you, is a bad man, an has likewise made a fool of you both." The king immediately ordered me to be put in irons ; which was accordingly done, and everything I had taken from me ; some were for killing me, and some for preserving my life.

The next morning early the king sent an army to a village called Boussa, near the river-side. There is before this village a rock across the whole breadth of the river. One part of the rocks is very high ; there is a large opening in that rock in the form of a door, which is the only passage for the water to pass through ; the tide-current is here very strong. This army went and took possession of the top of this opening. Mr. Park came there after the army had posted itself ; he nevertheless

* These words occasioned his death ; for the certainty of Mr. Park's not returning induced the chief to withhold the presents from the king.

attempted to pass.   The people began to attack him, throwing lances, pikes, arrows, and stones.   Mr. Park defended himself for a long time ; two of his slaves at the stern of the canoe were killed ; they threw everything they had in the canoe into the river, and kept firing ; but being overpowered by numbers and fatigue, and unable to keep up the canoe against the current, and no probability of escaping, Mr. Park took hold of one of the white men, and jumped into the water ; Martyn did the same, and they were drowned in the stream in attempting to escape.   The only slave remaining in the boat, seeing the natives persist in throwing weapons at the canoe without ceasing, stood up and said to them, "Stop throwing now, you see nothing in the canoe, and nobody but myself, therefore cease.   Take me and the canoe, but don't kill me."   They took possession of the canoe and the man, and carried them to the king.

I was kept in irons three months ; the king released me and gave me a slave (woman).   I immediately went to the slave taken in the canoe, who told me in what manner Mr. Park and all of them had died, and what I have related above. I asked him if he was sure nothing had been found in the canoe after its capture ; he said that nothing remained in the canoe but himself and a sword-belt.   I asked him where the sword-belt was ; he said the king took it, and had made a girth for his horse with it.

Thus perished Mungo Park (Dec. 1805), an example of those qualities of enterprising spirit, calm fortitude, and unshaken perseverance which have so often distinguished travellers of the British nation.

Conclusion

The people began to attack him, throwing lances, pikes, arrows, and stones.—Page 888.

ENDNOTES

1 (p. 4) *Feloops*   Actually the Jola; Park mistook their the common word for greeting for the name of this ethnic group.

2 (p. 13) *Jaloffs*   now written as Wolof

3 (p. 13) *Foulahs*   More commonly known as Fulani, though scholars now prefer the term Fulbe. Confusingly, in French scholarship they are known as Peuls.

4 (p. 18) *Ludamar*   a corruption of the name of the ruling family's clan, the Ahl-ould-Amar

5 (p. 20) *Francis Moore*   former factor of the Royal African Company who published his *Travels in the Inland Parts of Africa* in 1738

6 (p. 31) *Major Houghton*   The first of several references to Daniel Houghton (b. 1740) who preceded Park into the interior in late November 1790 and died (or was killed) the following September.

7 (p. 34) *Mumbo Jumbo*   Moore had also given an account of Mumbo Jumbo. The term was associated not only with the grotesque apparel described by Park but with what Moore called 'a cant language, entirely unknown to the women, being only spoken by the men, and is seldom used by them in any discourse than concerning a dreadful bugbear to the women . . . '

8 (p. 40) Park's letter to Laidley from Tallika never arrived (see Lupton, *Mungo Park*, p. 51).

9 (p. 42) *Maraboo*   More commonly written Marabout.

10 (p. 42) *Richardson's Arabic Grammar*   John Richardson (1741–1811) published his *Grammar of the Arabic Language* in 1776.

11 (p. 45) *corn*   In the late eighteenth-century usage denoted the local staple: in England wheat, in Scotland oats, in North America maize.

12 (p. 45) *Holcus cernuus*   a species of grain, resembling sorghum, colloquially known as Bulrush millet

13 (p. 56) *Serawoollies*   now usually referred to as the Serer

14 (p. 83) *Johars or Jowers*   now generally written as Diawara

15 (p. 85) *Daisy Koorabarri*   now written Desse Koulibali

16 (p. 90) *Rhamnus lotus*   colloquially known as the jujube tree

17 (p. 91) *Desfontaines*   René Louiche Desfontaines (1750–1833), distinguished French naturalist, author of *Flora atlantica*

18 (p. 91) *Pliny*   Pliny the Elder (AD 23–79), author of *Naturalis historia*

19 (p. 91) *Lotophagi*   in ancient legend, lotus eaters

20 (p. 102) *John Leo*   usually known as Leo Africanus (*c*.1483–*c*.1552), author of *Description of Africa* (1526)

21 (p. 105) *Asclepias giganteo*   the giant milkweed or swallow-wort

22 (p. 110) *succedaneum*   a substitute

23 (p. 118) *hope deferred maketh the heart sick*   from Proverbs 13:12

24 (p. 126) *the Mahomedan Lent*   Ramadan, the ninth month of the Muslim year, when fasting is prescribed during daylight

25 (p. 128) *a Shereef*   in this context, a Muslim priest, though *shereef* can mean noble or high-born

26 (p. 128) *Walet*   more commonly written Walata

27 (p. 175) *Sego*   in French written as Ségou, the principal river port and commercial centre on the Upper Niger

28 (p. 191) *cameleopard*   a giraffe

29 (p. 256) *lues*   in this context, syphilis

30 (p. 256) *phlebotomy*   bloodletting

31 (p. 268) *a drachm*   one sixteenth of an ounce

INDEX

Page references in *italic* refer to illustrations on the facing page

hippopotami 5, 366, 384
Hobart, Lord 341
honey 4, 277
horses 55, 95, 122–3
Houghton, Major Daniel 1, 31,
    32, 45, 47, 67, 77
    death of xi–xii, 94–5, 147, 331
    and the Niger 179
Houssa city 198
hunting 261
hyaenas 80

Illa-Compe (the corn town) 173
indigo 9, 264, 277
insolvency, slavery caused by 288
iron trade 22–3, 263–5, 323
Isaaco, Mandingo priest and
    trader xix, 350, 353, 354, 355,
    357, 367, 368, 370, 372, 374,
    377, 378
    and Park's letters and journal
    382
Islam xiii–xiv, 13, 45
    and the Arabian conquest of
        Africa 102
    conversions to 71, 93
    and the Foulahs 13, 40, 42,
        53–4
    itinerant bards 259
    in Kaarta 87–8
    in Kamalia 233–4, 291–5,
        298–9
    and the Mandingoes 16–17, 29
    and marriage 248
    and the Moors of Ludamar
        138–9
    mosques 179, 234

Ramadan 109, 126, 298–9
    in Sansanding 188–9
    in Timbuktu 198
ivory 5, 21, 40, 272–4, 276–7

Jaba 216
Jabbe 211
Jalacotta 327–8
Jallonka wilderness 234–5, 266,
    302, 305–15, 353
    Co-meissang stream 306
    Gadou 311
    Koba 314
    Kullo 311–12
    Lingicotta 315
    Manna 312–13, 314
    Melo 314–15
    Nunkolo stream 311
    Sooseeta 311–12
    Tinkingtang 315
Jaloffs (Yallofs) 13, 14–15
    king of 317–19
James's Island 3
Jarra 87, 88, 91, 94, 95, 100,
    101–4, 105, 150–6
    Banna Salee festival 152, 153
    houses 101
    journey to 135–6, 148—50
    Moorish inhabitants 101–2
    and the war with Kaarta 153–6
Jatta, king of Woolli 30–2
Jemaffo Mamadoo 26
Jenne (Djenne) xii, 183, 185–6,
    194, 196, 199
Jews
    in Sansanding 188
    in Timbuktu 128